To
Donny Spatafora, Richard Brown
and Terri Theis

CONFESSIONS
of a
TRANSYLVANIAN

a story of
SEX,
DRUGS
and
ROCKY
HORROR

by Kevin Theis
and Ron Fox

Everything in this book is based on real events, except those that aren't. Some of the names have been changed. Others are compilations of various people. Still others are simply the best we can remember. Many of the people discussed herein have, over the years, become fine, upstanding family role models. Others are still finding their way as they make their journey through life.

Berwick Court Publishing Company
Chicago, Illinois
http://www.berwickcourt.com

Cover design by Paul Stroili, Touchstone Graphic Design
Cover photograph by Johnny Knight

Theis, Kevin.
  Confessions of a Transylvanian : a story of sex, drugs and rocky horror / by Kevin Theis and Ron Fox.

  p. ; cm.

  ISBN: 978-0-9838846-4-4

  1. Rocky Horror picture show (Motion picture) 2. Theatrical companies--Florida--20th century. 3. Teenage boys--Florida--20th century. 4. Theater and youth--Florida--20th century. I. Fox, Ronald. II. Title. III. Title: Transylvanian

PN2298.R63 T44 2012
792.029   *2012937244*

Printed in the United States of America

Prologue

The first time I ever spoke to Donny, I lied to him. And all he did was ask my name.

Minutes after the Rocky show comes down and I'm standing in front of him practically kicking dirt clods, staring at the floor and sweating, I was so nervous. I had no idea what they'd want me to do before letting me join up. Was there a waiting list? Did I have to go through some kind of initiation? An elaborate, painful hazing ceremony that would leave me smarting in my hidey-hole? Who knew?

All I wanted was in. Whatever this was—this trippy, freaky, fucked-up thrill show I'd just witnessed for the past two hours—this was for me.

Yeah, it was weird. Absolutely. Way weirder than I thought it would be, even. But not granny-in-her-bra weird. It was 16-year-old-girls-in-fishnet-stockings weird, so hey, sign me up. If they wanted me to spit-shine shoes for a few months in order to get in the club, bring it. I got a rag. Let's go.

By the way, I was doing this—this signing up thing—without prior approval. The Mom hadn't yet given me a thumbs-up on this plan and I was taking a pretty big leap of faith that she would be cool with it. But, deep down? I wasn't too worried. Basically, it amounted to an irresistible trade-off: If she gave me permission to join the cast, I would guarantee that she would know *exactly* where I would be every Friday and Saturday night. What parent of a 16-year-old boy doesn't want that? Besides, she wasn't the "say no" type. I knew a few of them. Bitch moms. I didn't have one. Thank God.

So there I was, ready to set pen to paper and enlist. All I needed to know was: Where's the recruiting officer?

When the show came down and the lights bumped up, I felt a surge of panic. It was urgent that I find this person *now*. Before they left the theater for the night and my chance was blown. Working against the flow of traffic, I elbowed my way to the front of the theater and approached a girl from the cast as she was packing up her gear. She was one of the minion-looking types in the dark jackets.

"Hey, listen, what do you have to do to join the cast?"

She glanced up at me disinterestedly. "Talk to Donny," she said and went back to stuffing sequined costume pieces into a bag. Upon closer inspection, this girl was practically spilling out of her top. How could she even stand up straight?

Focus. Pay attention. She gave you a name. "Okay, Donny." I looked around. "Who's he?"

She jerked a thumb at a guy toward the front, murmured, "That's him. Can't miss him," and strolled away, swaying on her heels.

I turned and there he was. The biggest, meanest looking badass I'd ever laid eyes on. Two-seventy if he was a pound, and brother, was he a pound. Six-three and *huge*. Hair that practically shot out of his head. Arms like anacondas. Leather biker jacket, combat boots and a wallet strung on a chain that latched to his belt.

But the headline was *size*. This guy was gigantic in every conceivable way. Big like the U.S.S.R. was big. *Jupiter* big, get the picture?

I almost bailed out right there. Who needed this? I was not much inclined to make the acquaintance of a guy who looked like he could pop my head like a zit if I ticked him off.

But as I thought about retreating, I took another look around at the cast members as they swirled around me in a happy flurry of post-show activity. They were finished for the night, packing up and heading home but, even though the movie was over and the lights bumped up full, they hadn't lost their energy. They were still connected—talking, laughing, carrying props and costume pieces out the door.

They had purpose. Each of them seemed to know that they were a part of something that was bigger than they were and, clearly, they looked forward to the weekend for reasons that had little to do with simply sleeping until noon. Seeing the contented looks on their faces was all it took to straighten my spine. Whatever I had just seen, whatever this *thing* was, it seemed absolutely necessary that I become a part of it. In a way, I already was. The Rocky heroin had entered my bloodstream and I was hooked. I just needed to figure out how to get my weekly fix.

This, unfortunately, involved going through a gatekeeper who looked like a mountain crammed into a pair of denim trousers. And not a friendly mountain, either. More like the windswept, snow-capped K2 of human beings.

Gritting my teeth, I approached Mount Donny with what I hoped was a confident spring in my step. He was dealing with someone else as I walked up, so I had to wait to catch his eye. I had nothing but time. Finally, he seemed to notice me loitering and turned his bulk to face me.

Now, at this point, I wish I could say that there was this…I don't know… electric charge when he first laid eyes on me. You know, one of those "Where have you been all my life?" moments, like he'd been *waiting* for me to show up. Hoping for my arrival. I could have been the Rocky messiah for all I knew. The Chosen One.

Turns out, not so much.

"You here to join up?" he said. Kinda bored, really.

I nodded. Speaking wasn't required yet, apparently. Which was good.

"What's your name?"

I paused. And no, not because I temporarily forgot my name in all my flustered nervousness. This wasn't a sitcom, for fuck's sake. I knew my name. I just didn't want to *say* it.

Here's the thing: I had always wanted a cool name. A funky, kickass name. The kind of name that girls scream while they're clawing at your back. Like that.

My name, sadly, was anything but cool.

Kevin. Jesus. Could you get any more Irish Catholic dork than "Kevin"? I sure as hell didn't think so. Girls don't scream "Kevin" unless you spill something hot on their laps. Kevins didn't get their backs clawed. Ever. I wasn't about to hang that moniker around my neck.

So what did I do? I lied.

"Jack," I said. "I'm Jack." And immediately thought: Oooooh. Good choice.

Jack, see, that's a *name.* Jack commands respect, awe and admiration. The backs of guys named Jack are a goddamn mess, all the clawing.

Jack is also a no-nonsense, rebellion-is-my-business type of name. An "I had a bowl of anarchy for breakfast. What did *you* eat?" name. It says, "Listen up: I'm not *John.* John is what my *parents* named me, see? The real

vii

name is *Jack*. Don't forget it."

Donny? He didn't blink. He probably knew plenty of Jacks.

"Okay," he said, and then mechanically recited: "You start off as a Transylavanian. You know who they are, right? The Time Warpers?"

I nodded dumbly.

"Great. Here's the drill: black jacket, white shirt, black pants. Be here at 11 next Friday. And bring five bucks. See you then." He had barely looked at me and already he was done. Walking away.

I was jolted by his response. I had been expecting...something. Some resistance. At least a sense that joining up was an honor. A thing to be earned. Was he saying that just *anyone* could hop on board? I had to stop him.

"Wait," I called out. "You mean...just *show up*? That's it?"

Now he looked a little annoyed. "Yeah. Black jacket and pants, white shirt. Bring five bucks. We'll walk you through it. See you then." And he was gone.

Like he never expected to see me again. Like he'd forgotten me the second he turned his back. Like he'd been through this a thousand times before and seen idiots like me promise to show up the next weekend and then... *pffft*...disappear forever.

Which was, the more I thought about it, probably, entirely, completely true.

But still. The event had seemed so...unimportant. I mean, I didn't necessarily want a fanfare or for someone to roll out a red freakin' carpet but... some kind of "Welcome aboard" would have been nice.

No such luck. I'd come for information, I'd gotten it and now I was being shown the door.

So, for now, there was nothing left to do but...go shopping.

Black pants. Black jacket. White shirt.

See you on Friday, Donny. You won't forget me after that. Know why? That's right:

I'm *Jack*, motherfucker. I'm the guy you don't forget.

The Late Night, Double-Feature Picture Show

B efore we go any further, let's assume for the moment that if you're reading this book, you have already seen "The Rocky Horror Picture Show"
once if not several times. I mean, I don't want to leap to any huge conclu-
sions or anything, but that's a pretty safe bet, I figure.

What's more, if you *haven't* seen it, do me a favor: Close the book right
now, go see the movie, then come back and start reading. And no, I do *not*
mean rent the fucking DVD. I'm saying get out of the house one Friday or
Saturday at midnight and see the movie in a *theater*, the way God meant for
you to see it. With a cast, the flying props, the callbacks—the works.

Why? Because on DVD (and this is just between you and me) Rocky
Horror is one *unwatchable* movie. Truly, it is a real test of endurance.

Not that the acting is terrible. It really isn't. Hell, a Tony Award-winning actor and an Academy Award-winning actress are two of the leads, so
how bad could it be?

And it's not that the music isn't worth the price of admission either. It
is. The music is fantastic, actually. In fact, the soundtrack is arguably the best
thing about the movie.

But yeesh, the *plot*? Gimme a break. All hail to Richard O'Brien and all
that, but holy God...I wouldn't write the Cliff's Notes for this flick for all the
tea in the busiest tea market in Tealand on "Drink Your Tea Day."

And you know what? I'd be willing to bet that almost *nobody*, if they
can avoid it, watches this entire movie from beginning to end on DVD. At
least, I can't imagine why anyone would.

Sit down and listen to the whole soundtrack? Absolutely. I've done it
myself more times than can be calculated by NASA engineers. There's at

least some enjoyment to be derived from *that* experience. And, of course, you might do well to study the DVD to try to get one of the parts down *if* you're preparing to appear in the live show. I could see that, too.

But to sit and watch the whole movie alone in your apartment to perhaps enjoy the cinematic nuances of the film? No way, Spanish Joe. Makes no sense to me at all. And I've seen the damn thing over 300 times in theaters, so I know what I'm denigrating here, okay?

It's no wonder that when the movie was released to unsuspecting audiences back in 1975, there was basically a collective "Huh?" from the movie-going public. And it was a well-deserved "Huh?" The film is ridiculously off the wall and not merely in a John Waters kind of way (though it's ridiculous in that way, too). Hell, there's stuff in it that I *still* don't get and this movie is in my freakin' DNA.

So, if you haven't seen it and want to experience the whole Rocky experience, do yourself a favor and see it *live* and with a big cast acting it out in front of the screen. Shouldn't be hard to find. The midnight show is still running in most American cities even after thirty-five years. Freaky, huh?

At this point, I'm going to presume you're wondering: How did it all begin? How did the whole Rocky phenomenon start?

Well, here's the truth:

I don't really know.

Oh, I suppose that if I were so inclined, I could research it for you and give you a breakdown of the whole Rocky Horror history. I could study up, delve into all the historical facts and figgers about the Waverly Theatre and Sal and Dori and the rest and write you a little book report so you could know everything there is to know about How It All Began. Sure I could.

But, see, there's just two things: (1) Given its mysterious provenance, my version of the facts (even if I really stuck to the straight dope to the best of my ability) would, more likely than not, be totally and completely inaccurate; and, (2) this isn't a goddamn Rocky history book anyway. If you want to know the complete and total backstory of "The Rocky Horror Picture Show" phenomenon and how the live-show-in-front-of-the-screen thing all started, my advice would be to go to Wikipedia (or Rockypedia for that matter) and geek the fuck out. I'm not going to spell it all out for you here.

Instead, this is the story of how the downtrodden Hollywood, Florida, Rocky Horror castoffs became the one and only, high and mighty, Best Fucking Cast Ever inhabitants of the legendary Deerfield Ultravision movie theater in the Year of Our Lord 1982.

It's a tale of how this cast started from absolutely nothing and rose to...well, not *national* prominence (I don't want to oversell it), but *regional* prominence anyway.

It's a chronicle of how a disparate, unconnected band of weirdos, losers, sexy chicks, fat broads, geeks, faggots, dopers, freaks, criminals, complete dorks and goddesses (the underage *and* the legal kinds) were drawn together in the winter of '82 and somehow managed to create something so cool, it would freeze your balls off just to look at it.

So, pull up a chair. Here we go:

I first heard about the Rocky show in about 1979. My Uncle Mike owned the soundtrack album and, due perhaps to my younger brother's and my unmistakable maturity, he deemed us—then 12 and 14, respectively—old enough to share in the freakishness that was "The Rocky Horror Picture Show." Well, old enough to listen to the *music from* the Rocky show, anyway.

Uncle Mike, by the way, was not one of those weirdo, creepy, middle-aged-but-still-thinks-he's-a-teenager kind of uncles. In fact, Mike is only six years older than me, so that would put him at around 20 years old at the time. Still practically a kid himself.

But to be clear, he *was* a geek. Even at 14 (or maybe especially at 14) I could see that. He was a big science nerd, straight as an arrow, drug-free and proud of it. A total Poindexter.

David and I? We thought he was the bees' fuckin' knees.

He'd hang with us all the time and show us a bunch of shit the other grown-ups wouldn't let us get near (though rarely anything truly dangerous or, sadly, explosive). He'd perform science experiments that would amaze and confound our tiny minds. He'd take us on long nature hikes and magically prove to us that being surrounded by the great outdoors didn't have to mean being bored senseless. And, every once in a while, he would open our eyes to some kind of cultural phenomenon of which we had been tragically unaware.

Good example: One summer, Mike turned David and me on to Pink Floyd's "Dark Side of the Moon."

"Big deal," you might be thinking, right? Wrong. Because if you *really* want to properly appreciate "Dark Side of the Moon," there is truly only one way to do it:

First, your Uncle Mike must have a flawless, skip-free copy of the album in its original vinyl format.

Next, he must have a state-of-the-art sound system, including a perfectly balanced mixing board and a turntable that comes with a needle so sensitive that it can hear you *breathing* in the next room.

The final component is the most important, and without it your experience will be inadequate at best. You must have a pair of noise-canceling headphones that wrap around your ears like a giant, Pink Floyd-loving burrito. This. Is. Crucial.

Once all of these pieces are in place, you are ready to begin your introduction to "Dark Side." Here's how it goes down:

Your uncle will carefully place the cans over your ears (the volume having been pre-set and the levels balanced accordingly). He will then ease the needle onto the album, dim the lights and, presumably, go have lunch or something with your brother while you close your eyes and experience what can only be described as a sensory smorgasbord.

The notes slowly drift into your cerebrum. The album becomes a part of your circulatory system. Your pulse matches each tempo, changing from song to song. You're *breathing* sound. The world slowly dissolves away until the line between you and the music becomes blurred beyond recognition.

And, brother, when those bells go off at the beginning of "Time," good luck not jumping three feet in the air and soiling yourself. Fair warning.

My Uncle Mike, for this and for many other reasons, was the older brother I never had. To my little brother, Uncle Mike was the older brother he wished *I* had been. (I was a dick to David back in those days. Gotta cop to that.)

Mike was giving us a leg-up on adolescence and he was doing it at a time when my brother and I were basically functioning as human sponges, soaking up whatever was placed in our way. And among the things Uncle Mike placed in *my* way was a little thing called "The Rocky Horror Picture Show."

In doing so, whether he meant to do it or not, he changed my life.

Part of what made our relationship with our uncle so filled with indefinable awesomeness was the fact that my brother and I only saw him during the summer months and at Christmas and therefore never had an opportunity to grow bored with his company. (Teenage boys have the attention spans of kindergarteners on nitrous oxide.)

At the time, David and I were living in Florida with our mother. Uncle Mike—our father's youngest brother—lived with our grandmother in Colorado.

My Dad and Mom divorced when I was still a little, little kid. My brother, just a year and a half younger than me, was just a baby when they split. Accordingly, neither of us have any recollection of our folks ever having been together.

After they went their separate ways, the arrangement our parents settled on regarding visitation was that David and I would spend the school year with our Mom in Florida and then, during academic breaks, we'd go wherever our Dad happened to be.

However, if our Dad was traveling for work (a common occurrence), we didn't stay in Florida and cramp our mother's style. We would instead be shipped off to the Rockies to spend whatever time we had at my grandmother's place in Colorado.

Consequently, this meant a lot of vacations and holidays with Uncle Mike. And that, of course, was just hunky-dory with us.

Summer, 1979. Uncle Mike was home from college and we were in Colorado Springs for three months. At 14 and 12, my brother and I were starting to look at the world in an entirely new way. The hormones were practically bursting out of our eyeballs and, personally speaking, I could get a boner if a properly timed breeze shot through the window. To this pubescent mix, my uncle—for good or ill—deemed it appropriate for David and me to learn about Frank-N-Furter and his friends.

The Rocky experience was a phenomenon that, by the late '70s, was already in full swing. Someone (Mike could not say who) had discovered that if you ran this strange rock and roll movie late at night in a movie theater and yelled properly timed smartass comments at the screen as the story unfolded, it would be an enjoyable experience for the audience.

Merge that idea with the fact that some people (their origins were similarly vague) were actually willing to dress up as the characters in the movie and act out the plot in real time as the movie rolled on the screen above their heads.

Now, to that simmering brew of oddness, add the further participation of regular audience members who, at prearranged moments in the show, would throw items into the air (toast, cards, toilet paper, etc.) as the movie continues down the merry path of sexual ridiculousness. Mix these three ingredients together and, ladies and gentlemen, you've got yourself a cult film.

Mike explained all of this to David and me, who sat open-mouthed at this news. People brought *props* to the showings? And threw them in the air on cue? They yelled at the screen and nobody *cared*? Girls dressed up in little trashy outfits with fishnet stockings? And the *boys* did, too?

Amazing.

Then Mike said, "I've got the album. You want to hear it?"

We were, as you may imagine, mildly interested. He gave it a spin.

Now, for the record, listening to the Rocky soundtrack out of context won't help you with the story one little bit. I don't even think Mike bothered explaining the plot to us beyond, "These kids named Brad and Janet wander into a castle and things get weird."

We didn't care. The music was cool even without a corresponding storyline.

"Dammit Janet." "Over at the Frankenstein Place." "The Time Warp." It didn't get much better than that. And a sweet *what*? Did he say "transvestite"? Really? Plus a girl who begged you to touch-a, touch-a, touch her? Seriously?

It was unlike anything we'd ever heard before. In dropping that needle and exposing us to this truly bizarre series of songs, Mike had inadvertently kicked wide the door leading out of childhood and into the vast, steamy, whacked-out world of adolescence.

Listening to that soundtrack, we tasted blood and we wanted more.

Sadly, Mike had nothing more to give. He let us play the grooves off the album (you could do that in those days) but, tragically, there was no local Rocky show in Colorado Springs and, even if there were, my grandmother never would have let us go near one.

So, beyond the songs on the album, our Rocky initiation would have to wait.

But not, as the song says, for very much longer.

Flash forward three years. Well, don't *flash* forward. Let's fill in a few blanks before we take off on our all-Rocky adventure.

David and I are back in Florida and we're knee-deep in, respectively, our sophomore and junior years of high school.

And we're miserable. For different reasons and to different degrees, yes. But the truth was that life in Florida, to put it succinctly, sucked *balls*.

I don't know if you've spent any significant time in Florida. And if you haven't, what I'm about to describe might sound a little harsh. I assure you, from the bottom of my heart: It isn't harsh enough.

First and foremost, what you need to know about the state of Florida (and South Florida in particular) is that it is a swamp.

Exaggeration, right? "Swamp." C'mon now. How can it be a *swamp*? They've got highways and houses and luxury hotels and all that stuff. Can't build that on swamp, can you?

Well, if you truck in enough cement, buddy-boy, you bet your ass you can. Hell, with enough asphalt, concrete, rebar, plumbing fixtures and electricity, you can build just about anything anywhere.

And if it's located near a beach? You can charge top dollar for it. And *get* it, too.

But you don't want to *waste* that beachfront property. No, no. So when you're looking to build something, make sure it's a multi-story, thousand-unit condo complex. Or a clubhouse at a golf course. Or a bank. Or a strip club.

Not a museum. Jesus, whatever you do, don't build a *museum*. It's not like anyone will go to it anyway.

A theater? Puh-leeze. Tell you what: Put an auditorium out by the airport or something so that "Cats" or "Phantom" or whatever can stop off and do a few weeks of its tour there. People will like that. But don't build any actual *playhouses* or anything ridiculous like that. You don't want to throw your money away.

A library? Good God, fine. I'll tell you what: Build one library for every ten churches. How about that? Work for you? No?

Look, how about a pier? You can fish off that. Or just stand on it and get drunk. Sound good? And here's a marina for your enormous boat! And I'll throw in about a billion liquor stores, bars and nightclubs. Happy yet?

Boy, there's no pleasing some people.

Okay, final offer: the creation of not one, not two, but 5,000 old folks' homes. And not little ones, either! Whole *communities*, filled with millions and millions of little, tiny old people who have moved here from all over the country to live out their final days in alternating states of futility and rage.

I'm sorry, you had a question? You want to know why these old people would choose to live in this festering cesspool during the final few years of their lives?

Because they couldn't afford to retire to San Diego, why do you think?

To make things interesting, each of these old codgers will be supplied with keys to their own bright, shiny, two-ton killing machines called *automobiles*. Thus armed, these barely coherent octogenarians will head out on the road and zip around aimlessly all afternoon looking for early-bird specials at their favorite eateries. Because, really, what beats wolfing down a half-price three-course Chinese dinner at 3:30 in the afternoon? Nothing!

But wait! You can hardly be expected to live in this 150-degrees-in-the-shade paradise with just a bunch of old people, right? So before you call our toll-free number, we'll throw in a special bonus!

Snowbirds!

Yes, these lovely Northern wilting flowers will come pouring down into South Florida every year by the busload. They'll snatch up those newly constructed concrete houses, the little two- and three-bedroom monstrosities sequestered away in little private communities with clever little names like "The Glades of Emerald Cove" or "The Palms of Granny's Crotch" and they'll put down roots, change their party affiliation to Republican, learn how to make Mai Tais and slowly, but inevitably, turn into slovenly piles of goo.

Think of it—what type of person feels compelled to move into a humid, fetid sinkhole like this? Simple: They are the folks who can no longer stomach shoveling snow four months a year up in Brooklyn or Chicago or Denver. People whose balls retract up into their bodies if the temperature dips below 50. The kind of people who will leave behind their friends and family—the loved ones who have surrounded them all their lives—just to live in a state where the mean temperature is 85 degrees and the humidity hovers at about 90 percent year-round.

They are the weak. The thin-blooded. The lowest rung on the evolutionary scale.

Want to know why survival of the fittest is a thing of the past? Because people don't simply keel over into a snowbank and die at age 50 anymore the way they should. They move to *Florida*.

Exercise ceases. Air conditioning is the new religion. Their gathering places become these enormous indoor shopping malls where no one looks at you twice when you show up in a pink jogging suit that shows off your man-boobs. Why would they? Hell, everyone's wearing 'em!

They undergo complete transformations. They cultivate tans, learn how to smoke weed, snort coke, bang one another's spouses, tack on fifty pounds of ass fat and puff a few packs of smokes a day. Then, for kicks, they dial up the Weather Channel in mid-February, prop up their flip-flop clad feet and, when they see a blizzard clobbering Buffalo, they laugh their asses off at how much better they've got it.

And when they finally do shuffle off this mortal coil, their kids fly down to Florida, throw each and every item they ever owned into a dumpster, sell the condo (at a loss) to the next fresh-from-Minnesota retiree and...the circle of life continues.

This is where I grew up.

This is what I fled, the minute I had the chance.

This, my friends, is where our story begins.

It wasn't always thus. Nope, David and I began life up in Chicago, of all places. One of the coldest places on Earth most of the year. But since my folks decided to split up when my brother and I were young tadpoles, it was Mom who called the shots.

Here was the shot she called: When I was 8 and my brother was 6, she obeyed her thin-blooded genetic makeup and shipped us all down to the Sunshine State.

Zoom. Freeze-dried culture shock, delivered fresh to your door.

We woke up one day and we were in South Florida. Land of the dead, dying and constitutionally spineless.

And there we stayed. And there we festered.

Oh, sure—we got out of our humid prison for the occasional reprieve. Summers in Colorado with Uncle Mike. (Nature! Fresh air! Actual snow!)

Christmases in New York City with Dad and his new wife. (Broadway! Times Square! *Zabars*!)

Wonderful, memorable escapes.

But as suddenly as it began...it was over. The vacation would end and we would be banished back to the Swamp. To that citrus misery that was life in our little town of Deerfield Beach.

Cute name, isn't it? "Deerfield Beach." Do you know it? It's ideally situated, right between the world-famous retirement community of Boca Raton and the beloved tropical oasis known as Pompano Beach. Plus, it's only a few short miles north of Ft. Lauderdale itself and just an hour's drive away from beautiful, world-famous Miami Beach!

In other words:

It was a complete and utter shithole.

Deerfield Beach had a beach, all right. And it wasn't a bad one, if you're into that kind of thing.

I wasn't. Dirty, messy, appallingly hot places, beaches. You can have 'em. Besides, we didn't live *on* or even *near* the beach. We lived inland, a good five miles or so. So for me, going to the beach was a tremendous effort to get somewhere I didn't particularly want to be anyway. A few natives go all the time, but most don't. Too touristy anyway.

Oh, we had pools, though. Millions of 'em. Big business down there, the pool trade. Cleaning them, providing chemical products for them, building huge screened structures to enclose them, manufacturing floaty things that...you know...*float* in them. HUGE money in pools.

And just about everyone had one. The rich, the moderately wealthy, even the lower-middle class, like us. For just about everyone who lived in the Swamp, there was, more likely than not, a cement pond in the backyard. You had to be dirt poor not to have one.

Not all of them were *private* pools, of course. When we first moved to Florida, we lived in an apartment complex and had to swim in the building's community pool. And while it was incredibly cool to us, coming from the frozen north, to have a swimmin' hole we could dive into at our merest whim, to the locals it was pretty low-rent. Most people found the idea of a *community pool* distasteful.

In fact, it wasn't until years later, when our grandmother helped Mom to buy her first house, that we finally had a pool we could call our own. And once we got it, David and I practically lived in the thing.

I mean, honestly—what else was there to do? Taking part in outdoor sports was, for the most part, a horrifying experience in that climate. You couldn't run ten yards without having perspiration shoot out of your body like a geyser. It was *disgusting.*

That didn't stop anyone from offering plenty of options, though. There was Little League, school sports (especially indoor sports like basketball— very popular) and even live sporting events to attend if your idea of athletic participation was sitting still and watching others do all the running and sweating. But despite all my attempts to get interested in sports, nothing stuck. And I tried *everything*: baseball, soccer, volleyball...whatever they had. Nothing really caught fire.

David? He took another route to defeat boredom:

He took drugs.

Nothing really heavy, mind you. Just some pot. Okay, a *great deal* of pot. But that was his way of dealing with the stifling lethargy of the place. And this particular route was desperately hard to resist. I got sucked into that world for a while myself. You couldn't really help it.

See, Florida was *made* for stoners. You could get totally blasted, black out and fall asleep curled up on the lawn if you wanted. Why not? It's not like you had to worry about freezing to death or dying of exposure. Go ahead. Knock yourself out.

Besides, it wasn't as if most people had any real responsibilities down there. At least, nothing they couldn't accomplish *while* they were high.

So drugs were big down there. Bigger than pool care, even.

As a result of growing up in this climate, living as a stoner became a big part of my world for the majority of my sophomore year of high school.

Know what got me to stop? My Mom.

And no, she didn't sit me down one day and give me some big speech about how drugs were irresponsible and "that's why they called it dope" and all that. She didn't crack an egg in a frying pan and compare it to my brain. It wasn't really necessary.

She just gave me...The Look.

One day, I'm in the kitchen, I'm a little high, and I'm satisfying my stoner appetite by wolfing down a cold slice of pizza. All of a sudden, I catch my Mom's eye. And there it is. The Look.

The Look wasn't contemptuous. She wasn't trying to shame me or at- tack me or make me feel like a loser. Instead, The Look said: "Hey, kiddo. I'm really worried about you. You're a great kid and I love you and you're disappearing in a cloud of bong smoke. Where's my boy?"

And, hand to God, that did it. That's all it took to get me to quit.

Well, that coupled with the fact that, as a result of my descent into stonerland, I had almost no money. And I was eating absolute *crap* all day long. And I looked like shit.

Oh, and, maybe most importantly, the people I was hanging out with were the biggest collection of losers I'd ever met in my *life*.

Don't get me wrong. I'm not talking about recreational marijuana users or even mild potheads here. I know a few of both types and they live long, happy, interesting, productive lives. I'm talking about *stoners* here. Big, big difference.

See, a stoner is the type of guy who rolls out of bed every single day and engages in a ritual we used to call the Wake & Bake. You'd get up and you'd spark up. From the moment you opened your eyes in the a.m. until you finally passed out sometime late into the night, you were fried out of your gourd.

Mostly, the life of a stoner centers around a few basic needs: something to toke, something to munch, something to watch and, to make ends meet, something to sell. That, after all, is how stoners make a living. To scrape together rent money, they naturally deal pot.

This lifestyle, you can probably imagine, does not exactly result in the production of a well-rounded, fascinating human being. Not exactly. Living like this every day creates, instead, a person with the personality and intelligence of a fucking *turnip*.

Want to know what a conversation between two stoners is like? Here's a sampling:

Man, I am completely baked.

Me too. That's pretty good stuff.

Not as good as the stuff I had last week though, yo?

Nah. That was awesome.

Awesome.

Yeah.

Hey, you know what we did on Friday?

I can guess.

I'll bet you can.

Did you get wasted?

I totally did, man. It was this hash we got shipped in from Tur-

key. From actual Turkey, man. In <u>Africa</u>.

No way.

No lie. My guy knows this dude who makes his stuff special right on the Turkish border, in Bangkok.

Whoa.

Yeah. So we get it and we only broke off a couple of cubes, you know? And within a few, we were just <u>flying</u>, man. It was like nothing else.

Awesome.

And it goes on like that. The primary topic of stoner conversation centers around (a) how high you are at that particular moment, (b) how good that feels, (c) how truly enjoyable it was when you got really, really blasted at some time in the recent past, (d) how much more enjoyable *that* high was compared to your *current* high and, of course, (e) how completely out-of-your-mind-*mental* you plan to be at some point in the not-too-distant future.

Sometimes you talk about music, too. But mostly not.

And that's it. That's stoner life. Some folks can go on like that forever. And, you might be surprised to learn, they are tremendously happy people. Shallow as a saucer of hot nothing, yes. But happy.

For me, my little trip to Stonerville lasted about six months. Then, Mom gave me The Look and I was done. Oh, I still sparked up on occasion (I didn't become a monk or anything) but my hard-core stoner days were, blissfully, over.

It was time for something else.

I WOULD LIKE, IF I MAY, TO TAKE YOU ON A STRANGE JOURNEY

Monday

So here I am, two days after my first introduction to Donny at the Rocky show, and five days away from reporting for duty on Friday night.

It wasn't going to be easy, slogging through this week. School was back in session after Christmas break and the minutes seemed to crawl by like very, very slowly crawling creatures.

Where I went to school didn't help matters much. I mean, it wasn't that I hated going to school where I did. It wasn't great, but it wasn't awful. And I was the first to admit that it could have been much, much worse.

I went to this parochial school, which had its challenges, but overall beat the hell out of having to endure the South Florida public school system. The local public school, Deerfield High, was without question a triple-A-rated moron factory. So I was spared having to go there, at least.

My father insisted on sending us to private school and, what's more, made sure that we attend one with a religious affiliation. It was the way he was raised so he wanted the same for us. As a child, he had attended St. Ignatius College Prep, the renowned Catholic high school on Chicago's south side. Problem was, there was no Catholic school anywhere near where we lived in Deerfield Beach. So Mom looked around and discovered that the closest parochial school to our house was none other than the brand-spanking-new Zion Lutheran Christian School.

How brand-spanking-new was the place? Glad you asked.

This school was small. We're talking *really* little, okay?

I mean, our school was so small, our debate team consisted of one guy

15

with schizophrenia. It was *not* big.

No, seriously, you want to know just how little it was? The history class-es at our school only covered *yesterday*. I'm here to tell you: This was a small school.

Really, our school was so itsy-bitsy, my locker combination was *six*.

Okay, I think we've established that it wasn't an enormous place. When my class graduated in 1983, for example, we had a grand total of twenty-eight seniors. You could fit our entire class on a single bus and have room for the entire *junior* class.

That last paragraph, by the way, is the God's honest truth. There were, in fact, only twenty-eight of us in the Zion Lutheran class of '83. (Tiny, I believe, is the word you're looking for.)

Here's the thing—when you go to high school with a class as sparsely populated as ours, the school day isn't quite like it is at other, larger schools. For example, the students in my class didn't break apart and attend a variety of different classes all day, only seeing each other every once in a while. Nope. At our school, we all went to the same classes, all day long, without variation.

This meant that when I was in my junior year of high school, I spent seven hours a day with the same group of 16-year-old boys and girls. Day in. Day out. All. The. Time.

And when a group of kids see one another that often, work together that closely, share the same teachers, the same experiences, the same every-thing, all day long...

...they gradually grow to *fucking hate* one another.

Well, there are exceptions. I actually did have one good friend in high school. One. His name was Dean.

Dean was this Italian kid from Long Island (by way of Brooklyn) whose Mom, like mine, had finally given up on temperatures in the teens back home and headed South, dragging her kids down to the Swamp with her.

Having actually spent most of his life in the North, though, Dean was not cut from the same cloth as my other, raised-in-Florida classmates. I could, therefore, converse with him for more than ten minutes without hav-ing to resort to solely monosyllabic words.

I'm not saying my classmates were dumb, but if you said it was chilly outside, they'd bring bowls, spoons and sour cream. You get the idea.

Point is, there was really only one guy at my school I could talk to but... there was a problem. He was this tough guy, this New Yawker from freakin'

Brooklyn, so breaking the news to him that I was about to join a tribe of fishnet-stocking-wearing guys and gals for a little weekend fun was...risky. You might find this difficult to believe, but high school kids can be a trifle nasty to people who are different. They really can.

But, hell, I had to tell somebody.

"Hey." Between classes. Dean is digging books out of his locker.

"Hiya doin'?" he says. Accent so thick you could spread it on a bagel.

"You're from New York, right?"

He pauses, smiles. "You figured that out, huh?"

"Yeah, I have a sixth sense like that."

"Sherlock Holmes, practically."

"Yeah. So listen." Deep breath. "Have you ever heard of a thing called 'The Rocky Horror Picture Show'?"

His brow crinkles. I decide to help him out.

"It's a movie? Pretty big in New York, I think. You heard of it?"

He considers. "I think so, yeah. People dress up, dance around in front of a movie screen or something, right?"

See? Culturally educated. I had a feeling.

"Yeah, that's it."

"Okay, so what about it?"

"You know they're doing it here? Right up the street?"

"Really?"

"Yeah. At the Ultravision. Weekend nights at midnight."

"Uh-huh." I don't say anything, so he feels compelled to fill in the silence. "What about it? You go to see it or somethin'?"

Reluctant to admit it, I manage to say: "Yeah. I went last weekend."

He's waiting for the review and I'm not providing one. "So? Any good?"

I can't sound too enthusiastic, so it comes out: "Yeah, it was. It was, you know, pretty *weird* and all that."

"Weird?"

"Oh, yeah. You know. All those people, dressed up in...all kinds of strange outfits. Stockings and feather boas and stuff. Guys, too. Weird. But really kinda cool too, in a way."

"Wait, did you say *guys*?" Now I've really got his attention. And he's getting...a little *loud*, if you want the truth.

17

"Well, yeah." I'm sweating now. "Guys, sure. Like they do in the movie. I mean, the guys who do the show here, they kinda *have* to dress like that. Because it's the same as the characters in the movie. You know? It's not like they *want* to or anything."

"Oh, sure. They just show up on the weekend and dress up like that because they're under orders, right?" He's smiling, but he's serious too. What the hell, he's wondering, am I talking about?

And suddenly, I don't really know.

"Anyway, it was really crazy. Never seen anything like it really."

"Yeah, I'll bet." He slams the locker shut. "I'll see ya."

And he's off.

And I've got four days left and nobody to talk to.

And it's all I can think about.

Great.

Tuesday

Sleep didn't come all that easily the previous night but, by Tuesday morning, I had accomplished one small goal: I was twenty-four hours closer to my Rocky debut. Time to prepare.

In theory, it wouldn't take much. All I needed by Friday, I had been told, was five bucks and a spiffy new outfit. Well, a *used* outfit, at any rate. Who buys a brand-new black suit to do the Rocky show? I was off to Goodwill.

Not surprisingly, black jackets, matching pants and white button-down shirts are practically jumping off the rack at your average South Florida thrift store. They were everywhere you looked, and with good reason. This was the the first type of outfit Northern people donated to charity when they first arrived in Florida.

It went like this:

> "*Hershel! I'm heading to the Sal Army! You got anything to donate?*"
>
> "*Yeah! My black suit! Get rid of it! It makes me schvitz like an Armenian, it's so hot!*"

18

So, down at the Salvation Army, they had millions of cobalt-black suits for me to choose from. All shapes and sizes. Take your pick. I fit into a 40 skinny and after searching for a grand total of five seconds, I had put my hands on what I needed, parted ways with less than ten bucks and was now the proud owner of my first Transylvanian outfit. Niiice.

But there was something else I had noticed about Transylvanian costumes when I had seen the Rocky cast the previous week: The basic outfit—black jacket, white shirt and black pants—wasn't nearly enough.

All by itself, the look was way too funereal. You wear just a plain black jacket you're gonna look like a wedding usher, not a Time Warper. You need...stuff. A party hat, maybe. A colorful tie. Some buttons to pin all over the front of it. Maybe a pair of sunglasses.

Now, you might think that Transylvanians in the cast are under the obligation of trying to look like the corresponding Transylvanians on the screen just like everyone else in the cast. After all, the party guests at Frank-N-Furter's place are in the movie too, right? Why shouldn't we, the actors in the movie theater, be assigned certain partygoers and do our best to try to look like them?

There are many reasons why not.

First off, it's too much goddamn work.

Second, who can keep track?

Young people who play Transylvanians in the live Rocky show come and go week to week and cannot be counted upon to show up with anything even remotely resembling consistency. You gonna keep that list of Transylvanians and their corresponding on-screen doubles? Because I'm not.

So the solution is—no list. The normal rules of verisimilitude that are a hallmark of the Rocky shows don't apply in the case of the Transylvanians. Instead, you can wear whatever the hell you want, within these parameters:

Black jacket. Black pants. White shirt.

And bring your five bucks. You don't want to piss Donny off. Beyond that? Go nuts.

So I scoured my bedroom for something suitably Transylvanian. Did I have buttons? I did. But all my stuff was incredibly lame. There's an "I ♥ NY" button. Pathetic. My name tag from my brief career as a bagboy at Publix groceries. Even *more* pathetic. One from Disney World of a scowling Grumpy. Yeesh, this was useless. I grabbed some more of my few remaining dollars (setting aside five for Friday...mustn't forget that) and headed off to the mall.

19

The perfect store for finding appropriate Rocky buttons was located in the Pompano Fashion Square on Federal Highway. As you'd expect, the Fashion Square—being a typical American mall—had the usual selection of large-scale department stores (Sears, Penney's, Burdines) but it also had record stores, bookstores, shoe shops and, right in the center of the place, a quirky little store that every kid in South Florida loved to duck inside, called "The Barefoot Mailman."

I'll describe it a bit, but I think you know this place already. You've probably been to a million little knockoffs of the Barefoot Mailman at some point or another. Every tourist town has a version of it. They sell souvenir shirts from wherever the store happens to be (in this case, a lot of "Pompano Beach, Florida" and "Sunshine State" tees), cheesy junk like shells and pens and suchlike baubles. But in this particular place they also carried oddball stuff. Silly crap. Lowball humor kind of junk.

Here's what I mean: Imagine row upon row of signs to hang on your back deck that say things like "I Don't Swim In Your Toilet So Don't Pee In My Pool" and "Kiss the Chef!" and cornball garbage like that. Next to that, a section for gag gifts (fake vomit, whoopee cushions, etc.) for the fratboy set. Neon beer signs all over the place—some of which had...gasp!...dirty words on them (a prominent one declared "No Bullshit!"). Halloween costumes, crotchless panties and other sexy outfits for kinky couples. Handcuffs, beer bongs, ping-pong paddles, poker chips. The place had everything. And now that I've described it, you know what I mean, right? Walk down any beach-front in the world and you'll see a shop like it.

Okay, now whatever store you've got in your head? Picture it fifty times bigger and with a hundred times the silly crap scattered all over the place. The Walmart of American tourist garbage. *That* was the Barefoot Mailman. Great store.

I ducked inside and walked up to the clerk. "You guys sell buttons in here? Like, pin-on buttons?"

The guy looked at me like I walked into a strip club and asked if they were in any way involved in the naked-boob trade. "Yeah, we got a million stinkin' buttons. There's a bin of 'em over there." He gestured vaguely to a huge tub situated under a giant "NO FAT CHICKS" sign. "Knock yourself out."

I wandered over and...sure enough. There were buttons. Thousands of them. American-flag buttons, smiley-face buttons, some political stuff from the last election ("Carter for President!" "Vote Reagan!"). Buttons of every shape, size and description.

20

Most of them were the type that featured pseudo-witty sayings on them. "Allergic to Normal," "Bitch in Training," "Mustache Rides, 5 Cents." Stuff that seems absolutely *hilarious* right up until five seconds after you buy them.

So I bought a few.

Rooting around in the button bin, though, I came across...well what do you know?...*Rocky buttons*. I was stunned. They were all in there. Frank-N-Furter. Riff Raff. Magenta. Every single character. I'd hit the jackpot.

Still, I didn't want to go overboard. Buy too many of these and I'd risk looking like a Rocky nerd. (Do those exist?) Besides, I was on a budget. I couldn't afford to buy all of them even if I were so inclined. So I picked up a few buttons that appeared to have the *least* stupid sayings on them, three or so that were Rocky-themed (all, curiously, of Riff Raff) and, controlling my impulse to blow my whole wad, I headed to the cash register and home.

Back at my place, I locked myself in my room and began the time-honored tradition of all Transylvanians who have preceded me, preening in front of the mirror while I strategically placed the buttons up and down the lapels of my new/used jacket, and checking out the look.

It is judged to be "sweet."

Now we're cookin'. Now we're ready.

And...it's still *Tuesday.*

Wednesday

Today, I decided, would be devoted to my studies. I'd been messing around all week so far. Time to get serious.

So, in the interest of broadening my education, I broke out the Rocky Horror album and slid it onto the turntable.

Now, as I've said, I already knew the music. But I didn't really *know* it, you know? It wasn't second nature. Singing along seemed forced, not effortless. If I really wanted to be a part of this thing, I had to know this album backward. Which begins with learning it forward.

And I don't mean to get all grandfatherly here with the "you kids today have it so easy" stuff, but I feel the need to remind you: To prepare to do the show that weekend, it wasn't like I could run out to the video store or jump on the Internet and just watch the movie in the comfort of my own home. This was the '80s, okay? The *early* '80s.

Yes, at the time, we had videotapes and, yes, it was possible to watch movies at your house and all that. It wasn't the Stone Age. Like the '70s.

But Rocky hadn't been released on videotape in those days and wouldn't be for years. It had never once been broadcast on television. Hell, it hadn't even made an appearance on HBO because, technically, it was still in wide release. After almost *seven years*.

This meant the most I had seen of Rocky, the sum total of my viewing experience, had been the *one night* when I was actually in the theater. And that was all I would see of it until I actually performed *in the show* that Friday night.

So what did I have in my possession that would help me to properly prepare for my big debut? It turned out that my single source, my whole Rocky world, was confined to a single vinyl disc. I had the cast album and nothing else. And in order to get it down *perfectly*, I decided that I had to memorize it like I was trying to pass the Rocky bar exam.

I locked myself in my room and dropped the needle.

First side. Song number one: "Science Fiction / Double Feature."

This one was not really something I had to worry about, but I memorized it anyway. I had nothing better to do, so why not? But it wasn't like I'd have to perform it. In the film, all that appears on the screen during this song is a pair of lips, painted bright red and stretched across the screen, crooning the number. That's it.

Here was what the Deerfield cast chose to do during this song:

When the lips appeared and began singing, a spotlight shot across the theater and hit these two girls sitting cross-legged at the very center of the movie screen's base. As the song proceeded, the girls performed some very simple—yet intensely compelling—choreography to accompany the words.

They were perfectly matched, these two, movement-wise, but that's where the similarity ended. The girl on the left had long, curly hair that went down past her shoulders and these sultry, heavy-lidded eyes. She wore dark lipstick painted on a pair of lips that were perpetually pulled up into a secretive grin. It was as if she knew something very important but wasn't about to tell you a goddamn thing about it. Very pale skin, an hourglass body and a mysterious air.

The other was a raven-haired stunner whose black locks fell straight down everywhere but in the front. Here, she had pulled her hair into a part and feathered it off to the sides. Her eyes were enormous and she had accentuated this fact by making them pop with this thick (yet, somehow, not *too* thick) eyeliner. Her face was sharper than her partner's but her attitude was right up front. No subtext to this one. Her look said, very plainly, "You have no idea who you're fucking with." And you believed it.

So these two were the show's opening act. They went through their gestures, always seated, very economical, accentuating the lyrics, syncing up perfectly to the words until, finally, the song faded out...and the crowd went nuts.

I couldn't wait to see it again.

But, for now: work.

Song number two.

Next up on the Rocky hit parade: "Dammit Janet." Again, not a song I had to either sing or act out, but it was better to know it than not know it. Besides, the scene that took place *before* this song would be my first time on stage. Everyone in the show, including some of the principal performers, appeared in the opening sequence, when Ralph and Betty get their wedding photo and head off to their honeymoon.

As was the case with the Transylvanians, you weren't necessarily assigned a wedding guest to try to mimic (as far as I could tell) but you had to mill about and pretend to throw rice and all that.

I presumed I would have my duties in this scene explained to me when I arrived at the show on Friday.

Presumption is a funny thing, isn't it?

After "Dammit Janet" came "Over at the Frankenstein Place." I knew that one pretty well already and it didn't take much for me to get it solid. This is a three-hander, between Brad and Janet with a cameo from Riff Raff so, again, not a real problem to nail down.

I was three songs in and so far, so good.

But then, the big number: It was Time Warp time.

This is easily the most famous tune from the show, and I probably knew it better than any other. However, re-learning the song until it was second nature had to be a meticulous process, as this would be my big introduction to the corps of Transylvanians.

A group which would, for the first time, include me. This Friday. In front of a live audience. Just a few short days away—

Okay, *concentrate*. You've got a job to do, so do it.

So...I listened to "The Time Warp." Over and over.

What's fun about it, among other things, is the way the principal singers sort of pass the song back and forth. First it's Riff, then Magenta, then both, then Columbia...it's a real ensemble number. The Narrator sings, the Transylvanians sing...everybody sings.

Hell, even the *audience* sings it. And a lot of them got up and *danced* it, too, the night I was there.

Thing was, though, while I knew the song better than any song in the world by the time I'd gotten to the tenth repetition, I didn't know *any* of the choreography besides the main instructions (jump to the left...step to the right, etc.). What was the blocking? How do you avoid plowing into one of the principals?

I'd have to stay on my toes. I was hoping for someone to guide me.

Hope is a funny thing too, am I right?

On about the fifteenth iteration of the song, my mother knocked on the bedroom door and stuck her head in.

"I think you've listened to that one enough. I've memorized it myself. Move on."

I moved on.

"Sweet Transvestite." When they rank the top five oddest songs of all time, this one better be up there near the top. Totally bizarre tune.

This one involved some Transylvanian blocking, too, but what it was would remain a mystery until I got some sort of guidance. As it was my duty, I spent some time with that song as well, but not too much. My main work on the show was almost done.

Because after that number, the Transylvanians disappeared for a good long while, only to return to watch the big science experiment up in the lab. So no worries there, I thought.

Once we got to the lab, it looked to me like the Transylvanians did nothing more than a lot of watching. For example, there was a scene between Brad, Janet and Frank, followed by a short speech by Frank, then the birth of Rocky, Rocky's song, another scene, and then, finally, the number "I Can Make You a Man," which basically involved only Frank and Rocky, everyone else taking a little break.

After that, though, came "Hot Patootie." I figured this would be more difficult, as Eddie gets on his bike at the end of the song and basically drives it through the crowd of Transylvanians. Again, I'd have to wait and see what my movement was going to be. But the first order of business was knowing the song like I'd written it.

The reprise of "I Can Make You a Man" is trickier than the first, as it involves actual Frank-N-Furter/Transylvanian interaction but here's the good news: After that, I'd be done. No more work for the night. I could just sit back and enjoy the show.

So I had done my homework. I had committed even the smallest little lyrical oddities from the movie to memory and driven my family, listening in the next room, positively batshit in the process. I was as ready as anyone had ever been.

If. Only. Friday. Would. Arrive.

Thursday

As I may have mentioned, I had a really cool Mom. And many of you reading this are thinking: "Me too."

Here's the bad news: You didn't.

I mean, I'm sure you *think* you did. But the truth is you did not. I know this will come as a blow, but it's a simple fact: Your Mom was not cool. Mine was.

Don't get all defensive. Let's break it down: Your Mom was maybe really lax with the rules or totally flexible with the curfew, let you stay up until the wee hours, run wild in the house and live your own life. Therefore, this hands-off, do-what-you-will attitude made her cool, right?

No, actually, it didn't.

Maybe, instead, your Mom was incredibly strict, demanding that you get home early, homework done and in the sack by 9. Because she cared. It was her adherence to the rule of law, her deep, abiding love of *structure* that made her cool, am I right?

No, it decidedly did not. And I know that's tough to hear.

My mother, on the other hand, was cool. Here's why: First, she was on her own. Raising two young boys without any help at all and, most importantly, not fucking it up automatically gives you an aura of coolness. After all, you're stepping up, doing the right thing, proving that you're Superwoman. Single mothers who have their shit together? That's the essence of cool.

More than that, our Mom was this wonderfully affectionate person, in that unique, old-school, Irish mother kind of way. Man, try to leave my house without giving Mom a kiss goodbye, she'd flay you alive.

Best of all, she trusted us. Not to the point of, "Hey, here's the car keys, don't bother telling me where you're going," or anything. But she knew she hadn't raised morons and treated us accordingly.

Here's one of Mom's rules (Do yourself a favor—teach it to your kids. You'll thank me later): If you're at a party (she told us) and you find yourself messed up on either drugs or alcohol, *stay there*. Don't get in a car, don't try to hitchhike home or do anything stupid like that. Instead, perform two simple tasks: (1) Call home and let Mom know where you are and then (2) go pass out on a couch or something. Do *not* attempt to get home when you're all fucked up. That's how kids get killed. Try to *avoid* getting wasted if you could, she said, but if you suddenly found yourself on the other side of the street from sober? *Don't move.*

And what do you know? I'm still alive.

I always thought my Mom could have been anything she wanted to be. Sadly, however, my mother's strongest character trait was a complete and utter lack of ambition. Her idea of living a successful life was being able to afford to sit on the back deck of her house, crack open a can of beer, spark up a Virginia Slim and relax by the pool. Her opinion was that if she could enjoy these tiny luxuries and still manage to keep her kids clothed, fed and educated, she was way ahead of the game. Achieving these simple, modest goals—this was the sum total of her hopes and ambitions.

And she realized her dream without ever seeming to break a sweat.

For our part, David and I were latchkey kids. We came home to an empty house almost every day. The reason for this was that, in order to make the bacon, my Mom worked in a bar. She slung drinks at a joint called "Ed's Hideaway" from noon to 7 on weeknights, Sundays from 5 to midnight, the tip money going toward our daily fare. This schedule meant that, on most days, nobody would be home after school. We'd see her all day Saturday, but come Sunday night, we were on our own.

But while the house was indeed empty of parental units during these odd hours, it was not empty of the essentials.

See, Mom's main hobby was cooking. She was a maniac in the kitchen. Trouble was, she had no sense of proportion. There were only three of us in the house, yes. But it was simply not possible for my mother to cook a meal for less than a small army. So when she made a batch of Chicken Tetrazzini, it lasted for weeks. *Weeks.* And you never got tired of it, it was that good.

Her chili? It could have kept an entire regiment battle-ready for a fortnight. Her ox-tail soup, a particular specialty, was kept in gallon containers in the freezer, ready whenever we wanted a bowl or two.

And her smoked ham. Dear God. She actually had a hickory smoker built in the backyard out of an old oil drum, hinged in the middle and chock-full of hickory chips, and she regularly *smoked the hams herself.*

Suffice it to say, the woman liked to prepare *food.*

The only thing I can say against her—and as long as we're being honest I should just mention it and get it out of the way—is this: She was the worst judge of character imaginable. This failing of hers—her inability to spot bums, derelicts and con men—tended to make life a little tough for us. Her many friends, assorted confidants and, most especially, her occasional male companions...she really could pick the losers of the bunch, sad to say.

It killed me to witness the cast of sub-par characters that drifted through her life. And not a one...not a *single one* was worth the shovel-full of dirt it would have taken to bury them.

My Mom? She trusted them all implicitly. Right up until the day they disappointed her, cheated on her or ripped her off. It drove my brother and me completely nuts.

> *Charlie needed some money, so I lent it to him. Big deal. He'll pay me back.*
>
> *Mom, Charlie is a complete coke-head. You're never seeing that money again.*
>
> *Oh, stop being so cynical. He's a good guy. I know him. He'll pay me back, you watch.*

This happened a lot. There were a lot of Charlies. But what could you do? She had this completely unjustified, unwavering faith in human nature. Yes, she got burned and was abandoned by these people over and over again, but through it all she never lost her essential belief that, at the end of the day, people were good at heart and that, given the opportunity, they would step up and do the right thing.

My brother and I, in watching our mother, saw exactly what it meant to nurture a kindhearted and trusting spirit. And through her experiences, the two of us gleaned the most valuable life lesson of all. Here it is:

Trust no one. People are snakes. Be careful.

Is that a great teacher or *what*?

Needless to say, when it came time to get permission to do the Rocky show, I wasn't really that worried Mom would kill the idea. She was supportive, but careful. Fun-loving, but not reckless. And this sort of adventure was right up her alley.

The Rocky show, I explained to her, was slightly mischievous but still controlled. Sexually charged but not pornographic. And it took place late at night, sure, but...well, what 16-year-old doesn't blow their curfew?

She agreed, reluctantly, to let me join the cast and appeared happy to know that I'd be spending most of my weekends at the movie theater down the street. As long as my grades didn't suffer, she was all for it.

In other words, she was totally cool.

Unlike, for example, *your* mom.

I'm just saying.

Friday

The day had finally arrived and, to celebrate, I was up at dawn's crack.

This was mistake. After all, the show didn't even start until midnight, roughly eighteen hours away. By the time showtime finally rolled around, the likelihood was that I would be running on fumes. Falling asleep at my first Rocky show would not be an auspicious start.

On the other hand, there was a chance I'd be so ramped up, I wouldn't be able to sleep *after* the show either. Truth was, I didn't know what was going to happen and that's what made it so spine-tingling.

I was practically bouncing off the walls at breakfast and driving my Mom crazy.

"Knock off the coffee. You've had enough."

"Haven't touched it, Mom. I'm just keyed up about tonight."

"How are you getting there?"

I hadn't really thought about it. "Walking, I guess. It's only about a mile and a half."

"If you get a lift home, be careful who you ride with. You don't know these people."

"Gotcha."

My brother was a little mystified by all the hype. "What's the big deal?" he said. "It's just a movie."

I shook my head in disbelief. What is *wrong* with this kid? I just didn't get that he didn't get it. He had *been there* when Uncle Mike had spun that disc for us the very first time. Hell, he was there with me just last weekend and seen the show himself. How could he not have caught the same Rocky virus that infected me? How could that experience have seemed to him—or to *anyone*—to be so uninteresting?

But he could not have cared less. It was mystifying. So, since I couldn't fathom his complete apathy, I decided that he simply must have an immunity. He was able to resist the RHPS strain because of a Rocky vaccine he'd received as a child, perhaps.

Oddly, I was the one with the sickness, but I felt sorry for *him*.

Time for school. I kissed my Mom goodbye (rules are rules) and headed out the door.

School moved at a *glacial* pace. First period took hours, it seemed. Lunch was easily a month long. And the last class of the day was roughly the duration of the Cretaceous Period. I was living for nothing more than to hear the last bell ring.

I was strung tighter than a piano wire, but I shared nothing about the source of my tension with any of my classmates. They simply *would not* understand.

Just as the watched pot *will* eventually boil even if you stare at it, so the final bell will sound, even if you count the seconds. The buzzer finally, wonderfully went off, announcing the end of the school day and I blew home in a whirlwind.

As usual, I was alone at our place as Mom's shift didn't end until 7. But, of course, the refrigerator was chock-full of goodies and I was all set for dinner.

Until recently, my brother and I had been using the oven to heat up the dinners Mom left for us. But about six months earlier, Mom had come back from the store with that status symbol of the early '80s: a microwave oven. This, you may be surprised to learn, was a pretty extravagant purchase for us poor folk.

What it meant, though, was that David and I could now have meals that used to take half an hour to prepare ready-to-eat in about a minute. It was miraculous.

This was an early version of the microwave, though, not one of your tiny little modern gizmos. The thing was roughly the size of a big-screen television set. It heated up your food all right, but the way it went about its business was terrifying. The moment you turned it on, this monstrosity would roar to life, making a sound so horrifically loud that your first reaction was to back out of the room with a lead shield over your crotch, certain that the radio waves shooting out of this thing were strong enough to fry your gonads.

Still, it beat having to *wait*.

At the conclusion of my tasty little meal, I suddenly found myself with absolutely nothing to do and simply *hours* to do it in. In my haste and excitement, I had (a) arrived home, (b) eaten my dinner, (c) breezed through whatever homework I might have had for the weekend and (d) lined up all my Rocky clothes for the night all in the hope of keeping busy and making the time pass more quickly. Now I was done and it was...about 5:30 in the afternoon. The sun was just starting to set, for crying out loud, and I didn't need to be anywhere for more than five hours.

I couldn't just stare at the walls, but...what to do? Simple: I listened to the album. Again. By then, of course, I could sing along to every song from beginning to end and I didn't even have to think about them anymore. In fact, the only ones I didn't know letter-perfect were the songs where the lyrics are completely unintelligible.

"Hot Patootie" is a great example of this. Meatloaf sings the hell out of the song, but it was months before I knew what in the world he was saying. A sample of one of these indecipherable lyrics goes, in reality, like this:

> *My head used to swim from the perfume I smelled,*
> *My hands kind of fumbled with her white plastic belt.*
> *I'd taste her baby pink lipstick and that's when I'd melt.*
> *She whispered in my ear tonight she really was mi-ine.*

However, it is sung at a machine-gun pace, so I couldn't possibly catch the real words. To me, it was more like:

> *My hair kinda stank from the purseful of smelt*
> *My pants had a rumble, it's a wide jazzy belt.*
> *I'd tape on Mr. Mxyzptlk and that's when I felt*
> *She weetzie beanie pixie stick, she really was fi-ine.*

Hell, I didn't get ANY of it.

Most of the songbook, though, I had down cold. Frigid, baby. I was ready. Sharp set. Let's go.

But now the album was over and showtime was still *hours* away.

I killed time. Watched TV. Dressed up in my Transylvanian outfit. Took it off again. I was fidgety. Restless. Bored as shit.

Finally, as the time to leave approached, I realized I had a conundrum: Do I change into the Transylvanian outfit here at the house and walk over to the theater *in costume* or...do I bring my clothes to the theater and change there? It was a real puzzle. My concern was that I would arrive in full regalia and be the only one all dressed up. Nothing like starting off your first day looking like a total tool. Equally upsetting was the idea that I would be the only one to show up *without* my outfit and...I'd look like an equally humungous tool.

I decided to split the difference. I'd wear my black pants and white shirt to the theater but carry the Transylvanian jacket in a bag. This seemed the wisest move, as pedestrians wandering about at night on the South Florida streets might not cotton to guys strolling down the sidewalk wearing buttons on their lapels asking, "If I Said You Had a Great Body, Would You Hold It Against Me?"

Incognito seemed the way to go.

Even walking as slowly as I possibly could, I got to the theater twenty minutes earlier than my 11:00 call time. The main feature at the movie house hadn't even let out yet. The current movie playing at the Ultravision was the dark comedy "Neighbors," starring John Belushi and Dan Aykroyd. I had seen it the previous week. Meh. Not much to it.

With time to kill (and not wanting to be the first one to arrive for the show), I wandered over to the taco joint situated on the north side of the movie theater parking lot. The restaurant had a big window, which allowed me to sit and watch for the cast to arrive from a safe distance and not look too anxious.

I nibbled a quesadilla and watched the clock. The minute hand was torturing me, appearing not to move at all. Finally, I noticed that feature had let out. People streamed out the exit doors and drifted to their cars. They piled in. Pulled away. All typical, Friday night, nothing-to-see-here behavior.

And then...the Rocky people started to arrive.

You could tell exactly who they were. They didn't wear cotton print dresses and polo shirts. No sensible shoes, oversized purses and gold necklaces on these people. No, that was how the folks getting in their cars and *leaving* were dressed.

31

The Rocky folks, the ones getting *out* of their cars, wore tight leather pants and leopard-print shirts. They sported feathered roach clips as hair accessories. They wore too much eye makeup, blasted "Bat Out of Hell" from their car windows and talked way too loud.

And they *all* smoked.

The regular folks, the ones pulling out of the lot after a lovely evening at the movies, looked pretty much done-in for the day. They looked like they wanted nothing more than to get home, crawl into bed and conk-out for the night.

They were done. Spent. Their evening was finished.

But the people they left behind in the lot? *My* people?

They looked *ready*.

In The Velvet Darkness

After about a dozen or so of the Rocky folks had arrived in the parking lot, I figured it was safe to drift over and begin to mingle with the crowd. I grabbed my bag and headed toward the theater, strolling as casually as I could.

The closer I got, the more gun-shy I became about simply walking up and introducing myself to someone. Luckily, I saw that Donny had also arrived (it was hard to miss him) and, despite his fearsome appearance, I felt the most comfortable approaching him. The two of us, at least, had conversed before.

As I neared the cast, I tried to take them in and absorb every detail about them. Theoretically, assuming things worked out, this was to be my new crowd. The sooner I got to know them, the better.

It was a mixed bunch, age-wise. All the girls and most of the boys looked to be in their teens, but there were guys who were clearly in their early 20s here, too. One of them looked to be pushing 30 by my reckoning, and there was one old man. (By old, I mean he was in his 50s. A coot.)

I skirted the main crowd and sort of sidled up to Donny.

"Hey," I said. I really know how to kick off a conversation.

"Hey yourself," he said, looking me over. "You here to join up?"

At this, I'll admit, I was a little disappointed. He clearly didn't remember me at all from the previous week. Then it occurred to me: Why should he? He ran a thirty-person cast that probably featured a revolving door of young punks like me drifting in and out of the show. Add to this the fact that, in our one and only encounter, we had talked for about ten seconds, max, and it made perfect sense. In actuality, it would have been pretty damned impressive if he *had* remembered me.

"Yeah, I am. Should I get a ticket, or...?"

"No, no. If you're in the cast, you're in for free. Don't worry about it."

There was an awkward moment. I struggled to fill the void. "You said to bring five bucks...?" I offered.

"Oh, right. That's just your initiation fee. One time only. We also have cast dues, but it's only a buck a week. What's your name again?"

"I'm Jack." Man, it felt good saying that. *Jack.*

"Right, Jack. I'm Donny," he waved a massive arm toward the small crowd. "You'll get to know everyone eventually, if you stick around long enough."

"Great." Donny took a pull on a long cigarette, relaxed.

I was antsy. "So, can I help with the setup or anything?"

"In a minute, yeah," said Donny, then he called out, "Hey, Doc!" The older guy jerked his head around. He was barrel-chested with a gray-white crew cut and a Hemingway beard. It was 11 at night and the guy sported tinted shades and a military bearing.

Donny motioned to me. "Got a new kid. Have him help you with the props and shit, okay?"

"Sure," the guy looked me over and stuck out a meaty paw. "I'm Doc."

I shook. "Jack." Now it was official. Two people knew my new name.

Doc glanced at his watch. "Better get a move on, I guess. The theater should be empty by now." Doc looked over to this younger, good-looking kid with hair down to his shoulders and said, "Go in with Don and open the door. I'll get the stuff."

The young kid nodded and drifted off with Donny and the rest of the cast as they moved toward the front of the theater. Doc motioned to me.

"This way, kid. We got storage around back." He tapped another young guy on the shoulder, a shiny-faced kid with dark hair and big eyes, just a little older than me. "You too. Come on."

As the young kid and I followed Doc around to the back of the theater, he stuck out a hand.

"I'm Steve."

"Jack. Good to meet you."

"You too. Your first night?"

"Yeah, you?"

"Yup. I saw it last week and thought I'd give it a try."

34

For one thing, we knew there was the possibility that Doc was having a laugh at our expense. Maybe this was some kind of Rocky hazing, Doc's hilarious play-a-joke-on-the-rookies gag. "Hey, I got the newbies to go change in the women's toilet!"

Har-de-fuckin'-har-har.

So we stood there for a few minutes, looking completely moronic, until at last one of the older guys from the show, a guy I hadn't met yet, came out of the theater, walked straight across the lobby and, as naturally as you please, walked right into the ladies' room without a second thought.

That was all the prompting we needed. Steve and I followed him in as casually as if we were walking into an elevator.

An elevator full of half-naked teenage girls, that is.

Here's a tip: When you walk into a room and find yourself surrounded by a gaggle of young ladies you've never met before standing around in their underwear, the best thing you can do is to remain *cool*. Try to act as if this is a commonplace occurrence in your life. In fact, reacting *in any way* is something you want to avoid altogether. Any slight reaction, no matter how small, will not go unnoticed.

To our credit, Steve and I managed not to point or stare or say, "Holy shit, I can totally see your boobs," or anything *untoward*. We just went about our business getting ready for the show and completely ignored the fleshy, undulating surroundings in which we suddenly found ourselves. We just did our best to tune it out.

Well, I mean...not *completely*. But we did pretty well, considering.

One of the things that Donny hadn't mentioned to me about appearing as a Transylvanian (and something I probably should have figured out for myself) is that every one of them is expected to appear in whiteface, along with lipstick and eyeliner to accentuate the features. Due to his omission of this fact, I had, therefore, committed a minor Rocky *faux pas* by not showing up with the proper makeup.

Fortunately, there was plenty of extra to go around (Steve had brought his own and was nice enough to offer it) and pretty soon—after some careful application—I had the Transylvanian greasepaint in place. The result was that you basically appeared as if you were an actor from the silent film era. Mack Sennett would have been proud. And while the look itself isn't all that attractive up close, it's effective as hell once you're on stage.

As we went about the business of applying the face paint, Steve and I slowly realized that there was a backstage patter going on that was well worth a listen. The nonstop back-and-forth of the cast was hard to ignore.

"I about wrenched my fuckin' neck on that twirl last week. Donny's gotta learn to slow the hell down." This from one of the girls that did the opening "Science Fiction" number in front of the screen. I think she also doubled as Columbia, but I couldn't be sure. Her voice had a slight New York twang to it, but running across a New York accent in South Florida is more common than finding sand in your crotch after a trip to the beach.

"So talk to him. Don't just bitch about it." This came from her top-of-the-show partner, whom I recognized as the girl who also played Magenta. There was no mistaking her.

Both of these girls had different versions of the same basic persona: tough as nails and completely unapproachable.

I was content just to listen.

Next to them was the guy who played Frank-N-Furter and he was applying his makeup the way DaVinci must have painted the Mona Lisa. Sllooowly. Carefully. Like he had all year. (He had a later entrance than most of the cast and could get away with taking his time.) And his patience was paying off. Frank's makeup is, until the finale, sharp, clean and perfect, and watching him carefully etch it onto his face was mesmerizing. When he was done, this guy was going to look amazing.

He added his two cents to the conversation. "Someone's got to tell Jackie to change her panties before the show if she's going to fuck Barry on the way here. By the time we get to the bedroom scene it's like a goddamn fish market down there."

Everyone laughed. I could hardly believe what I was hearing. Did they always talk like this?

Next to "Frank" (I didn't know anyone's names yet) was the guy getting ready to play Riff Raff. Silent, but no less intent at putting on his makeup, he exuded the kind of calm coolness that comes from both (a) not giving a shit about the drama swirling around him and (b) secretly really giving a shit but hiding it really well.

He was tall—almost a head taller than anyone else in the room—but rail thin. He had enormous eyes and an equally huge nose that he was accentuating with some brown blush. When he was done with the makeup, he reached over and pulled a bald-cap wig from this little mannequin head on the counter and slipped it onto his head. He centered it on his cranium, arranged the wisps of hair and in less than a minute, *voila*, he was Riff Raff.

I hoped these people didn't mind that I was eyeballing them so shamelessly but, the truth is, I might as well have been invisible. This was the locker room before the big game and they had better things to do than worry about the towel boy.

Finally, word drifted in that they were going to open up the house to the audience. Steve and I, now suited up, drifted back toward the theater.

As we passed through the lobby I saw the line outside. It looked like a good crowd. I'm not much at estimating these things, but it appeared to be easily a couple hundred people. The manager of the theater got the high sign from Doc that we were ready and the gates were opened.

As we walked into the theater, I heard the words, "*Check! Check! This is a fucking sound check!*" boom over the speakers and saw this tough-looking, bearded Italian guy standing at the front of the house with a big microphone stand, testing the equipment. The pre-show was about to start.

In groups of twos and threes, the audience members slowly made their way into the theater and down the aisles. As they entered they were greeted by their host—who introduced himself as Tony—calling out to everyone as they entered the auditorium, "*Welcome to 'The Rocky Horror Picture Show,' ladies and gentlemen! Have a seat anywhere! We'll get to you in just a minute!*" He wore a dark suit, a red ascot and a no-nonsense expression. "*Sit the fuck down, I said! We've got a lot to do and very little time to do it in!*"

The seating area filled up fast. Some of the patrons, though not many, were dressed up in character costumes. I saw a Magenta (sexy maid) and a Columbia (though she appeared to have gotten the costume wrong) and there was one brave guy in a Frank-N-Furter bustier and face makeup, but the poor guy looked like he had applied the makeup with a spatula.

The rest of the crowd was a real demographic mix. There didn't appear to be a specific Rocky "type" in the audience; they came in all shapes and sizes. Some were young, some old; some cute, a few scary; a couple that were big and fat and a few who were sexy as hell. And they just kept coming.

Tony, for his part, was whipping up the crowd.

"*Gimme an R!*"

The crowd roared back "*R!*"

"*Gimme an O!*"

"*O!*"

"*Gimme a C!*"

"C!"

"Gimme a K!"

"K!"

"Gimme a Y!"

"Y!"

"What's that spell?"

"Rocky!"

"I can't hear you!" Tony bellowed.

"ROCKY!"

"WHAT?!?!"

"ROCKY!!!!" Now they were howling. Tony looked unimpressed. That was his job. The audience had to *earn* his respect.

In addition to revving the assembled patrons into a frenzy before the show began, Tony clearly had a set list of things he needed to run through, including some rules (which seemed very important) and a few announcements. One such announcement was that a young lady would be walking among the crowd soliciting donations for the cast.

"We might do this shit for free, but it doesn't mean it don't cost nothing," Tony informed the audience. "So if you can spare a couple of bucks to keep the props and costumes looking good, we'd appreciate it. Hell, Jackie might just show you her tits if you're lucky."

"Fuck you, Tony!" yelled the girl from across the theater who was, presumably, Jackie.

"Sorry, my fault," Tony yelled back. "The tits cost you five."

"You're goddamn right!"

The rules of the house, which Tony took pains to impart, were pretty straightforward. You could throw stuff, but nothing dangerous. Stay out of the aisles when people are running around the theater in costume (this happened a couple times during the show). And if you get a little wet or hit by a piece of toast or something, try not to be a big pussy about it.

Then, as he seemed to near the end of his spiel, Tony asked, very casually, "Say, is anybody here for the first time?"

A few hands, maybe twenty or so, shot up. Why not? What did they know?

Tony's eyes suddenly burned red as he leaped into action. He jabbed a finger at the Transylvanians and hollered, *"Go get 'em, girls! Bring me those goddamn virgins right this fucking second!"*

Three or four cast members, all ladies, swarmed into the crowd and plucked the first-timers out of their chairs, dragging them to the front of the theater. (This had happened to me the previous week and I had *loved* it.) Most of the patrons being pulled onto the stage seemed perfectly happy to come, as this ritual was either expected or seemed harmless. Tony had them all line up in front of the crowd.

"Let's hear it for our virgins, ladies and gentlemen, aren't they great?"

The crowd went wild.

The method of deflowering virgins at Rocky shows varies from cast to cast. Some are more daring than others in what they demand of their virgins but, at the Deerfield show, the ceremony was pretty tame. The participants had to pledge their undying fealty to the Rocky show, of course. They were given a rudimentary Time Warp lesson. Ceremonial paddlings were threatened, but never administered. Finally, they had to swear not to reveal anything about the show to their virgin friends. All told, it was nothing more than a semi-formal "Welcome to Rocky, get ready to enjoy yourselves" kind of thing.

Finally, the initiation was over and the no-longer virgins were led back to their seats. The performers filed into the room as Tony finished up the pre-show with a final, cacophonous cheer, bringing the energy level in the auditorium to its peak.

The show was about to begin.

So...pop quiz: What *didn't* happen before the show? Did you catch it? Did you notice the *one thing* that appeared to be missing from the whole pre-show business?

That's right: Nobody had explained to me or to Steve just *what the hell we were supposed to do during the performance.*

Clearly, joining the Rocky cast involved on-the-job training. We were going to learn how to swim, but the teaching method this cast employed was to throw you in the deep end of the pool, lob an anvil at you and wish you good luck.

Needless to say, when we realized that we would be improvising as we went along, the blood froze in our veins. The very idea was utterly terrifying. Terrifying *and* exciting, perhaps. But definitely equal parts of both.

I checked in with Steve to see if he had been given any sort of guidance or advice to which I remained ignorant. "Do you have a clue what to...you know...*do*?" I asked him. "I mean, once the show begins? Anything?"

Steve looked about as shit-scared as I was. "No way," he said. "I guess we just...figure it out, huh?"

Our eyes must have been as big as saucers when the lights went down.

Donny spotted the two of us huddled off to the side and corralled us just as the projector flickered to life.

"Hey, listen," he said. "You're gonna be fine. Just find a few other Transylvanians and follow their lead. And try not to get in anyone's way. Understand?"

Steve and I bobbed our heads up and down vigorously. "Absolutely," I stammered out. "No problem."

"Great. Have fun." Donny stalked away.

Steve and I looked at each other, each attempting to look calm.

"Here we go," he said.

The lights had faded entirely. The projector was alive. The crowd roared.

It had begun.

Unconventional Conventionists

O h, you thought the Rocky movie was going to start right then, didn't you?

Not quite. I mean, whenever you go to the movies, just before the feature begins, you've got to have coming attractions, right? Things were no different at the Rocky show.

Well, things were slightly different. See, before *this* movie began, you didn't watch previews for movies that were *about* to come out. You watched previews for movies that came out years and years ago.

The coming attractions at the Deerfield Ultravision midnight movie were all classic trailers. They ran previews for "The Blues Brothers," "Animal House," the Beatles' "Help!"; films that most of us had already seen a dozen times. The audience went crazy for them. It put them right in the mood.

All during the previews, cast members scurried around in the dark getting ready. I didn't really get a sense that the main event was about to begin until, at last, everybody stopped fussing and finally settled down. Half of the cast was making their way to the ramp under the screen so they could look up at the two girls performing the opening number. Steve and I, lemmings that we were, joined them. Donny himself was perched dead center. His approach to this ritual was almost religious, the way he sat cross-legged at the bottom of the ramp staring placidly up at the screen, a contented smile plastered across his face.

All of a sudden, the screen went black and the crowd started chanting, *"We want lips! We want lips! We want lips!"*

Then the opening music kicked in, and the bright red lips appeared, very small, on the screen. They continued to swell in size until the smile was fifty, sixty, seventy feet across. The audience was howling their approval.

Very slowly, the spotlight came up on the two girls center stage. At that moment, the lips on the screen parted...and started to sing.

The previous week, I had seen this pair go through their rendition of "Science Fiction / Double Feature" from about halfway back in the theater. It was a sight to behold, even at that distance.

But now, practically sitting in their laps, I could hardly stand it. They had sexual vibes pouring off them in waves and I was sitting at the epicenter of this erotic tsunami.

As before, they were sharply in sync with each other. They seemed to sense the other's precise movements, down to the last detail, even before either of them moved. And it wasn't simply that they were performing pre-arranged choreography. It was more intricately detailed than that, their symmetry. There was the slight flick of the wrist here. A momentary turn of the head there. Their timing was impeccable. Watching them move together was a study in precision.

Despite all this, they each somehow managed to maintain their own individual style throughout the entire song. The one on the right, the smaller one, had this bad-girl, dangerous thing going on (which, um, really worked on many levels). She was the more aggressive of the two, slightly sharper in her movements but, in every way, completely sensual. But for all her obvious attractions I was—for reasons I could not explain—falling madly, deeply in love with the girl on the left. The Magenta. A girl whose name I didn't even know.

Her hair was impossibly curly and just rained down around her shoulders. She had a thin, aquiline nose and these secretive eyes that looked right through you. Her face, as was required of Magentas, was a deathly pale, slashed through with a bloody red mouth. And while she was deadly serious at her task, moving through her movements to accompany and accentuate the song, there was a smile playing around her lips that seemed to say, "Hey, is this fun or what?"

I understood Donny's attraction immediately. Who wouldn't want to spend the rest of their lives sitting here, drinking in this smoldering post-pubescent display of forbidden desire?

For my part, I wanted nothing more than to stay right where I was for the whole number, but about three-quarters through the song, I felt a tug on my jacket. Steve was motioning to me to follow him, so I reluctantly scooted down the ramp and made my way to the stage-left side.

Steve hissed at me, "*The wedding!*"

I had completely forgotten, in my reverie, that I actually had a show to perform.

"*Right!*" I whispered back. "*I'm all set. Where do we go?*"

I stumped him there. He hadn't the slightest idea.

We looked around and finally spotted a cluster of people gathering in the dark at the top of the ramp to our right. We thought it best to join them and sidled over. And since no one screamed, "What the fuck are you doing here?" we figured we were in the right place.

And, you want to know something? That, in a nutshell, is exactly how a young performer learns to do the Rocky show. You get up on stage, you go where you think you should go and, unless someone says, "What the fuck are you doing here?" you're doing an excellent job.

Apparently, we did an excellent job. Well, through the wedding scene, anyway. Steve and I stayed in our little cluster of guests and when the others on stage posed for the wedding picture, we struck a pose and smiled. When they waved to Ralph and Betty as they "drove" off, we waved, too. And when the other guests eventually wandered away, we wandered with them.

Then…the scene was over. We had survived. We didn't bump into Brad or Janet or anyone else. We hadn't engendered any harsh, urgent whispers, we had managed not to step on anyone and, best of all, we had not been invited to go fuck ourselves. Steve and I, for the first time in our lives, had performed in a scene in "The Rocky Horror Picture Show"…

…and we had not, as far as we knew, sucked at it.

Before we move on to the rest of this evening's festivities, there is another very important thing about the Rocky experience that I feel compelled to relate and, really, there cannot be too much emphasis placed upon this aspect of the performance:

The costumes. The costumes have to be absolutely, dead-on right.

Now, Steve and I—like most of the people up on the stage—were dressed similarly at the top of the show. We had the Transylvanian uniform I've already described: black jackets and pants, white shirts and neckties, various party hats, dark sunglasses and, of course, our buttons. Our hundreds and hundreds of buttons. But our pseudo-uniformity should have been the big tip-off that we were the lowest rung on the ladder. After all, we weren't even under an obligation to bother looking like anyone in particular on the screen. We just had to look like we'd *fit in* with that crowd. We were the Rocky equivalent of wallpaper.

But the principals? Well. That was another story altogether.

In case you need one last refresher, here are the main characters in the movie, in no particular order: Brad and Janet (the hapless couple who stumble into this adventure), Riff Raff and Magenta (the servants at the castle), Columbia and Eddie (a groupie and her beloved biker dude), Dr. Scott (a professor), Rocky (the Creation), the Narrator (a narrator) and, of course, the Big Kahuna himself, Dr. Frank-N-Furter. As I said, there were some additional incidental players, like Ralph and Betty Hapschatt (the couple who get married at the top of the film), but the principals were- forever and always- the primary focus.

This was the varsity squad. And as with any group of A-Listers, you had to *earn* a spot on that team. I very soon discovered that achieving this goal could take months. Years, even. If it happened at all.

But back to the costumes: If the Transylvanians' outfits were acceptably slapdash (nobody seemed to care if, for example, your suit jacket even matched your pants or gave a flying crap what your buttons said), the principals' costumes were subject to a level of exactitude that would have impressed a drill sergeant.

Obviously, the goal was to look as much like the on-screen character as possible. Janet, up on the screen, walks through the rain in a pink dress and white sweater so, naturally, the goal of our Janet was to find a similar pink dress and white sweater. Sounds easy, right?

Not quite. Janet's pink dress also had to have a pink gingham collar, feature a gold script "Janet" necklace and had to unzip down the back (let me emphasize: *had* to unzip down the back). Plus the barrettes. And the *collarless* white sweater. Not to mention the underwear. Once could write a book about the underwear *alone*. (In fact, one should.)

So, while I had spent two minutes, tops, in the thrift store looking for my black suit, young girls aspiring to be up-and-coming Janets would spend months scouring South Florida's second-hand stores for just the right dress, hat and underwear combo. For them, nailing Janet's look *precisely* was serious business and they did everything they could to look as much like Susan Sarandon as it was possible to look.

Then there was Brad. Brad's jacket and plaid cummerbund had to be the *exact* design as the one Barry Bostwick wore. What's more, for the approach to the castle, the windbreaker Brad sported in the rainstorm had to match up perfectly, down to the Denton High School patch on the front. Ditto the tighty-whitey underpants revealed in the undressing scene. And, of course, the glasses.

But for the really, really serious Brads, you also had to have a picture-perfect blue kimono to be worn in the latter half of the film (the post-bedroom scenes). The *truly* efficient and studious Brads even went so far as to find the exact same pair of *socks*. (Come to think of it, Brad had a *lot* of costume changes. That's a ton of work for a guy who gets called an asshole all night.)

The character of Rocky was a breeze, comparatively. All he needed was a pair of skin-tight, gold hot pants. Pretty easy there. But the part also required a nice pair of pectoral muscles as well and let me tell you—those aren't easy to find.

Magenta needed a hot maid outfit but, happily, they're sold everywhere. Sexy maid outfits, it will not surprise you to learn, are *very* popular. But the trick was: You had to look *good* in it. Think that's easy? Try it.

Riff Raff sported a ripped-up tux jacket—with tails—and a white vest that looked as if you had pulled it out of the wrong end of a rhino. Cool boots were also a big plus. The skull cap was optional, but preferred. And brown gloves with no fingers. Those were a necessity.

Eddie sported a basic biker look. Motorcycle boots, jeans, leather jacket and a Gestapo-looking helmet. But the jacket had to be tricked out just right—sleeveless, with a sun flare painted on the back along with the word "BABY" across the top, the chains draped below and, if you could manage it, a bit of leopard fur peeking out the front. Most important, the saxophone, which Eddie uses to great effect during his song. A final touch is a bizarre slingshot-looking necklace draped on his chest, but only the hardcore Eddies remember to include it.

Dr. Scott? Piece of cake: button-down shirt, tie, dark suit, glasses, mustache. Oh, and one fishnet stocking. Just one. (Keep Dr. Scott's fishnet stocking in mind, if you would. It will figure prominently later in the story.)

So clearly (and to varying degrees), the costumes for the Rocky principals are extremely difficult to put together. That said, there is no question that the toughest costumes to acquire in the entire cast were the outfits worn by Columbia, Frank-N-Furter and the performers in the Floor Show.

Columbia was, essentially, a walking sequin. She sported a rainbow-sequined vertically striped tube top, vertically striped rainbow shorts, flawless fishnet stockings (no rips), black-rhinestone-studded tap shoes, a gold-sequined tuxedo jacket with black trim, pink-sequined bowtie and a gold-sequined top hat. Oh, and if you could manage it, shocking pink-red hair.

These days, you can find an outfit like that on eBay and in a few clicks have it delivered to your doorstep. But back then, girls had to *make* them.

Frank-N-Furter was clad in full-on transvestite gear, of course. From bottom to top, it went a little something like this: black and silver high-heeled platform shoes, fishnet stockings, garters, black underwear, black bustier (red corset for the Floor Show), long, black fingerless gloves, a string of oversized white pearls around your neck and, naturally, a black wig that did *not*, if you could avoid it, make you look like Cher after a round of shock therapy. Plus-sized actors playing Frank had a hard time finding appropriate outfits for the show. But somehow or other, they appeared.

Those were the principals. But we're not done.

Something else I found out at that first show: Half of the principals had doubles for the Floor Show. (For you virgins or forgetful types: The "Floor Show" is the final dance number/orgy that Frank puts together with tarted-up versions of Janet, Brad, Columbia, and Rocky.)

The doubling makes sense for this scene due to the virtual impossibility of getting any actor, even a speedy one, to change from the last scene where the characters are turned into statues and into the fishnets and corsets required to participate properly in the final scenes. Plus, it would have been *inconceivable* to get the makeup just right, even if you succeeded on the costume front.

So the remedy was: Brad, Janet and Rocky were played, in the Floor Show, by substitutes. And those jobs weren't easy to get, either. After all, you were dancing around in your underwear and leaping into the midst of an orgy in a swimming pool, so, simply put, you had to look *really, really, awesomely good* to play those roles.

Generally speaking, if you want to locate the sexiest members of any Rocky cast, start with the Floor Show. You won't be disappointed.

I suppose you've gathered by now that the cast was pretty huge. There were the ten principals, plus three Floor Show doubles and at least a dozen Transylvanians. Add to this the usual one or two additional members of the team, like Doc, who didn't perform but, instead, handled the crew work— loading and storing the set pieces and working the lights. Put 'em all together and, collectively, the cast would usually fluctuate between twenty-five and thirty members at any given time.

The median age in the cast was roughly 17. Most everyone involved in the show was still in high school or—in many cases—had recently dropped out. There were a few of them in their 20s but, to most of us, anyone old enough to be of legal drinking age was over the hill. Ancient.

I thought it was pretty astounding, looking around, that a cast this large could even be assembled, considering how many teenagers seemed to be required to do the job. After all, these shows took place at midnight every Friday and Saturday night and the evening didn't usually conclude until the show had been over for a couple of hours and the cast finally decided to stagger home (if they even *went* home).

So it begged the question: What kind of parent lets their 16-year-old kid stay up half the night every weekend with a bunch of barely clad, sexually aggressive fellow teenagers acting out a movie that celebrated transsexuality, space aliens and depravity? Who in their right mind would go along with this?

The answer was: not too goddamn many.

And that is why most of the kids in the Rocky cast had no parents to answer to. A large percentage of them no longer lived at home. I soon learned that a lot of the cast, even some of the really young ones, had been on their own for two, three, even four years. They were kids in the technical sense. But they had grown up fast. A hell of a lot faster than a lot of them would have preferred.

My mother—my tolerant, cool but still loving and affectionate mother—was the exception. Not the rule. The rule was actually pretty goddamn grim for a lot of these kids.

So this theater—this was their home. Doing this show every weekend was their life. And this cast was their family.

Not their parents, their siblings or their friends from school. Nope. Just this cast.

This was their entire world.

Back to the show:

After the Hapschatt/Munroe wedding scene was over, the Transylvanians could basically knock off until "The Time Warp" started, so I took a seat in the theater with Steve and watched the cast do their stuff. The scenes that occurred during this interim included both the Janet and Brad car scene and the cast's staging of the number "Over at the Frankenstein Place."

By this time, Steve and I had got up the nerve to introduce ourselves to some of our fellow Transylvanians (the principals were too intimidating to approach). There was Cheryl, the girl who had directed me to Donny the previous week (and who seemed barely able to keep the buttons on her Transylvanian shirt from popping off, her chest was so enormous); Trey, this older guy with a huge afro, a stoner's bloodshot eyes and a perpetual smell of clove cigarettes; and finally, there was this little brunette named Tracey who, like Steve and I, was here for the first time. We hit it off immediately.

Tracey didn't seem nearly as intimidated by the whole process as I was. She was there for the pure enjoyment of participating and didn't seem to worry about finding herself in the wrong place at the wrong time.

I found her attitude healthy, if not adoptable. I wanted to get it *right*. Nailing this thing down had become an obsession. Tracey's outlook seemed to be, "Let's dive in and have some *fun*. What's the worst that can happen?" Since the choice seemed to be between hating her perky guts and admiring her spunk, I went with spunk.

The time for chitchat was drawing to a close, however, because by this point, Brad and Janet were in the castle, Riff and Magenta were grinning mischievously and the clock was chiming. That, my friends, could only mean one thing:

Time Warp time.

The rule for the newbie Transylvanians, as far as I could tell, was Follow the Leader. But as no clear leader had ever been established, it was really a much shorter rule: Follow.

Easier said than done, I'll give you that...but when the familiar opening guitar riff of "The Time Warp" began and the other Transylvanians jumped up and headed to the stage, Steve, Tracey and I didn't hesitate. We stuck to them like a commercial adhesive product and, one eye on the screen and the other on our castmates, we readied ourselves.

Soon, Riff and Magenta burst into the room full of party guests, the light hit us...and we were on.

Now, it is tempting to say that we did an absolutely wonderful job (because we really did), but the problem with bragging about your Time Warping skills is that the minute you get done, someone is bound to point out that the dance itself *could not be simpler*. If you start patting yourself on the back for your truly first-rate Time Warp abilities, some smartass is undoubtedly going to pipe up and say, "Uh, guys? The dance steps are in the *lyrics to the song*. This is not a difficult piece of choreography to master. Get over yourselves."

And, to be fair, there is some truth to that. Anyone—and I mean *anyone*—can learn how to do the Time Warp.

But there's a lot more to being a truly successful Time Warper, in my opinion, than simply jumping to the left, stepping to the right and making with the pelvic thrusts.

No, you also need to bring a certain Transylvanian *essence* to what you do in order to be deemed a top-tier Time Warp dancer. You must show a little transsexual *joie de vivre*. In brief, if you truly want to rock the Rocky house as a Time Warper...you had to be on *fire*, baby.

Us? Hell, it's a wonder our costumes didn't burst into flames. All inhibition was banished. We leaped about with reckless abandon. We jumped, stepped and thrust like there was no tomorrow.

In other words: We Time Warped the *bejesus* out of that place.

Thankfully, the song ends with everyone collapsing to the floor, which was a relief because by the end, we were completely spent. We'd been dancing for less than two minutes but we had put so much energy into it that we had nothing left when we were done. Also, those of us who were up there for the first time were extremely happy that we had performed the entire song and had not managed to trip up either Riff, Magenta or Columbia during their portions of the song (the latter of whom does a spinning tap dance midway through it). So we were, I have to say, pretty pleased with ourselves.

And our reward for having not screwed up our all-important number was:

We got a front-row seat to see the all-time best Tim Curry impersonator you ever saw in your life. For, within just a few seconds...

...the Deerfield Ultravision Frank-N-Furter was going to make his entrance. And that's when the party *really* began.

In the history of film, there have been some great match-ups of character to actor. Sometimes the heavenly stars align, the right script goes to the right performer and the result is a truly unforgettable performance. When this happens—and it is a rare occurrence—the characters portrayed become iconic cultural touchstones.

Who, after all, was better suited to play Terry Malloy in "On the Waterfront" than Marlon Brando? Then there's Charles Foster Kane. Orson Welles wrote the damn part for himself at the age of *twenty-five* and the performance is now legendary.

Fast Eddie Felson and Paul Newman. Rick Blane and Humphrey Bogart. Michael Corleone and Al Pacino. Randall Patrick McMurphy and Jack Nicholson. The characters work as brilliantly as they do because the actor chosen to play the part was *perfect*. No question about it.

That said, I defy you to come up with a better match of character to actor in *movie history* than the casting of Tim Curry as Dr. Frank-N-Furter in "The Rocky Horror Picture Show." I issue this challenge without reservation because it simply cannot be done.

Without Curry, this ridiculous, mindfuck of a movie remains nothing more than a failed experiment in cinematic audacity. Hell, if he hadn't been involved, this wacko flick never gets made in the first place. I'll go even further than that: The *stage* show wouldn't have worked without him either. If Curry hadn't been born, the world would never have heard of such things as Brad and Janet, the Time Warp or the Sonic Transducer.

I sincerely hope that Richard O'Brien sends a phenomenal Christmas basket to Mr. Curry every year with a *really* nice card and an Ikea gift certificate or something because if it hadn't been for Tim, Richard isn't living comfortably off of his Rocky Horror royalties. No, sir. He's writing commercial jingles for a living and wondering, "Why me, Lord?" That's the sad truth.

Thankfully, however, the two of them—Tim and Frank—were drawn together by the mystic forces of artistic fortune (which must never be questioned) and...all was right with the world.

So, here you have this one-of-a-kind actor in this never-to-be-seen-again role, and what happens? Miracle of miracles, the movie featuring this character becomes the first live-action, interactive movie experience in all of recorded history. Suddenly, the action taking place on screen is being performed *live* coast-to-coast, with young actors attempting to play the characters from the film *in real time* as the movie spools out onto the screen above them. And, naturally, these young performers attempt to do everything they can to precisely mimic the performers who are appearing, simultaneously, on seventy-foot screens behind them.

This development, perversely, necessitates that you (when you are trying to cast the role of Frank-N-Furter for the live show) somehow manage to put your hands on Tim Curry's doppelgänger. Someone who can perfectly imitate one of the most original performances in cinematic history. And in this particular scenario, you have to find this person in, of all places, South Florida. The Swamp that Time Forgot.

So give that a few moments' thought. What are the odds you're going to succeed in your quest? You think Tim Curry doubles grow on trees, do you?

Well, in this case, the Deerfield Ultravision hit the Mega-Super-Power-Gigantic-Bonus-Über-Lotto, ladies and gents.

Because the Ultravision...had Mark.

Now, I had seen this young actor perform this exact role only a week earlier, so there was no reason why I should have been as blown away as I was on this particular evening. So what made this night so special? A little thing called *proximity*.

There was something about seeing what Mark was doing from this unique, in-your-face perspective, that I finally realized what was so transfixing about the guy: He wasn't simply better than I remembered him.

He was better than I remembered *Curry* being.

And while it might appear that I am overstating this guy's abilities, I'm really, really not. I have seen the Rocky show many times since those early days and have witnessed dozens of Frank-N-Furters and I'm here to tell you: Nobody ever got anywhere near what Mark did at the Ultravision week after week. There have been a number of pretenders to the throne, but not one of them got within a country mile of Mark's Frank. That's how good he was.

Mark became Exhibit A of how to properly perform the live Rocky show. It wasn't simply a matter of mimicking what you saw on the screen. You had to actually *inhabit* the character you were portraying. It was rooted in mimicry, yes. But if you just robotically mirrored the moves (even if your physical gestures matched the screen exactly) and didn't give the character a *soul*, the result was completely uninspiring.

Mark, however, gave his Frank a soul and a half. He moved in perfect harmony with the Frank on the screen, but he also, somehow, managed to make the character his own. At times, you could swear that Tim Curry was following *him*. It was astonishing.

Now, being just three feet away from this blistering performer, I found myself staring in awe. And in truth, I didn't really have time to stare, and awe wasn't exactly budgeted for either. Instead of watching the performers, I was supposed to be keeping up with what my fellow Transylvanians were doing. After all, while Mark was doing his thing, I was on stage, too. *Supposedly* delivering a performance of my own.

It suddenly occurred to me that perhaps I should start paying attention to what I was doing. Surely, I thought to myself, you can watch and act at the same time, right?

So I did my best to go with the crowd. It wasn't hard. The basic rule of finding your own way through the Rocky show without any guidance was to meld into the background and keep a weather eye out for what the rest of the Transylvanians were up to.

Also, if one of the main characters was headed toward you, I discovered that a good idea was to *get the living fuck out of the way.*

The show proceeded apace. Frank got on his elevator, my fellow Transylvanians and I disappeared and re-formed as a group up in the lab. We clapped and laughed on cue during the following scene (where Frank reveals his new experiment) and screamed with horror when Eddie burst through the freezer wall and began his song.

It should go without saying, based on my description of the guy, that Donny played Eddie in the show. It is the fate of any plus-size man in a Rocky cast that—if you get to play a main character of any kind—it's either going to be Eddie, Dr. Scott or both. Donny played both.

This is by no means a bad deal for the actor. Sure, if you play Eddie you only get to be on stage for the one song. But the song...well, it's not simply one of the best songs in the show. It also involves, during the course of this one number, dancing with, getting smooched by, and, basically, getting down and dirty with the actress playing Columbia.

Men have killed for less.

Donny was a kick-ass Eddie, too. Born to play the role. He had (if such a thing exists) the perfect Meatloaf attitude. The trick to Eddie is intensity and Donny managed to bring an energy to the character that he utterly lacked while off stage. Talking with him in the parking lot, he came off as your mellow, slightly high uncle. But here, he was a head-stomping biker god with a "Don't fuck with me" sneer.

Donny made what he did as Eddie look effortless and it was anything but. He danced, sang, jumped around, played the saxophone; he never stopped moving. An added benefit: Because of his enormous strength, Donny was able to toss the girl playing Columbia around the stage like she was a rag doll.

It looked to me like he was having the time of his life.

Then the song wound to a close, Frank got his ax out of the freezer and—chop, chop—goodbye Eddie. It was a shame to see him go.

After that was the reconciliation scene between Frank and Rocky, during which the Transylvanians had a tricky bit of choreography, getting set up for the exit into the "bridal" chamber. Again, I found myself directionless and in danger of getting in the way, but someone eventually prodded and poked me into the right place. Frank and Rocky were provided with a clear path to make their exit, they sidled up the aisle, Frank jumped, the light winked out and...

...I was pretty much done for the night. The rest of the movie is Transylvanian-free, so I had little else to contribute. Every once in a while a prop or set piece would need to be moved so I pitched in when needed, but mostly I just watched.

And listened. It was very, very important to *listen* as carefully as I could.

Because, see, apart from the costumes, the lights, the sets, the crap you throw around during the show and all that other ridiculousness, there is one final, essential component to the Rocky experience:

Yelling back at the screen.

In case you're not familiar with the concept, here's how it worked:

During the course of the movie, certain moments would crop up that seemed to *demand* a reaction from the audience. The most familiar of these are when Janet first appears on screen or someone says her name (at which point you yell, as loud as you can, "Slut!"). Similarly, when Brad appears, he is welcomed with the catcall "Asshole!" This continues for the entire film, or until it gets boring. Even the most virginal of virgins knows enough to at least yell out these two callbacks. "Slut!" and "Asshole!" are the bedrock of the Rocky audience-participation script. Just so we're clear on that.

In addition, however, there are smartass comments you can jam in between or on top of almost every line in the film. These change from theater to theater (and have a multitude of variations), but it is how the Rocky experience first got started and it is what keeps the audience engaged. At the Rocky show, you are not simply a passive viewer, after all. You are a *participant*. So yelling at the screen becomes a communal experience.

Again, there are no hard-and-fast rules about when and where to yell things, but some moments simply beg for a catcall. For example, the lines at the beginning of "Dammit Janet" go something like this:

Brad : *Janet?*
Janet: *Yes, Brad?*
Brad: *I've got something to say.*
Janet: *Uh-huh.* [Pause.]
Brad: *I really love the* [pause] *skillful way* [pause] *you beat the other girls* [pause] *to the bride's bouquet.*

Pretty simple, right? But when you saw the Rocky show live, at least at our theater, here is what you generally heard. The audience lines are in **BOLD CAPS.**

Brad: *Janet?*
Janet: *Yes, Brad?* **YOU ASSHOLE.**
Brad: *I've got something to say.*
Janet: *Uh-huh.* **SO SAY IT, DIPSHIT!**
Brad: *I really love the* **STARTS WITH AN S, RHYMES WITH KILLFUL..***skillful way* **LOSER** *you beat the other girls* **WITH WHIPS AND CHAINS** *to the bride's bouquet.*

That's the basic idea. And this sort of thing continues throughout the movie and never, ever stops. Most of the callbacks are just yelling for the sake of yelling, but some of it is actually pretty clever. The best lines, the *really* funny ones, live on at almost every theater where the movie is performed. I won't do the whole movie for you (though you can find that kind of thing online these days), but I will share one of my favorite sections.

The following speech, with my additions, is the first monologue delivered by the Narrator (called, in the movie, the "Criminologist" but affectionately known to Rocky folk as "Chucky Gray," after the actor who plays the

58

role).

This character suffers from what appears to be a physical abnormality. He is missing, as far as we can tell, any discernible *neck* whatsoever. (His collar seems to climb right up to his ears.) Therefore, the callbacks for this scene go generally thisaways:

> Criminologist: *I would like,* **A NECK!** *if I may,* **YOU MAY** *to take you* **WHERE?** *on a strange journey.* **HOW STRANGE WAS IT? IT WAS SO STRANGE, THEY MADE A MOVIE OUT OF IT.** [He picks up a large book.] **NOT A BOOK! A MOVIE!** *It seemed a fairly ordinary night.* **ORDINARY?** [As he turns the pages:] **THREE PAGES TO ASSHOLE. THREE, TWO, ONE...** [He turns to a page with Brad's picture.] *Brad Majors,* **ASSHOLE!** [Turns to the next page, with Janet.] *and his fiancé, Janet Weiss.* **SLUT!** *Two young, ordinary, healthy kids* **ORDINARY?** *left Denton that late November evening, to visit a Dr. Everett Scott,* **SIEG HEIL!** *ex-tutor, now friend to both of them.* **IS IT TRUE YOU LIKE LITTLE BOYS?** *It's true, there were dark storm clouds,* **DESCRIBE YOUR BALLS.** *heavy black and pendulous, towards which they were driving.* **IS IT ALSO TRUE YOU LIKE GLADIATORS?** *It's true also, that the spare tire they were carrying was badly in need of some air.* **LIKE YOUR NECK.** *But they, being two normal kids* **NORMAL?** *on a night out, were not going to let a storm spoil the events of their evening. On a night out,* **WHAT KIND OF NIGHT OUT WAS IT?** *it was a night out they were going to remember,* **FOR HOW LONG?** *for a very long time.* **DO YOUR RICHARD NIXON IMPRESSION AND DISAPPEAR.** [He does.]

It's funnier when you hear it live. Trust me.

Every cast has its own particular set of callbacks and Deerfield's was no different. Where these lines originated I couldn't tell you, but we picked and chose from the best. No two Rocky shows were the same, callback-wise, nor should they be. It's a free-form audience ritual and it constantly evolved. Good lines would come and go, some would be timely and then...not so timely. When they reached their sell-by date, they were abandoned. Also, there weren't any rules about callbacks. If something funny occurred to you, you were encouraged to shout it out. Maybe it would stick. Maybe not. You never knew.

Still, it didn't hurt to know what the basic callbacks for this cast were so that you could join in with everyone else.

So I listened.

And learned.

Another thing you need to know about Rocky tradition: what to throw. Or, in some cases, squirt.

The following audience-participation moments have evolved over the years and have become fairly commonplace at every Rocky show. Each show develops its own traditions, of course, but here are the basics:

When Ralph and Betty come out of the church after their wedding, throw rice. (Some people brought, and threw, entire *bags* of rice. What else you gonna do with it?)

When Janet gets out of the car to walk to the castle in the rain, put a newspaper over your head, mirroring her. This is a good idea, because at the same moment, you are supposed to:

Pull out your squirt gun and shoot water into the air until it is empty. Some people shot the squirt gun at *one another*, but I gotta tell you: That's just childish. Grow up, people.

When Brad and Janet begin singing "There's a light…" in this scene, pull out a lighter, spark it up and hold it high.

Later, when Dr. Scott bursts through the wall and Brad yells, "Great Scott!" throw toilet paper. (Get it? Scott…toilet paper? I know, high-larious.) By the way, when you throw it, you should try to toss it so it unravels as it flies through the air. This is a skill few can master. I have seen grown men who can chuck a roll of toilet paper in the air and do it in such a way that the goddamn cardboard tube would land in your lap. It should be an Olympic event, really.

In the dinner scene, when Frank says, "A toast," throw toast in the air. Most people forget to *bring* toast and they just throw bread instead. Now ask yourself: Why throw bread? The man said *toast*. Throw toast or nothing. Sheesh.

And, finally, when Frank-N-Furter, in his song "I'm Going Home," sings "Cards for sorrow, cards for pain," throw playing cards in the air.

And those are the basics. Rice, water, newspapers, lighter, toilet paper, toast and cards. Show up with those, you're fine.

Back to the evening at hand:

The only truly memorable thing about the rest of the night was getting a front-row seat to the Floor Show finale. On screen, the song "Don't Dream It, Be It" ends with an orgy in the swimming pool. All of the characters jump in the pool and spend a few minutes kissing, groping and clawing at each other.

The previous week, when I first attended the live show at the Ultravision, I couldn't really see what had happened once they all dropped to the floor. This time, I was right up front and could see that, as suspected, what happened on the screen happened on the floor of the theater as well: These scantily clad youngsters, who had been dancing about in their underwear, wound up in a flesh-pile that would have made Hugh Hefner blush. It was a sight to behold. Also, it was the only part of the show I could not imagine doing...and yet, I could not imagine wanting to do anything else.

Minutes later, it was all over. The credits ran, the lights came up, the audience cheered and then headed for the doors. This cued the clean-up crew (meaning the Transylvanians) to spring into action. Steve and I, with about five or six others, jumped up and got to work, directed by Doc, our new drill sergeant.

As I loaded up the wheelchairs and pushed them back to the storage area, it occurred to me: I now had two Rocky shows under my belt. One as an audience member, and one as an actual part of the cast.

And with that first night on stage at last behind me, one question remained:

What next?

Fantasy Free Me

The show was over, so I figured it was time to get home. After all, it was around 2 in the morning and I'd been up since dawn, had gone to school, spent the afternoon freaking out about the night ahead and then attended and performed in a midnight movie showing. To most people, that's a pretty full day.

These weren't most people.

Now that the show had come down and all their friends were in the same place, it was time for this cast to have a bit of fun.

I caught wind of this as I was shuttling props back and forth.

"You coming out?" asked Cheryl.

"Out? Out where?" My ears must have shot up. Was there a party? Were we heading over to the beach? What was the Rocky cast's idea of a post-show get together?

Cheryl filled me in: "We're going over to Denny's. We meet over there after every show. Get something to eat. Cast meeting. That kinda thing."

I was stunned. *Denny's*? This was where the glorious Rocky after-party was scheduled to take place? Really? Sitting around a diner eating open-faced tuna sandwiches and cottage fries?

It was, to say the least, a bit of a letdown. I had expected...I don't know... naked Jell-O shots or something. Hookah pipes and raunchy videos. Not onion rings.

As disappointing as it sounded, I felt compelled to check it out. There was always a chance that "going to Denny's" was really code for "strip poker and whip-its," so why not have a look? Quick as I could, I finished up storing the props and sets backstage and caught a ride with Steve over to the restaurant. At the very least, it would finally be my chance to meet and talk with some of the people I had only seen on stage.

Now, I don't know how much experience you have hanging out in late-night eateries, but one of the best things about Denny's (perhaps the only thing, come to think of it) is the fact that they are open twenty-four hours a day. This, by process of elimination, made it the ideal option for a Rocky post-show gathering.

I can't imagine what the management of the place must have thought of this gang of freaks when they first walked through the door but, surprisingly, the Rocky cast turned out to be a late-night manager's wet dream. Here was a group of people who showed up *hungry*, didn't shirk when it came to tipping and could not have been a friendlier bunch to have in your restaurant in the wee small hours.

All anarchy-loving, free-wheeling, bohemian-ness aside, we were a very well-behaved group. Nothing was destroyed, no fights broke out and, thinking in terms of pure dollars and cents, we were a group of thirty people (a number of whom suffered from a severe case of the munchies) showing up right in the middle of the night shift. What's not to love?

By the time Steve and I joined up, the Rocky cast was on a first-name basis with the entire staff.

When we walked in, we were directed to the back of the restaurant where the Rocky group had been provided with what amounted to a private dining room. About ten tables had been shoved together end-to-end forming one long banquet-style table (not unlike Frank's dinner table in the movie). Most of the principal cast members were already gathered and, since only Transylvanians are expected to do the grunt work, Steve and I were the last to arrive.

Donny, as cast manager, was holding court, taking care of cast business. He had a natural authority and, either because of the respect he'd earned from his fellow cast members or the fact that it looked like he could rip off your arm and pick his teeth with your nails, he was given everyone's utmost attention.

Steve and I took seats toward the end, furthest away from Donny. I sat down next to Tony, the bearded, pre-show loudmouth who had played the Criminologist in the show. He introduced himself to me brusquely and then quieted down for the weekly meeting.

The actual business of being a cast manager basically involved (a) checking with the cast for any problems, (b) making sure the assignments for the next show were clear, (c) collecting dues, (d) enforcing rules, (e) welcoming new cast members and (f) ensuring the general smoothness of the Rocky ride.

Donny got right to it:

He was looking ahead to the following evening's Saturday night performance. There were to be no new assignments for this show, cast-wise. Everyone who played the roles earlier that night would reprise them the next day. But in running through the cast by name, I was finally able to figure out who was who. For that first month at the Ultravision, the regular (let's call them "A-list") cast was as follows:

Frank-N-Furter – Mark
Brad – Ron
Janet – Jackie
Riff – Kenny
Magenta – Andrea
Columbia – Sunday
Eddie – Donny
The Criminologist – Tony
Rocky – Barry
Dr. Scott – Donny, again
Floor Show Brad – Russ
Floor Show Janet – Iris
Floor Show Rocky – Jeff

I tried to commit all their names to memory, but it took about a week or so to finally get them all straight. It took even longer to introduce myself to the whole gang. I didn't want to appear too eager, for one thing, and for another…they were incredibly intimidating. Part of me was afraid that I would blurt out something like, "You guys are *so awesome*," or something similarly lame. Remember, I told myself, the word of the day was "cool." Gushing at them wasn't going to get me anywhere. I was in the end zone. Best to pretend I'd been there before.

Dues were collected (I forked over my initiation fee), a few complaints were dealt with and either dismissed or addressed. Then it was our turn.

"We've got three new cast members tonight. Stand up if you're here." We did. "This is Tracey, Steve and Jack. Make 'em feel welcome."

"Go fuck yourselves!" was offered by someone, to general laughter. We smiled and sat down. It was pretty much the welcome we had expected.

After Donny wrapped up the meeting, I chatted up Tony a bit, who introduced me to his buddy, a guy named Tom. Tom worked as a full-time member of the crew and was solely responsible for running the spotlight, an extremely important job. He and Tony seemed like old friends and both were about four to five years older than the rest of the cast. I pegged them to be about 23 or so, a good seven years my senior.

They were polite enough, I suppose, though they didn't seem in the least bit interested in me. No "where do you go to school?" or "did you have fun tonight?" chit-chat. They were too busy recounting the bits that had gone wrong or right during the show that evening. As I took in their conversation, I tried to get a bead on who they were and where they were from.

Tony was pretty easy to peg. He had a New York vibe that was practically pouring off him. As Brooklyn as the day is long. Loud, brash and extremely quick-witted, he had an answer for everything, this guy. And he always got in the last word.

Tom, however, was another story. This guy didn't have four words out of his mouth before I knew exactly who he was. See, Tom was a rarity in those Southern climes: He was a native. Born and bred in South Florida, no question about it. I would have taken good odds that he had never set foot outside of Dade and Broward counties. Well, okay—maybe a day trip or two to Disney World. But this guy had never traveled north of Lake Okeechobee, I'd have bet my life on it.

The two of them had the kind of back-and-forth banter that only comes from long acquaintance. And while Tom may have lacked Tony's razor-sharp tongue, he seconded everything his friend said with gusto. They were quite a pair.

Steve and I didn't say much in our little corner, but the table didn't suffer from any awkward silences. They were talkers, this group. No one lacked an opinion or seemed completely satisfied unless they had weighed in on whatever topic was being discussed.

Most of the commentary had to do with busting one another's balls. If someone had made a mistake during the show, they were now catching hell about it. Or a prop had been missing and the resulting fiasco had *ruined the show* for this or that person. Nothing was too trivial not to bitch about, so the fight was joined every couple of minutes on a new topic.

The principals held court, with a primary focus on the two girls from the "Science Fiction" duet. The Columbia half of the pair, a girl named Sunday, was the smaller, more caustic of the two. And while Tony had impressed me with his quick-wittedness, this chick was the Speedy Gonzalez of repartee. She was tossing out zingers without inhibition, laying her fellow cast members low with each remark. If she hadn't been so smoking hot, they probably would have thrown her out a window.

The other one, though, was the one I couldn't rip my eyes off of. This was Andrea, the A-list Magenta, and the second pea in the "Science Fiction" pod. She wasn't as incisively pointed with her commentary as Sunday was, but she had the foulest mouth of any girl I had ever seen. She used the word "fuck" like most people use conjunctions and she spoke with such unflinching authority that the idea of butting heads with her was utterly terrifying. I sincerely hoped that she didn't notice me staring at her the whole night, but I couldn't help myself.

Between them, these two projected an unmistakable message: In case anyone was wondering, they were the rulers of this little kingdom and the rest of the cast members were expected to treat them accordingly. If you didn't (and some clearly didn't), you had to be ready to lock horns.

Fascinating as it was to watch the group dynamic develop, I really couldn't stay for long. It was already approaching 3 a.m. and I hadn't expected to be out much later than 2. I was both itching to get home and unwilling to leave. Finally, Steve offered me a lift and that settled it. I didn't want to go but, hey—this was to be the first of many nights, right? No harm in heading out early for once (if this could be considered "early"). We paid our check and started for the door.

Sunday, who didn't miss much, spied us making our way out. "Look at these pussies," she called out. "First day on the job and they skip out while the night is still young. What's the matter? Your mommas waiting up for you?"

Everyone turned our way. It was like getting hit with a spotlight, having this girl call attention to you. Steve and I froze in our tracks.

"Yeah, I..." I started. How did you answer that? "I've gotta go. See you tomorrow?"

"If you're lucky," she shot back. "Good night, ladies."

Andrea remained quiet, her eyes tracking the two of us as we made for the exit.

I didn't live that far away, so Steve and I only had a few minutes to re-count our own impressions of how the night had gone before we arrived at my place. We were in agreement: It had been better than we'd hoped and we wanted more. We also seemed to be in total harmony when it came to our opinions of our fellow cast members.

Sunday and Andrea, we concluded, were as terrifying as young girls were capable of being. Donny, on the other hand, seemed totally approach-able and very cool. Tracey, the other rookie that night, was adorable and we both hoped that she'd come back the following night, too.

Steve mentioned he had met a guy earlier that evening named Russ who had made a big impression. Somehow, I had missed out on running into him. According to Steve, Russ was a real character and, from his brief experience with him, he appeared to be one of the most unusual, if friendli-est, guys in the cast. Steve couldn't really elaborate, but promised to intro-duce me to Russ the next night.

We pulled up in front of my pitch-dark house and I got out of the car as slowly and quietly as I could. It being the middle of the night, the entire neighborhood was ghostly quiet. Every footstep I took sounded deafening. I crept in by the back door, tiptoed into my bedroom and slid silently into bed.

The clock on the nightstand said 3:24. I had been up for nearly twenty-four hours. Oddly, though, I didn't feel in the least bit tired.

Which was why, thirty seconds later, it surprised the hell out of me when I fell crashing into a deep, restful sleep.

My Mom, who I may have mentioned was really cool, did not come barging into my room at the crack of dawn and demand a report of the previous night. She let me sleep in, but only until she deemed my rest to be more slothful than rejuvenating.

"Up and at 'em, sport," she finally called into my room at about 9:30.

I wrenched myself out of bed (no easy task) and made my way to the living room.

"What time did you get in?" she asked, sliding a cup of coffee across to me.

"About 3:30, almost."

"Why so late?"

"They go out to the Denny's on Federal Highway after the show and have a cast meeting, so I went to that."

"Denny's?" she said, incredulously. "Really?"

"Yeah, that's what I thought. But it wasn't too bad."

We sipped our coffee.

"So? How was it?"

I paused. How do you describe it? "It was...awesome." I was a regular wordsmith in those days.

I related the story of the previous evening to her, not really feeling the need to edit it all that much. First, most of what had happened was pretty tame, really. And what hadn't been rated PG was not going to be shocking to *my* mother. She worked in a bar, after all, and had seen far worse than I felt capable of telling her.

When I was done with my story, she seemed pleased by my interpretation of the whole experience. "So this cast, they're okay, then? They seem like people you want to hang out with?"

I smiled at her. "Like you wouldn't believe."

And, just like that, I was cleared for my second night. All systems go.

Night two wasn't all that different from night one, except the terror of committing some horrifying mistake had (almost) entirely disappeared. A few things about the Saturday night show, though, are worth mentioning.

First, Steve introduced me to Russ in the parking lot before the show. I liked the guy immediately and, within a few minutes, understood perfectly why Steve had described him as being such an unforgettable personality.

Russ was a compact guy—not short, but concentrated. Like orange juice. He had dark, curly hair, a ready smile and was toasted as brown as a berry from the Florida sun. I judged him to be only a few years older than me, but he talked as if he were the wizened old Mayor of Rockytown. Like Doc, Russ wore dark shades, even at night, which covered up the tiniest pin-prick eyes I had ever seen.

That night, standing in the parking lot, Russ was shirtless, but had a black bow-tie around his neck, a dark-brown fedora cocked jauntily over his eye and sported a silky-smooth Members Only jacket. He had a cigarette in his hand and always seemed on the verge of lighting it, when something would occur to him and he'd start talking and forget all about it.

There was never a moment's stillness with Russ. He was in constant motion; gesticulating, nodding, objecting, agreeing, contradicting, laughing, crowing with indignation and shaking his head in disbelief. I hadn't been talking with him for five minutes before he started treating me as if he'd known me for years. The guy was a riot.

He and Donny were apparently old buddies. But where Donny was laid back and relaxed, Russ was hyped up and ready for action. Not tense, mind you. That's the wrong word for it. But Russ was, at all times, ready to go. Go where? Well, where did you need him? His whole manner said, "What's next on the agenda, people?"

That Saturday was also the night I decided which character I ultimately wanted to play in the show. It is, from my experience, a good idea to set your sights early on a specific goal and then do everything you can to make it a reality. The power of positive thinking, right?

So that night I looked around and made my decision.

My character of choice: Riff Raff.

There was something about him—Riff's innate coolness, his seeming subservience that turned to sly cunning or apoplectic rage at a moment's notice. He isn't overt or over-the-top. Instead, he lurks in the background, ready to strike. And when he does...*whammo!* He knocks off half the cast with a laser gun. Plus, he sings the best song in the movie.

And if you think about it: The author of the whole film had written the role *for himself*, so how could it not be a choice part?

Trouble was, there was someone standing in my way. And what's worse:

He was really good.

Kenny, my Riff Raff nemesis, may have been at least a foot-and-a-half taller than his on-screen counterpart, but other than that he was perfectly suited to the role. For one thing, Kenny was one of the least "colorful" members of the cast. He didn't seem to thrive on the drama and fireworks that appeared to motivate practically everyone else. He was above that petty bullshit, apparently. Who needed it? It was this aloof, I-don't-need-this-b.s. coolness on Kenny's part that made his Riff so watchable.

That's not to say he blended into the background or was a non-entity by any means. But Kenny was practical, reasonable and well-grounded, which, in a Rocky cast, was as rare as a talking albino howler monkey.

He was going to be a tough guy to depose, I figured. But I had made up my mind. Riff was going to be mine and Kenny was clearly in the way.

Like him or not, Kenny had to *go*.

There were no new cast members that first Saturday night, so we (the Transylvanian crew) fell into our respective roles without any muss or fuss and managed not to trip over one another during the course of the show.

I had learned some new Time Warp moves (when to wave your arms to and fro or left and right...it was slightly more complicated than it appeared) and had the opportunity to actually chat up some more cast members than I had the previous evening. Of course, none of what we had to say to one another about our respective lives was really all that interesting. We all went to different high schools, most of us lived at home and, oh yeah, we were having a really excellent time doing the show.

Clearly, the details would have to come later.

It was still far too early to try to actually meet or (God forbid) interact with any of the principals, so I basically stuck to my own caste. The Transylvanians were a very friendly bunch and we stayed together out of equal parts fear and camaraderie. We knew we were a part of a community of sorts, but we were keenly aware of our status on the food chain.

We were the gerbils. Wait. Are they lowest on the food chain? Maybe not. Okay, we were the plankton. There we go.

And while clinging to the lowest rung on the ladder was a degrading place to be, it did come with this comforting thought: There was no place to go but up.

The top of the show began and, again, I camped out in front of Andrea and Sunday for the opening number, once more filled with post-pubescent wonder at the pure sexual attractiveness on display just a few feet away. Then it was off to the wedding scene. Then a break. Then "The Time Warp." Then Frank's song. Then the lab. Then Eddie. Then the newlyweds' trip to the boudoir. Then...clock out and wait for clean-up time, honing my callback skills along the way.

There wasn't a moment during the show where I wasn't still keyed up. I was like a Transylvanian sponge, soaking everything up at once. I spent the show hanging out with Steve, but Tracey soon joined us. The rookies felt it was important to hang close together, I suppose.

But the experience itself no longer felt completely foreign. Even though it was only the second night, I already felt like I was merging with my surroundings. There was still a lot to learn, a great many hurdles to overcome as far as ingratiating myself with the headliners and a lot more viewings to get under my belt before I could be called a veteran. But there wasn't a question in my mind as to whether or not I had made the right decision.

I was home.

After the film came down, there wasn't that awkward, "What now?" feeling either. When all was said, done and safely stored away, I piled into Steve's car and we were off to Denny's for the post-show gathering. The seating at the restaurant was slightly different than the night before (there didn't seem to be a pre-arranged arrangement) and I found myself seated next to Russ instead of Tony and Tom. Worked for me.

Once Donny's portion of the evening was finished and the official cast business was put to rest, the sparks began to fly.

Russ, along with a couple of other Rocky veterans, was more than willing to mix it up with Sunday and Andrea, if only to wind them up and watch them go. The veteran cast members were always spoiling for a fight, it seemed, and it wasn't exactly comfortable to be caught in the crossfire. My proximity to Russ meant that I was going to catch a lot of shrapnel that wasn't necessarily meant for me.

Tonight, Sunday and Andrea were joined in their evening banter by the girl who played the Floor Show Janet, and she was just as whip-smart and devastatingly quick as the other two. Her name was Iris and she was this tall girl—not much older than me—with long, wavy blonde hair down past her shoulders and this positively enormous pair of bright-blue eyes. Iris was thin but, like many of the young ladies in the cast, had a balcony that you could do Shakespeare from. The girl knew how to enter a room, is what I'm saying. Also, she had a laugh that exploded from her like a cannon and, since she found a lot of what was said at the table hilariously funny, her outbursts were enough to rattle the windows.

The banter usually revolved around a specific topic and this evening the subject was music. The debate swiftly grew fast and fierce.

Russ seemed to be the non-partisan arbitrator, as there wasn't much music he *didn't* seem to like. But the rest of the people at the table had very strong opinions about what music did (or did not) totally and completely suck balls.

Iris was a huge Van Halen fan and she was catching a lot of flak for that. Most of the people at the table seemed willing to concede that Eddie was an impressive guitar player, but that David Lee Roth was horrifying—an egotistical, preening idiot. The guys all *hated* him and took turns trashing Roth. Iris, for her part, was having none of it.

Someone dared to call him a showboating asshole and most of the table agreed. "Fuck you all," Iris shot back. "Not one of you is worth a hair on his nut sack, so get bent."

But if the Van Halen front man proved to be a divisive topic, he was nothing compared to the singer Sunday and Andrea were currently swooning over. In fact, I'd go so far as to say that there were few lead singers in the early '80s who caused more friction by the mere mention of their names.

Who was this mystery man who was so capable of creating such a vast cultural divide?

Steve "Don't Stop Believin'" Perry.

The lead singer for Journey was a unique persona in the way that he inspired either complete and total devotion on the part of his fans or, conversely, caused his detractors to involuntarily vomit into their own mouths.

Sunday and Andrea rose to Perry's defense valiantly, but they were clearly convincing no one.

"Nobody else sings like that. Nobody," Sunday offered on his behalf.

"Thank God for that," answered Tony.

"Hey, fuck you, Tony. Who else in music has a better voice than him? He's got more range than anybody in rock and roll right now," Andrea volleyed back.

The table erupted.

"Complete bullshit!"

"Are you fucking *kidding* me?"

"Who?" Sunday demanded. "Give me a name, assholes!"

Russ knew his music, so he offered a few names. "Rod Stewart, Bob Seger, Robert Plant..."

Andrea dismissed them out of hand, "Absolutely not. Perry is better than any of them. Nice try, Russ, but no dice."

"That's what I said," Sunday was nailing down the lid of the coffin. "There's not one singer out there who gets anywhere near Perry, so get used to it."

In the silence that followed, a thought occurred to me and, though every instinct in my body *should* have warned me to keep my Transylvanian mouth shut, I piped up, offering the following observation in an apologetic tone: "Well…there's Freddy Mercury."

Well, that did it.

Sunday and Andrea knew, the moment I said it, that they had lost the argument. The Perry-haters at the other end of the table knew it, too. At the mention of Freddy, they smelled the blood in the water and went in for the kill. I had given them an Arthur capable of defeating Andrea and Sunday's Black Knight, and they had the time of their lives rubbing it in the girls' faces for the rest of the evening.

As the abuse rained down on them, the two young ladies turned to me and gave me a pair of stares so intense, I was surprised I didn't turn to stone.

I wasn't exactly making friends with the two Rocky divas. Must get to work on that.

Not wanting to look like a lightweight for two nights running, I stayed out that Saturday until everyone was heading out the door. Steve again offered me a ride and I took him up on it.

As we were walking out of the restaurant, Russ (who was climbing into Donny's car) said something that puzzled me the entire week.

"Hey, you guys. Party at the Orphanage next Friday. Try to make it. Should be a lot of fun."

"Okay," I said, as if this made perfect sense. "Can't wait."

"Later," said Donny. "Hope you boys had a good time this weekend."

"Absolutely," Steve said.

I was nodding my head in agreement. "No question."

"So…we'll see you next week?"

I frowned, not quite understanding what he meant. Then it hit me: Donny was actually questioning whether we had enjoyed ourselves enough to justify a return to the show. Inexplicably, he seemed to have some doubt as to whether the Rocky experience had lived up to *our* expectations.

We both practically fell over ourselves assuring him that we would most definitely be back.

"Cool," said Donny. He and Russ piled into his car and took off.

On the ride back to my place, Steve and I tried to make sense of what Russ had mentioned just before he left.

"Did he say party...at the 'Orphanage'?" I asked Steve.

"Sounded like that to me."

We pondered that one for a moment.

"Any clue what that could mean?"

"Your guess is as good as mine."

Guess I'd have to wait until Friday to find out.

It would be worth the wait.

Over At The Frankenstein Place

The Orphanage, I soon learned, came into being entirely by accident. Here's the scoop:

Years before I ever set foot in the place, Russ and Donny began dating these two girls, Christie and Bea, who happened to be roommates. After a while, they all decided it would be a good idea for them to live together in one place and, to that end, started hunting around for a suitable residence.

They eventually found a house (not an apartment mind you—a house) that they could all rent together. And it was a big one, too—four bedrooms in all—that lay in the shadow of the Hollywood Bread building in Downtown Hollywood, Florida. (Hollywood Bread is now a defunct baking company. More about the building, if not the company, later.)

As it happened, the house was also just a mile or so from the Florida Twin, where Russ and Donny first performed the Rocky show, so the price and the location could not have been better.

But, as these things happen, almost immediately after the two couples had signed the lease, but days before they were to move in, Donny and Bea split up. Suddenly, it looked as if the three roommates would be short on the rent. So they decided to start looking for a new tenant or two. After all, they had plenty of room.

Thus began the round-robin subletting of the rooms at the place that would very soon be dubbed "the Orphanage." Russ, Donny and Christie found a roommate, but...it didn't last. Then Russ and Christie broke up. Another roommate was needed. People began moving in and out at a furious pace. Donny eventually drifted away, too, leaving Russ to rule the roost.

Pretty soon, it became a refuge of last resort. If you were in the Rocky cast and your life hit the skids, you usually wound up at the Orphanage. If you got kicked out of your house by your parents, or you ran away from an abusive home, or your folks found out you were gay and tossed you out on your ass, or even if you simply broke up with your current live-in partner,— whatever the reason—you could give Russ a call and, before you knew it, you had a place to stay.

Lord knows how many people lived there over the years. Some would stay a week, some a few months. But no one had squatter's rights. If you didn't pony up the dough to Russ when the rent came due, he might cut you some slack for day or so, but rules were rules. Under the Orphanage's roof, you could live whatever way you chose but, man, don't you *ever* try to stiff Russ on the rent. You'd find yourself back out on the street.

Simply put, as long as you paid your bills, you could marry a Vietnamese pig and get Pacific-rimmed in your room at all hours of the day or night for all Russ cared. He wasn't one to judge.

The relaxed rules at the Orphanage also allowed for parties to occur there at any hour of the day and at a moment's notice. These parties didn't happen nightly (they couldn't—no one could sustain such an effort), but when a party began, it would often last for days. This meant that it was possible for you to go to the Rocky show on Friday night, stop off at Denny's for a bite and then drive down to the Orphanage and join the party already in progress. Once there, you would stay up all night and all of the following day, go to the Saturday night Rocky show and...repeat. Most folks didn't last all the way until Sunday night, but it sure was fun to try.

The architecture of the Orphanage also lent itself to being a party house. When you entered the front door, you immediately found yourself in a large, open room. To your right, in the front, was a huge rectangular table. This was, ostensibly, the "dining room" but there was no dividing wall between it and the "living room." This area, just past the table, featured a few couches that faced a large fireplace (though, what a fireplace was doing in South Florida was anyone's guess). In front of the couches was an enormous square coffee table, usually strewn with all manner of detritus from the various tenants (unpaid bills, lighters, half-smoked joints, porn mags, etc.) and above it loomed a large skylight.

Continue through this room and you'd walk into a big kitchen with an enormous refrigerator and a perfectly hideous sink full of dirty dishes. (I understand they took them out back and hosed them off in the lawn when it got really bad in there.)

Every room was painted the same dingy-white and the only artwork was a few posters that had been slapped up on the wall by tenants who had long since departed. There was a communal bathroom that served whomever lived in the front three rooms. (Russ was smart enough to commandeer the master bedroom, which sported its own facilities). The bedrooms all branched off of the main room. And that was it.

So generally, when you arrived, you would join the party taking place in the main room and for the rest of your stay that was about as far as you needed to go, unless it was for a bathroom break or to get more beer from the kitchen. Music poured in an unending stream from the radio. Revelers floated in and out, some into the bedrooms for brief periods, but always returning to the central area.

It was, as one might expect, a complete mess. Ashtrays piled high with butts, similarly overflowing garbage cans, stacks of beer cans, piles of pizza boxes, empty fast-food bags, and bits and pieces of clothing (and underclothing) could be found everywhere. Props from the Rocky show were also stored there: wheelchairs, laser guns, feather dusters, steering wheels, copies of the Cleveland *Plain Dealer*, electric carving knives, hair dryers and costumes of all sorts, including what must have been the most elaborate collection of fishnet stockings in the lower forty-eight states.

Plus, there were the souvenirs people would find and bring to the Orphanage just for the hell of it. Supermarket carts, stand-up movie promotions, elaborate homemade bongs, blow-up dolls, broken TVs, chairs and tables of all kinds, lamps of every description, neon beer signs (some of which actually worked), car parts, sex toys, handcuffs, motorcycle helmets, a weight bench with various dumbbells and free-weights, stash boxes and a million different ashtrays and shot glasses...it was a veritable flea market of discarded goods. When prompted (or simply bored) we could often put these items to good, or at least *entertaining*, use.

The best part about the place was: Virtually nobody lived nearby. The Orphanage was surrounded on three sides by empty lots and the closest house was almost a block away. Federal Highway was about a hundred yards to the west, but the passing cars didn't seem to mind the loud music. The Hollywood Bread Building was right across the street, but the entrance to the building faced the highway, so all you could see when you walked out the front door of the Orphanage was the outside of Bread Building's parking garage.

All in all, the Orphanage was perfectly situated to serve as Rocky Horror Cast Party Central. We could do whatever we wanted, to whomever we wanted at whatever time of the day or night suited our mood and we never,

ever had the police show up to put an end to our fun.

Well, except that one time…but I'll get to that.

After the excitement of that first weekend, the school days seemed to limp by. I was living for Friday again, but this time knowing exactly what I was missing made the wait even worse. I needed a distraction and, since my grades were the thing that would guarantee my continued work with the cast (per my deal with Mom), I decided to hit the books.

But my arrival back at school that Monday felt different somehow. There was something about having experienced my first couple of shows in the clutches of Rocky fever that had brightened my outlook in general. For example, I began, for the first time, to look around at the girls at school and see them not as unattainable creatures to be gazed upon from afar but, instead, as actual human beings that could be approached and, perhaps, enticed into going out with me.

That's not to say that I hadn't dated any girls until I was 16. Things weren't *that* bad. But for some reason the entire process had been, up to now, an utter disaster. I would no sooner get some girl to agree to go out with me than I would begin convincing myself that the relationship was doomed. As self-fulfilling prophecies go, these were *amazingly* self-fulfilling. The brief relationships I had tried to kindle to life had suddenly burst into flames and had to be stomped out with flame-resistant combat boots. These failures had made me understandably gun-shy about dating.

Part of it was insecurity, of course. What teenage boy who is *not* on the varsity team doesn't suffer from insecurity? But there was also this nagging fear that there were not any girls my age—or close to it—that were interested in having an actual, physical relationship with a guy like me and, if they were, they were *already* in long-term relationships with guys like me and had been for some time.

And it wasn't just sex that I wanted. Not at all. I wanted to have a loving, genuine relationship with a girl, first and foremost. To form a kinship wherein we could open up to each other in a safe, affectionate environment. A close, emotional attachment that can only arise from a personal, respectful connection of souls.

In addition, I also wanted to have hours and hours of sweaty, torrid sexual congress with this girl until we fell back onto the bed, entirely spent.

You know. The whole package.

Until then, something like that actually happening to me seemed an impossibility.

But my acceptance into the Rocky fold (well, if not my complete *acceptance*, at least my *lack of rejection*) gave me the confidence to believe that, just maybe, somewhere out there was this mythical girl who was nice, sweet, interested in me and, when all was said and done...*willing*.

I thought of my own class, the junior girls of Zion Lutheran, and then immediately dismissed them. There was not a single girl in my own grade that I was the least bit interested in dating. Our constant contact with each other, day after day, class after class, had resulted in our finding each other repulsive and horrifying. The idea of attempting to be *intimate* with one of them was...unspeakable.

The senior class was similarly out of the question. They were *way* out of my league. I don't know what it was, specifically, but there was definitely something that happened to girls between their 16th and their 17th birthdays. At 16, they were girls. At 17, they were *women*. And I knew that, at my tender age, I was not even remotely ready to handle a woman. Not even close.

That left, by process of elimination, the sophomore class. My brother's class, in fact. And while the tenth grade at Zion wasn't as teensy-tiny as mine was, David's class wasn't exactly Woodstock. He had thirty-three classmates, seventeen of whom were girls. That's all, folks.

Fortunately, the sophomore class (as compared to my grade full of shrieking harpies) was fairly jumping with good-looking, funny, sweet young things. What's more, I already knew most of them either through my brother or from the fact that, in a school that size, you couldn't help but know everyone's names. And the names of their brothers, sisters, pets and interestingly shaped birthmarks. We're talking about a *small school here, people*.

I spent the week, therefore, casting an eye around the sophomore class. There were a lot of possibilities, but most of the real knockouts were already dating upperclassmen. (Ain't it always the way?) Still, there weren't all that many of *them* either, so that left plenty of unattached young ladies. And one in particular seemed responsive to the attention I was suddenly starting to pay.

Holly was a lot like the other kids at my school in that she came from privileged stock. Zion, being a private parochial school, was not cheap. If my

Dad hadn't been footing the bill for my brother and me to attend, my mother would have had no choice but to enroll us in the local public school and pray that we, someday, with a great deal of luck, became fortunate enough to get promoted to Burger King manager.

Our comparative poverty occasionally made things awkward at the school for me and my brother but we usually didn't let it bother us.

However, on the scale of affluence at the school (and it was a pretty big scale), Holly was a cut above the rest. Her parents weren't merely rich. They were *loaded*. They lived in this huge mansion situated on the Intracoastal Waterway that ran through Pompano Beach, had a simply gigantic swimming pool in their backyard (with a hot tub attached) and a dock on the water where they could tie up their speedboat. No shit. A freakin' *speedboat*.

I knew Holly through David and she had always seemed like a nice girl, but with my post-Rocky girl-goggles on, she suddenly appeared to be something much more. In fact, I started to wish with every fiber of my being that Holly, underneath it all, was not a nice girl *in any way*.

Holly had dark, curly hair that fell to just above her shoulders and a bright, open, freckly face that usually had an enormous smile planted in the middle of it. She was shorter than me by about three inches and was the first girl I ever knew that had a particular *scent* that set her apart from all the other girls. I don't know what it was she used—a body wash, a shampoo, a lotion, conditioner—I really have no clue. But you could tell Holly was standing behind you just by breathing her in. It was floral, her scent, but not pungent or overpowering.

And, um, it worked.

We danced around each other that whole week and I soon discovered that I was not particularly skilled in the ways of *amour*. If flirting was supposed to be a balletic duet of discreet, coy subtleties and shy innuendo, I was wearing clown shoes and tap dancing until I fell ass-first into a tub of chocolate pudding.

Fortunately, Holly was just as new to this sort of thing as I was, so our awkwardness was mutually charming rather than simply embarrassing. On some level, though, it must have been successful because by the time Thursday rolled around, we had agreed to go out on an actual date. The plan was to see a movie that Sunday night and then…see where it went from there. She had even offered to pick me up, as her parents had given her a car when she turned 16 and mine…had not.

In the interest of full disclosure, I had made sure to tell her that I did the Rocky show on the weekends and, to my surprise, she didn't seem to think that my joining the cast was bizarre or strange at all. I didn't actually invite her to see the show that weekend (a bit much for a relationship that was still in its infancy) but I wanted her to be clear about who I was and what I was into.

She not only understood, but she made it clear that, for her part, what she was into was....me.

The first time I set foot in the Orphanage that Friday night, I had no idea what I was getting myself into. For one thing, it was eerily quiet at the house when we arrived at about 2:45 a.m. I pulled up with Russ and Donny, who had offered me a ride down to Hollywood after the show. On the way there, the two of them had filled me in on the history of the place, so by the time we arrived, I was expecting it to look like a Vegas casino—bustling with life, music and flashing lights.

But no, the place was silent as the grave by the time Russ wheeled the car into his drive. None of his roommates were home yet, by the looks of things.

The house was dark, clearly an unusual occurrence. The only light came from a dim chandelier that hung over the dining room table, so as we entered I was unable to gape in wonder at the collection of oddities that lined the walls. Russ sat me down at the table, broke out a joint and started describing his current roommates to me. Donny joined us at the table but seemed content with letting Russ do all the talking.

Russ had just finished up telling me about Phillip, this runaway who was currently camping in the front room, when all hell broke loose.

The phone rang and Russ snatched the receiver from its cradle. "Orphanage," he barked.

He listened for a moment and then his eyebrows shot up in alarm. "No shit," he said.

"What's up?" asked Donny.

Russ cupped his hand over the receiver and matter-of-factly said, "Ron's been in a car accident."

Donny seemed unimpressed. "Again?"

"Again," Russ confirmed. "But he's in the ICU this time. Sounds pretty serious."

Donny frowned. "No shit." He sparked up a cigarette as Russ continued listening on the phone. Obviously, Russ was being given elaborate details about the accident but wasn't writing anything down. He didn't need to. He'd remember everything.

I turned to Donny. "Which one is Ron again?"

Before he could answer, the door burst open and a group of Rocky cast members and hangers-on arrived. It consisted mostly of girls from the show who had tagged along with Jackie for the ride down from Deerfield. Russ hung up the phone and steeled himself for what he knew would be an overblown reaction to Ron's accident. He was right to be as apprehensive as he was. Jackie no sooner got the bad news about Ron before she went, in a word, bananas.

After that, things became a blur. Jackie was ranting and raving about poor, unfortunate Ron and how horrible the whole thing was, and the other girls served as a sort of Greek chorus, matching Jackie howl for howl. They demanded to know where Ron was being treated and launched into another cacophony of wailing and keening before Russ could answer. Eventually, Russ explained from memory where Ron was being treated, what room he was occupying and the name of his physician. Thus armed, the girls promptly marched out of the house, presumably to descend upon the hospital and give the nursing staff a taste of their hysteria.

This sort of thing continued over the next few hours. Another group would arrive, Russ would tender his report, half of them would erupt with disbelief and shock, run around screaming for a while, wringing their hands and rending their clothes and then they would all troop off to the hospital.

Russ, Donny and I were the only ones who stayed put that night, sitting at the table, smoking joint after joint and watching the parade of grief roll by.

Eventually, the groups started staggering back from the hospital, each bearing a different version of events.

"Ron was hit by a drunk driver and isn't expected to live," one would say.

Minutes later, someone else would barge in, "He's in surgery now and he's going to be okay. The police car that rammed into him is totaled, though."

In an unending stream, the ill-informed gossips kept pouring through the door. Ron was fine, we were told. Ron was close to death. Ron stopped breathing. Ron was sitting up and talking. Ron was on a respirator. No one agreed on a single detail but each of them was convinced that they had the straight dope.

I eventually got someone to properly identify Ron. He was the young, long-haired kid I had met briefly on my first night. He played Brad in the show and brought this terrific, sincere, goofy quality to the character. In addition, he appeared to have slept with almost every girl in the Rocky cast. Well, the ones that were actually having sex, that is. I hadn't really gotten to know him, though, because when the show came down, he generally wouldn't join us at Denny's, opting instead to disappear with one or another girl from the show. Can't say as I blamed him, really.

Russ, Donny and I stayed up the whole night and finally, when the sun had begun to peek over the horizon and our heads began to droop, Russ picked up the phone and, through a haze of cigarette smoke and dope, he dialed up the hospital.

"Yeah, I'm calling about a patient admitted last night." He gave Ron's name. "I'm just checking on his condition." Russ paused. "I'm his grandfather," he coolly lied, "I need to know how he's doing. Yeah, I'll hold." He took a drag on his smoke and drummed his fingers on the table impatiently. After a few minutes, they came back on the line. "Uh-huh. Yeah. Okay. Thanks." Russ hung up and reached for the bong.

"He'll be fine," Russ said.

And that was that. I drifted off to sleep on one of the couches. Russ and Donny kept the vigil.

My first night in the Orphanage was over.

When I awoke that afternoon the party was in full swing. Apparently, while I had been passed out on Russ's couch the house had filled up with people, some of whom had gotten some rest during the previous night and some who didn't seem to need sleep at all. The Ron hysteria had finally passed (the word had gone out that he would fully recover), so everyone was coming down hard from all the excitement.

The previous night at the Rocky show, we had been joined by two new cast members—a guy named Jimmy, this dark-haired dude with a stocky build (a future Eddie, if he stuck around) and a flaxen-haired young girl named Felicia who had sparkling blue eyes, a sunny smile and a sweet, if cautious, disposition.

It had clearly been an interesting twenty-four hours for the both of them. They had spent the previous night on stage at the Ultravision in Transylvanian jackets being yanked this way and that (as I had been the previous week), then ordered about as crew minions when the movie came to an end and now suddenly found themselves down in Hollywood confronting the gang at the Orphanage, likely with no sleep whatsoever under their belts. It was the equivalent of being thrown out of the frying pan and into a blazing pit of hell.

I felt almost bad for them. At least in my case I had been given a week to get to know most of the cast before landing in this zoo of a place; I couldn't imagine what it must have been like for them. Jimmy actually didn't seem all that fazed, but he didn't strike me as the overly expressive type anyway. Felicia, on the other hand, looked like she'd been walloped in the back of the head with a hammer. "Gobsmacked" is the correct term, I think.

Everyone seemed to be there. Russ and Donny, of course, but also Mark, Sunday, Andrea, Tony, Tom, Kenny, Iris...the whole gang, plus a bunch of Transylvanians, now out of their uniforms and in their civvies. Some of the folks were drinking beer or were sampling this ferocious rum/vodka punch-like concoction that had been dreamed up in the kitchen. Some were smoking, some were toking up, others were just sitting back looking dazed and tired. I was still a little unfocused myself and I sort of wandered about, trying to achieve some measure of balance.

It was my first chance to really take in the environs of the Orphanage during the daytime hours and what I saw just knocked me out. My mother's house had never been a place you would describe as "pristine" (there were two teenage boys living there, after all), but compared to the Orphanage, our place was a freakin' hospital.

Piles of everything lay everywhere. It was how I always imagined a fraternity house to look, but with far more sex toys and far fewer rich kids. To put it mildly, it was a disaster. I supposed that once or twice a year the mess would eventually reach a tipping point, at which time the tenants would have no choice but to fumigate, de-louse and scrub the place down, but the last time that occurred had clearly been a while ago.

Disaster or not, though, it was a very cool place to hang out. If there was ever a joint to let your hair down, this was it. Packed with people of every shape, size and persuasion, you either left your inhibitions at the door or you walked around with your eyes bugging out. Playing the part of Unruffled Cool Guy, I chose not to gape.

I don't mean to make it sound like Sodom and Gomorrah in there, but let's just say that Caligula would have had a *fine* time chilling at the Orphanage. I slid from room to room, just watching.

There was a large group huddled around the front dining room table at which joints were being rolled and consumed at a steady rate. As I took this in, Donny wandered out of the back room with a tallboy in his grip. Upon seeing him, the folks around the pot table requested that he open something called "Donny's Shotgun Booth." Donny smiled and said he'd be happy to oblige. Even I, who had some experience in matters THC, hadn't the slightest idea what they were talking about.

Turns out that when you're smoking pot, there are many ways in which you can take the smoke into your lungs. There is the traditional method of lighting a joint and smoking it like a cigarette, there is the use of pipes or bongs (which came, I knew from my short time as a stoner, in a myriad of shapes and sizes), there's the classical hookah (they had one at the Orphanage, in fact, but it wasn't in use at the time) and then...there is the shotgun.

A shotgun is typically delivered thusly: The shotgunner—in this case, Donny—sits backward in a chair and lights up a joint. (In Donny's case, he would instead squeeze himself into an antique wooden school desk, his girth bulging out on all sides.) A line forms in front of him. Donny takes a drag of the joint and, while the smoke is still in his lungs, turns the joint around and sticks the lighted end in his mouth. At this point, the shotgunee leans forward and positions himself directly in front of Donny, who would then *blow* on the joint sticking the wrong way out of his mouth. A stream of smoke would shoot out the end, to be inhaled in by the eager recipient.

If this sounds like a somewhat convoluted method of getting stoned, I'd have to say: I agree with you. But Donny's Shotgun Booth had become a tradition with this crowd and they all swore by its effectiveness. Who was I to argue? When in Rome, keep your gladiator criticism to yourself.

Tempting as it was, though, I did not get in line. I had given up the Wake & Bake a long while back and wasn't about to fall back on my youthful indiscretions. Besides, I was still soaking up the whole carnival freakshow that surrounded me. With that kind of entertainment bubbling all around, drugs became redundant.

Music blared almost constantly as you moved from room to room, but it all came from televisions rather than from the stereo. Every room had its own set and each and every one was tuned to MTV. A constant stream of music videos played all day. (This was back when MTV showed actual music videos instead of "reality" TV shows. Pretty radical concept, isn't it? We called it "music television." But I mustn't digress.)

The only areas that were off-limits in the place were the bedrooms themselves, and those weren't exactly empty. People were clearly making good use of them, but you had to be *invited* in. These folks may have been exhibitionists, but there were limits.

Russ's bedroom, though, had an open-door policy and there were a lot of people crowded in there, forming a semicircle on and around his bed. Russ himself was sitting up, leaning against the headboard, dressed only in his fedora, a tight pair of red Speedo underpants and, unsurprisingly, a bow-tie around his neck. He was holding court, as was his custom, but hailed me the moment he saw me.

"Jack!" he hollered out. "Finally back in the land of the living! About time, too. Have a seat." I spent the next hour or so sitting at the foot of his bed, listening to him regale his fellow orphans with tales of Rocky shows gone by. He was a natural raconteur and he held the room spellbound with stories of his Rocky exploits. I'll bet a lot of his stories were true, even.

At one point, when he seemed to have paused for breath, I saw my opportunity. I blurted out the question I'd been wanting to ask Russ since I'd first seen the cast perform at the Ultravision.

"Hey," I piped up. "How did you all wind up in Deerfield anyway?"

The room went completely silent. It felt as if all the TV sets in the house had suddenly gone dead and the party ground to a halt. Looking around, I realized that everyone was looking at me as if I'd let out a fart in front of the Pope.

Russ leveled his narrow eyes in my direction and smiled. "That's a good story, Jack." He leaned forward, lit up a smoke, took a long drag and said, "Lemme tell it to you."

The Wild and Untamed Things

"Once upon a time, young Jack, there was a theater in North Hollywood, Florida, called the Florida Twin. It's still there, actually, but that's not the point. A few years ago, this theater was offered a first-run copy of 'The Rocky Horror Picture Show' to be shown on weekends, at midnight, the first such midnight show in all of South Florida. Now, the manager of the theater, who had heard a little something about the Rocky show making big money all over the country, had absolutely no idea how to organize an actual cast. So the word went out that some qualified person was needed to put the cast together and the guy chosen to perform this task was named…" Here, Russ lowered his voice dramatically, "…Marshall Douglas."

At this, a voice rose in anger from the next room, "*Who said that fucking name?*" There was no mistaking who it was. Moments later, Sunday charged into Russ's bedroom, steam practically shooting out of her ears. "I heard that, goddammit! Who said that asshole's name? Speak up, motherfuckers!"

Russ was unfazed, "Relax, Sunday. Jesus. Take a pill or something, will ya? Young Jack here asked me to tell the story about how we wound up at Deerfield and I'm telling him."

"Oh *really*," Sunday seethed. She was supremely pissed off and darted a glance my way to let me know she was none too pleased with me for having opened this can of worms. "Look, I thought we agreed when we got out of there never to mention that fucking walrus's name again. It's been, like, four weeks, Russ. What the fuck?"

"The man asks me a question, I'm gonna answer it," Russ replied, undaunted by her bubbling wrath. "I can talk about who I want in my own goddamn bedroom." Sunday was shooting daggers at him with her mag-

89

nificent eyes. I don't know how Russ stood up under the pressure. It was a stalemate.

"Tell you what," Russ finally said in a conciliatory tone, "I'll tell the story once, and that's it. Okay? One time and I'm done. Stick around, you can tell me if I miss something." He paused. Sunday continued to smolder. "Okay?"

"Fine," Sunday said, slightly mollified. She waved someone away from the end of the bed and sat down next to me. "But this is it, Russ. Never again."

"Whatever you say. After this, I'll lock it in the vault. It'll be gone. Gone in the vault." Russ squared his shoulders. "Okay, here we go...."

As Russ related it to me that day, the story went like this:

The first Rocky Horror show in South Florida was started up at the Florida Twin theater in Hollywood by a guy named Marshall Douglas. Marshall was this huge, behemoth of a guy who, from his description, made Jabba the Hutt look like Christie Freakin' Brinkley. Even Donny conceded that Marshall had a "bit of a weight problem." He was tall, too, about six-foot three, but he had this annoying little reedy voice that didn't match his look in the slightest bit. With a shock of dark curly hair on top, a perpetual five o'clock shadow and an advanced case of halitosis, he sounded like a real piece of work.

Marshall, thus enlisted by the Twin management to bring together a Rocky cast, was further informed that he only had three weeks to make it happen. This he did, but with decidedly mixed results.

Casting a wide net, Marshall made an announcement by way of a D.J. buddy at a local radio station that he was looking for cast members for a live Rocky show and that he would be making his choice on a first-come, first-serve basis. Tryouts were set to take place at the Twin in seven days.

A week later, Marshall waded down into the group of prospective cast members in the Twin lobby and, in just a few minutes, cast the show. He was able to do this quickly due to the unique and novel approach he took to casting: He assigned them roles based on *what they looked like*.

No auditions. No pre-performance viewings of the film. Nothing of the kind. Marshall just walked around the lobby saying, "You're Frank, you're

Riff Raff, you're a Transylvanian, you're Magenta, you're also a Transylvanian, you're Columbia…" until he ran out of people.

And, thus, the Hollywood Twin cast came into existence.

Russ rattled off the names of all the actors who, as a result of this random process, wound up playing the principals down at the Florida Twin. To my great surprise, there were only three people in the Florida Twin A-list cast whose names I knew: Mark, Ron and Iris (who played, respectively, Frank, Brad and Floor Show Janet).

Then came the real shock. After he was done summarizing the Twin varsity players, Russ revealed to me that Sunday, Andrea, Kenny, even Donny…almost the entire Deerfield cast whose performances I had been admiring for weeks…had all been *understudies* at the Twin show. Other than Mark, Iris and Ron, none of the others—not *one*—performed regularly as a main character in Hollywood. It was, to me, inexplicable.

Russ explained that this situation had come about due to what Marshall called his "loyalty" to his cast. Once he had hired his starting lineup, he had thrown them up on the stage and…there they had remained. When it turned out that most of the young "actors" he hired were actually pretty terrible for the parts he had given them, Marshall did absolutely nothing about it. No rehearsals to help them improve, no helpful notes at the end of the performance, no suggestions that they find a different weekend hobby. Zippo.

What's worse, when someone came along who could really knock the socks off the audience in a chosen role…they were out of luck, as far as taking over the part was concerned. In Marshall's opinion, once you had been given a specific character in the Rocky show, you had it for life. Even if you really, really, really sucked. Which, apparently, many did.

As far as the attendance went, though, the Twin show was a hit. This was due, in part, to the fact that there was no competition whatsoever within 500 miles. The fact that the cast was (mostly) awful mattered not one little bit. If you wanted to see Rocky Horror, there was only one place to go, so people flocked to the Twin.

It was, essentially, a Rocky monopoly.

As the months passed and interest in the show grew, many young wannabes joined up with the cast hoping, as I had when I signed on in Deerfield, that they would eventually be given the opportunity to move up the ranks into one of the principal's roles.

They swiftly learned: no such luck. If you were really good—I mean terrifically amazing—you might be allowed to serve as an understudy, to fill in for the regular performer if they were sick or out of town. But you would *never* get to play the part full time unless the owner of the role left the show. Or was killed. Which, I'm sure, was contemplated.

After this had gone on for about a year or so, Marshall found he had a real problem on his hands.

On one side of the room, he had a cast of performers who had been with him from the very beginning and whom he had gone out of his way to protect. He had shown them his deepest devotion and they loved him for it.

On the other side of the room, however, was a large group of extremely talented and *indescribably* dissatisfied performers who had banded together out of shared frustration into a demonstrably bitter clique of tight-knit malcontents. And they were growing restless. Something had to give.

Turned out, what gave was Marshall. But *what* he gave was completely unexpected.

One night, in late December 1981, Marshall called a cast meeting. The whole group assembled in the Twin lobby. On one side were Marshall's loyalists and on the other was the Clique (as it was called), the disgruntled group of Marshall haters. Marshall ran through the normal cast bullshit, finances, old business, new business, etc., and then he dropped the bombshell:

It seemed that another print of the Rocky film had become available. Marshall had gotten word that the management at the Deerfield Ultravision had decided to rent the film and start up a Rocky cast of their own the following week. Being the only Rocky game in town, they had naturally contacted Marshall about fielding a new cast up in Deerfield.

Seeing an opportunity to kill two birds with one stone, Marshall then announced that, seven days later, on January 1, 1982, there would be a group of former Florida Twin cast members up in Deerfield appearing in the new show.

And to ensure that this would happen the way he had described it, Marshall promptly fired half of the Hollywood cast on the spot.

"The following people are no longer in the Hollywood cast and will be sent to Deerfield." He turned to the Clique. "Sunday, you're fired," he called out in his little sing-song voice. "Russ, you're fired. Donny, you're fired. Skinny Kenny, you're fired. Andrea, you're fired..."

He had meant to continue this list, but those were the last words to pass his lips that night. Andrea, in a blaze of fury, leaped to her feet. She then proceeded to hit Marshall with a double-barrel full of vitriol at the top of her lungs and did not stop hollering at him until she was dragged, bodily, from the room.

What Andrea actually said cannot be transcribed, however, because from what I understand, if the actual quotes were ever committed to paper, the page would collapse in on itself and form a black hole of nothingness and despair. Suffice it to say that Andrea tore Marshall a new one and, while Andrea ranted, the rest of the Clique picked up their gear and marched out of the Twin, never to return.

The Clique had been banished. Marshall's nightmare appeared to be over.

His master plan had not been without its sacrifices, however. Iris, one of his best performers, was extremely close friends with Andrea and Sunday and so, when they were thrown out, Iris blew out the door with them. As if that weren't bad enough, since Iris had gone to pre-school with Mark and the two of them had remained the best of friends their entire lives, Mark had responded to the mass firings by quitting the show outright, causing Marshall to lose the best Frank-N-Furter on the planet whose last name wasn't "Curry." These are the lumps one has to take when making difficult decisions, I suppose, but it had to hurt, losing Mark.

But while Iris and Mark's departures had been anticipated by Marshall, what he didn't see coming was that two additional cast members, Ron and Jackie—his Brad and his understudy Janet no less—would also quit under protest and walk out with the rest of the banished cast.

Despite these losses, Marshall's evil plan had worked brilliantly. He had gotten his wish. The thorn in his side, his albatross, his *bête noire*, the dreaded Clique...

...was gone.

That night, the newly discarded Rocky cast members gathered at the Hollywood Denny's to vent about what had just happened. Many of them were in favor of just quitting the whole thing outright and never going near a Rocky show again. They were furious at Marshall and spent the evening trading fantasies about what they would do to him if they had him at their mercy. His head on a pike was among the kindest suggestions.

Finally, when the storm subsided, Donny spoke up.

"Listen, I'm just as pissed about this whole situation as you are, but...I gotta tell ya: You guys are kind of missing the point of what just happened here tonight."

"He fucking fired us, Donny," Andrea shot back. "That fat fuck threw us *out*. I'm done with his bullshit. *Done*. I don't need this anymore. I'm finished with this shit."

"You think that's going to teach him a lesson, Andy? Hell, that's just what he wants," said Donny in his calm way. He knew he was basically talking her off a ledge so he spoke as evenly as he could. "He *wants* us to give up. That's his plan. He's hoping that half of us just go home and never do Rocky again and that the other half head up to Deerfield, put on a crappy show and then, when the whole thing comes crashing down, that we'll come crawling back, begging him to let us back into his cast."

A few ears pricked up at this. He *what*?

"If you really want to get back at this asshole, there's only one thing to do." Donny looked around at each of them. "We go up to Deerfield and we do the best goddamn Rocky show anyone has ever seen. We blow the fucking doors off this thing like we *know* we can and we show Marshall Fucking Douglas exactly what this show can look like if you put up a cast who knows what the hell they're doing."

An electric charge was thrumming through the room. Donny knew he had their attention now and he pressed his advantage.

"We can do this. And it'll belong to *us*. And we'll never have to deal with that motherfucker ever again in our lives."

They looked around at one another, wondering to themselves: *Can we really make this happen?*

"So," said Donny at last. "Who wants to go?"

Turned out, all of them did. In fact, in addition to the group that Marshall had fired, they even managed to pick up two new guys at Denny's that night who had been watching the show from the audience for the past few weeks and hadn't yet gotten up the nerve to join the cast. The guys' names: Tony and Tom.

Jackie said she was pretty sure she could convince her boyfriend Barry to join the cast as their Rocky and, looking around, this group of rejects suddenly realized that they had a fully formed Rocky cast sitting right in front of them. The decision was made. They would go to Deerfield and try to make history. Everyone was on board.

Within minutes, their new roles had been cemented, Donny was unanimously elected Cast Manager and they had given their new cast a name.

The Wild and Untamed Things was born.

Well, almost. Because, in truth, live Rocky shows don't just materialize out of thin air just because you have a cast of characters. There's a hell of a lot that goes into putting on a performance in front of a live audience and this newly formed cast had only had six days to make it happen. Time to get crackin'.

Donny and Russ called in every favor they had and the mad scramble began. Everyone sprang into action and did what they could. While some people were busy gluing PVC pipe together to make a control panel, others were filching wheelchairs from hospital waiting rooms, commandeering motorcycle helmets or trying to scare up actual spotlights. It was a team effort and they were racing against the clock.

One lucky break they caught was that Bernie, the projectionist at the Hollywood Twin, had heard about their expulsion and invited Donny and Russ over to the theater one last time to commiserate and, not incidentally, to get really high with the two of them.

It turned out, after about the third joint or so, that Bernie the Projectionist was no fan of Marshall's either. Hated the guy, in fact, ever since Marshall banned his young, female cast members from the projection booth soon after catching Bernie handling some girl's second reel.

To stick a well-placed knife in Marshall's back, Bernie made a presentation to Donny and Russ to commemorate their departure: It was a film canister containing the previews they played at the Twin before the Rocky show began. They were all there: "Animal House," "The Blues Brothers," "Help!"... everything. Russ and Donny were very touched.

"And guess what?" said Bernie. "I even tossed in a little Lynyrd Skynyrd-tribute flick as a bonus. If you haven't seen it yet, you're gonna *love* it." He wished the new cast well and sent Donny and Russ on their way, loaded with goodies.

Meanwhile, the rest of the cast were making sure they had the costume situation straightened out. Most of them seemed to be fine, as they already had the outfits they wore as understudies, but a lot of necessary costume pieces—like the Riff and Magenta space suits—had been owned outright by the Twin cast. Replacements either had to be located or constructed in time for that Friday's show.

Little things proved even more difficult to find, like Riff's feather duster (which he brandishes during his intro to "The Time Warp"), the oversized, four-foot-tall candelabra Riff uses to torture Rocky, the fishnets stockings for Dr. Scott (which, you'll remember, had to somehow be big enough to fit *Donny*) and a laundry list of other items that had to be secured in the very little time they had left.

Couple this dilemma with the fact that Donny and Russ were attempting to pull off this stunt by mobilizing a bunch of people who had never organized anything in their lives. Most of them were still in high school, many of them didn't even *drive* and, to make matters worse, the list of items to be collected was *totally bizarre*. It wasn't as if they were being asked to come up with a series of normal household items. Pitchfork-shaped laser guns and hinged-lid wooden coffins with skeletons inside do not exactly grow on trees.

But they persevered, if only out of a sense that if they were successful, Marshall would somehow suffer. This work ethic seemed to drive them all relentlessly and by Friday night, January 1, 1982, they were ready.

The big night had finally arrived. The cast gathered. Makeup was applied, the colored spotlight was in place, and props were placed strategically around the theater. It was showtime at the Ultravision. Everything appeared to be in place.

Despite their fears that no one would show up to see them, the place was packed for the Wild and Untamed Things' debut. The throng was admitted and Tony—chosen to run the Deerfield pre-show—proved to be the ideal greeter. Virgins were trotted up on stage, money was collected, announcements were made. The Rocky machine was humming along.

People kept filing in as the pre-show buzz continued to grow. With showtime only minutes away, it looked as if they would get about 300 people into the place, a gigantic turnout by any standard.

The electricity was palpable. They were ready.

Finally, at about ten after 12, Russ signaled the projectionist in the Ultravision booth, the lights dimmed and they were off and running. The audience cheered. It was all about to come together.

The first thing to hit the screen was the Lynyrd Skynyrd-tribute film that had been lovingly bequeathed to Donny and Russ the previous week.

Within seconds, the entire cast knew...

....that they had made a terrible, *terrible* mistake.

For one thing, the story that was related in the film was incredibly depressing. It was all about the plane crash that had occurred five years earlier that had killed three of the band members. It was a tribute to these lost artists and the story of how, despite this terrible tragedy, the band's legacy lived on. It was a tale of survival, friendship and endurance in the face of long odds.

And it was *awful*. Halfway into it, you began to wish you were on that plane too.

The audience began to get restless, then agitated. I mean, people are supposed to throw stuff at a Rocky show, but not *before* the movie. These people were pissed.

Another problem: It apparently had not occurred to anyone that there wasn't a single Lynyrd Skynyrd fan in the entire cast or, for that matter, in the audience. Southern rock and Rocky Horror, it turns out, did not mix. Not one little bit. So, in addition to the throwing of objects at the screen, the catcalls also starting raining down about thirty seconds into the film and didn't let up. In fact, one could say that they *escalated*.

Worst of all, the video was *endless*. All told, the film lasted only about twenty minutes. But when you're watching something you truly hate, every second is an eternity. By the time this cinematic abomination finally ground to a halt, half the Rocky cast members were so disheartened, they just wanted to pack up and go home. The rest were demanding to know why the hell Donny and Russ hadn't bothered to *watch* the fucking thing before allowing it to be shown. The response? "We've been a little busy."

At last, "Lynyrd Skynyrd, Forever in Our Hearts," or whatever the hell it was called, finally, mercifully ended. The audience cheered derisively as the credits rolled. It was now 12:30 and, so far, things could not have gone worse.

Finally, the previews that had been pilfered from Marshall's theater kicked in. And for the first time that night, the audience saw something on screen that they could cheer about. During the brief few minutes that the previews ran, the audience's mood appeared to shift back out of the red zone and some of them actually appeared to be happy that they had chosen to come to the show.

Then the previews petered out, the screen went black and the familiar chant began.

"We want lips! We want lips! We want lips!"

97

And when those cherry-red lips finally appeared on the screen, something very unusual happened:

On this night, for one night only, never seen before and never to be seen again, "Science Fiction / Double Feature" was performed—not by Sunday and Andrea alone—but by the entire cast of the Rocky Horror show. They sat, this cast of castaways, side by side, stretching across the entire length of the enormous Ultravision screen and, as one, they carefully, meticulously lip-synced along with the giant lips above them and performed the refashioned choreography that Sunday and Andrea had prepared for the opening number.

The rest, Russ told me, is history.

"There," Russ said when he was done. "That wasn't so fucking bad, was it?"

By the time he had finished the story, Russ's bedroom was packed. Most of the people in the room knew the story already (having lived it) but it was news to us greenhorns. I just couldn't fathom how the Deerfield cast—these amazing people—had been benchwarmers at the Twin while Marshall's supposed "A-Team" went out and screwed up the show every night. It was beyond me.

Sunday weighed in: "I never said you couldn't tell a nice fuckin' story, Russ," she said, in her matter-of-fact way, "I just don't like hearing that douchebag's name. Is that too much to ask?"

"That's it! I'm done! Story told," said Russ, throwing his hands up in surrender. "I had a job to do....and I *done* it. On your way, boys and girls." Russ blessed the crowd, they disbursed and the bunch of us started to get ready.

After all...we had a show that night.

I'm Sure You're Not Spent Yet

Sunday night and my first date with Holly. Going strictly by hours slept during the two days leading up to this event, by the time the date finally rolled around I should have been dragging a great deal of ass. Instead, I was wide awake and raring to go.

It had simply been an incredible weekend. Friday night had featured the show, followed by my night (and day) at the Orphanage. Then Saturday night's show, the post-show Denny's pow-wow and then, at last, home. Mom had not only given her blessing to my outing at the Orphanage that weekend, she even let me sleep in again on Sunday morning. It seemed like God was in his heaven and all was right with the world. (That's the kind of thing that occurs to you when you wake up at noon.)

As for the shows themselves, they were very well-attended for both performances and the turnout had resulted in a dramatic and very positive uptick in mood for the whole Rocky gang. Looking out at the sea of people each night allowed the ex-Hollywood cast to finally let go of their unspoken fear that the first couple of weeks' attendance figures had been a fluke.

Now that I knew the full history of this cast and how they got here, I understood their uneasiness. If the Deerfield show fizzled out after just a few weeks, Marshall would be judged as having been right all along about the inferiority of this group. They would be seen as failures. No question about it.

Worse, if the show closed down, these people would be stuck. The choices would be to either (a) hope for another show to crop up somewhere (an unlikely prospect if this one was a bust), (b) go crawling back to Marshall (an abhorrent thought to all present), or (c) give up doing the Rocky show altogether. All three options were vying for the top spot on the "suck" list.

If, however, the Ultravision show was a big, fat hit, the Wild and Untamed Things would be vindicated and would, presumably, live happily ever after in a world of sunshine, flowers and unicorns and would one day dance the Time Warp on Marshall's grave. Or something like that.

Thus, the throngs who elbowed their way into the show that weekend—along with the fabulous gathering at the Orphanage—had lifted everyone's spirits. This euphoric feeling, contagious as it was, meant that by Sunday, when Holly picked me up for our date, I was flying.

And yeah, I know. Picked *me* up for our date? I couldn't pick *her* up like a normal human being? Well, here's the thing:

I didn't have a car. My Mom did, of course, but she drove this old MG that was either in the shop or, when running, completely off-limits. She would sooner have allowed me to pilot a homemade jet-pack than hand me the keys to her beloved set of wheels.

Also, my school (my *tiny* school, as I may have mentioned) didn't have a driver's ed. course. This meant, I am sorry to admit, that at the age of 16 (and dating a girl almost a full-year younger than me), Holly was the only one of us with a driver's license. Shocking, I know. Especially in Florida, where you don't get the newspaper in the morning without hopping in the car for the trip to the end of the driveway.

So, times being what they were, Holly picked *me* up. Go on. Sue me.

When she pulled up outside, I was out the door like a shot. Before she could even set foot outside the car, I had jerked open the passenger door and hopped inside. It wasn't that I didn't want her to come inside the house and meet my mother or anything, but I was acutely aware of the difference in our social stations and I wasn't crazy about Holly seeing our humblest-of-the-humble abode. She lived in a freakin' mansion for crying out loud. I had anticipated (perhaps unfairly) that she would be dismayed at the way we lived. This is called, I believe, reverse snobbery.

Neither of us was particularly hungry, but we had an hour or so to kill before the movie so we opted for a couple hot-wing appetizers at Tark's to start off the night. One could weigh the pros and cons of consuming spicy-hot barbecued wings on a first date, but Tark's had what were arguably the best wings in the hemisphere, so we rolled the culinary dice and gave it a shot.

Aside from our brief encounters at school, this was the first one-on-one time I had really had the chance to spend with Holly. Talking with her, one of the first things I discovered was that, despite her obviously privileged background, Holly was anything but a snob. Her family's wealth and prestige (and they had a lot of both) did not seem to have affected her personality adversely in any way. She was this really sweet girl who took my comparative poverty in stride. She even tried to pay her own way that night but I wasn't about to let *that* happen. Drive me around, sure, but go Dutch? Please.

The movie we picked to see was the new Steve Martin film, "Pennies from Heaven." While I thought it was really great (if completely different than the movie I expected), the story turned out to be a lot heavier than I thought appropriate for a date movie. Holly didn't seem to think so, though, and as the evening progressed, I got the distinct impression that everything was going really well.

This feeling was reinforced when Holly went to drop me off at my house and, instead of booting me out of her car, we wound up lip-locked in her front seat for a few minutes before calling it a night. Nothing out of the ordinary (rated PG, our little front-seat romp would have been), but if what had happened with my Rocky friends earlier that weekend hadn't already put me in the greatest mood imaginable, this certainly would have done the trick.

We decided to start seeing each other on a regular basis and there were, as far as I could tell, no foreseeable obstacles to our making a real go of it.

Well, except the fact that I would, eventually, have to introduce her to my friends. The ones with the leather bustiers and the fishnet stockings. But really:

How bad could it be?

The weekly routine became familiar, if difficult to endure.

Boring week, followed by two weekend nights of fun and excitement in and around the movie theater (with the occasional jaunt down to the Orphanage). Then a night to recover and another week of tedium. Rinse and repeat.

It was tough going. Thankfully, as our relationship got more and more serious, my time with Holly slowly made the weekdays' boredom far less boring. And while Holly, despite my diligent attempts, wasn't quite willing to advance to DEFCON 1, I was willing to wait. Hell, I'd waited this long.

So we developed a routine of our own:

We would hang out after school every day, most times winding up at my house for a little innocent bout of "what can I get away with today" and then we'd part, each gratified for the time we'd spent together and (pleasantly) sexually frustrated. Most of our afternoons had been spent in spirited but good-natured wrestling matches on my Mom's couch, but never advanced much beyond that. At least, not yet.

My opinion was, we were more than ready.

We were willing, even.

And able. Let's not forget able.

But I was also keenly aware that the worst thing you can do in a relationship where you're looking to advance things beyond the comfortable and into the brand-spanking-new is to push. So I did not push. I may have wheedled, cajoled and even begged a bit. But push? I did not.

Whatever was going to happen was going to happen in its own sweet time and I would wait patiently to see how things developed. Well, *patiently* is perhaps too strong a word. But I waited anyway. And I had little in the way of expectations.

Which is why no one was more surprised than I was the night Holly decided that the time was right, the waiting had been sufficient and my restraint in not pressing her had finally made me worthy of a great reward.

Thus, about five weeks or so after we started dating each other, in March of 1982, I was given one of those rare gifts that a truly generous young woman can bestow on her beloved:

I received an actual, real-life blow job. Live, in-person and in Technicolor.

How did I react? Honestly, it left me utterly and completely speechless.

Luckily for me, this was one of those rare instances where speech is *entirely* unnecessary. In fact, at moments like this, speaking is not only redundant but, from what I've heard, far more distracting than helpful. All that was required of me was to shut up, sit back and be grateful.

And you know what?

It was awful.

Well, not *awful*, really. "Awful" is smacking your thumb with a hammer or having someone walk into your stall in a public toilet. So it wasn't *awful*, really.

But...it wasn't great.

Okay, that's not really true either. Because what was occurring was that, for the first time in my existence, I had a girl who was actually coming in contact with me *down below the equator* and, what's more, it turned out that the sole purpose of the visit was to give me and me alone sexual gratification. So, when you put it in perspective it was, in point of fact, pretty great.

But let's get this out into the open—girls who have no experience in such matters are not going to hit the ball out of the park (for lack of a better expression) on their first try. Not even close. Oh, sure, the final outcome (for lack of an even *better* expression) might indicate that things had gone terrifically well, but don't be fooled.

Here's the simple truth: Blow jobs are not for amateurs. And truly excellent fellators, if I may coin a phrase, are made, not born. It is a skill that is learned and not, at least in my experience, innate.

So while I was immensely grateful, and expressed my thanks effusively, I couldn't help but think, in the back of my mind:

That's not really how that's supposed to go, is it?

Turns out, it isn't. But I wouldn't learn that for a long, long time.

Back at the show, life was proceeding apace. That next weekend, with Ron still recovering from his car accident, Russ had graduated briefly from Floor Show Brad to full-time Brad and it turned out he had a real knack for it. He may not have had Ron's ability to capture the full "Bostwick experience" but, from what we saw, Russ was pretty damned impressive.

Another development: Jackie and Barry left the show, never to return. No explanation given, just....poof! They were off like the proverbial post-prom frock.

It was a little unnerving, watching someone just...*leave* like that. And yet, that's just how it happened. They simply disappeared and we were left to reshuffle the cast. This meant that Iris would step up to the role of full-time Janet and that we would have a big hole in the Rocky department. Namely, Rocky himself.

Enter Billy.

Billy was Tom's younger brother and I'm here to tell you—there have rarely been two brothers in the history of the world who were less alike. Think Randy and Dennis Quaid, but not nearly as similar.

Tom, the older brother (and Tony's boon companion), was a good ol' boy, as I've previously mentioned. He liked to accompany Tony to the shootin' range or break out the ATVs and go freewheelin' or tune-up their trucks and vote Republican and stuff like that. Tom had yellow-tinted glasses, a big toothy grin and a soup-strainer of a curly mustache. "Distinctive" I think is the word I'm searching for.

Billy, on the other hand, was this soft-spoken, really good-looking young guy with a laid-back, surfer-boy attitude he must have picked up down at the beach. He looked, physically, just as you'd hope a guy playing Rocky would look. Well built, unabashed and willing to strip down to his skivvies at a moment's notice.

Plus, he pulled off this singular style that reigned supreme back in the '80s: His brown hair drifted almost down to his shoulders but was feathered back (as was done in those days) giving him an almost feminine aura. It was the full Sean Cassidy look and Billy nailed it.

This, of course, explained why all of the young ladies in the cast, if they weren't already sleeping with Ron, immediately gravitated to Billy.

And just like that, we had a new set of principals. Jackie and Barry were gone and Iris and Billy stepped up.

It was about this time that Donny, seeing how quickly this change had occurred, realized that we were severely lacking in the understudy department. Mulling this over, and completely unbeknownst to us, Donny began to look around.

Let's not kid ourselves. I know, deep down, if you're curious about this cast at all, you're curious about their sex lives. God knows I was. But let's make something clear:

I could, if I were so inclined, very easily take you through the cast and tell you who was sleeping with whom at various points during our time at the Ultravision, but here's the problem: To accomplish this task correctly and provide the detail necessary to be fully accurate about the whole thing, I'd have to employ pie charts and bar graphs and multi-level 3D dramatizations and honestly, who has the time? Suffice it to say that some relationships between cast members were a bit more relevant (and colorful) than others and I will, I swear, get to that.

For the time being, let's just say that these people got *around*. Most of the rest, I leave entirely to your imagination.

Another thing: Given that the movie unapologetically involved transvestites and featured explicit homoerotic behavior, there was a general assumption that everyone involved in the whole Rocky experience was sexually confused, bi-curious or simply gay. This assumption was, in actuality, very far from true.

Most of the young men who got involved with Rocky were straight as a plumb line. And to tell you the truth, this made things a bit frustrating. When you're surrounded by beautiful girls and you want to get their attention, believe me, it really pays to have a lot of homosexuals around. I mean, think about it. Your odds of scoring with one of the girls increase exponentially with the inclusion of each gay dude. That's just simple mathematics.

But at the Ultravision, almost all of the guys lusted after the fairer sex.

While we're on the subject, I should mention that at the time that this story takes place, there was still a huge social stigma attached to being homosexual. Thanks to the efforts of Anita Bryant, this was especially true in South Florida. Still, by the time I joined the Rocky cast, I had known some adults who were openly gay and—due no doubt to the fact that my folks were old-school liberal Democrats—I had been raised not to fear or loathe my same-sex-preferring brothers and sisters. No big deal, I thought.

However, my experience at the Rocky show marked the first time I had ever met anyone *my own age* who was actually out of the closet. Most gay high-schoolers, purely out of self-preservation, usually did everything they could to hide their true identities. I was shocked, therefore, to discover that Mark, our stellar Frank-N-Furter, made no secret of the fact that he was gay. This might seem like an odd statement, considering that he dressed up in ladies underwear and flounced around the stage every weekend night proclaiming his lust for a muscleman. Of *course* he was gay, you might be thinking.

The truth was, though, that most of the guys I knew who played Frank over the years were straight, despite their impulse to don the bustier. Go figure.

So another important lesson that I picked up doing this show was: Being in the Rocky Horror show didn't make you gay. Dressing up in women's clothing didn't make you gay. Playing Frank didn't make you gay.

Having sex with another guy? *That* made you gay.

Ron returned to the show quicker than I would have thought possible after everything that I had heard about his injuries. When he showed up at the theater ready to resume his Brad duties after only a few weeks, there was much fanfare and tossing of confetti and the usual ball-busting about having gotten into the smash-up in the first place.

But it was actually pretty gentle, as ball-busting goes, and the cast's restraint was due in part to the fact that the accident had left him with some pretty serious scars along the right side of his neck and up behind the ear. He wore his hair long, which helped, but there was no mistaking that he'd obviously been in a very serious wreck.

Don't get me wrong: He remained an unstoppable lady-killing machine, and now he had battle scars to show off, which doesn't exactly hurt.

Doc had been gone from the show the entire time Ron was recuperating and I hadn't really connected these two events until two weeks after the both of them had disappeared. When I finally asked after Doc, I was informed that he was more than just a guy working the crew. He was Ron's foster father.

When I learned this, a lot of pieces fell into place: Doc's presence at the show had always seemed a bit strange, but I now understood why an old guy like him would hang around the Rocky cast. He was looking after Ron.

And when I finally put it all together, I was also able to grasp, a bit more accurately anyway, why Ron was such a fruitcake.

Up until this time, I didn't really know Ron all that well. He was one of the principals, of course, which carried a certain mystique for us lowly Transylvanians, so I had kept my distance for that reason. But Ron was also, by far, the wildest cast member of the bunch. There wasn't anything he wouldn't do on a dare, no girl he would not approach, no man or woman in the cast he wouldn't clamp into his arms and afflict a ghastly hickey upon, no stunt or physical challenge he would reject as being too risky or dangerous. He was absolutely fearless.

Ron was also the only Rocky cast member who seemed to have *carte blanche* about breaking character on stage. If he was in the Dr. Scott/Frank scene and got nailed with a roll of toilet paper (an occupational hazard common to Brads, I'm sure), Ron would drop his Brad impersonation like a hot rock, scoop up the toilet paper and furiously hurl it back into the crowd. Or if something unexpected or funny happened on stage, Ron wouldn't even attempt to keep from breaking up. He'd just burst out laughing and recover his composure in his own good time. He embodied a strain of the Rocky ethos that said, "Hey, don't take yourself too seriously. This is supposed to be fun."

And I despised it.

To me, sticking as close as possible to the character and *never* losing your concentration was paramount to all other concerns. Your job—your *only* job—was to try to embody whatever actor you were supposed to be mimicking on the screen and that's it. If you can't do that much? You don't belong on the stage.

The trouble was, when Ron was actually concentrating, really trying, there was no Brad like him. He was *exact*. He was precise. He had it down cold. He *was* Brad. And then, in the blink of an eye, Brad would disappear. For a few fleeting seconds, it was like Ron didn't care at all. He was just this kid on stage, goofing around. Then, just as suddenly...BAM. He's back in it. He's 100 percent Brad. And you'd never guess he dropped the persona even for a moment.

It was maddening to watch. All that talent going to waste because the guy had no control.

Once I got a handle on his background, though, it seemed to bring everything into focus. Foster kid, didn't know his folks probably, living this tough life, so he escapes to Rocky. I was putting on my Sigmund Freud hat and really enjoying picking apart Ron's psyche from afar.

I didn't know him, I told myself. But, on some level, I *knew* him.

Pretty nauseating, huh?

Anyway, you'd think that flying through a windshield and almost dying in the middle of the road—as Ron had—would mellow a guy out, wouldn't you? Not him. He was just as wild, just as freakishly daring as he had been before the accident. He seemed to want to assure everyone that the crash hadn't caused him to lose a step. Ron was back and he was better than ever.

This became apparent that weekend, when I finally attended my first Orphanage party where Ron was in attendance.

But before we get to that, you have to know about Storme.

It occurs to me, at this juncture, that I've introduced a lot of folks so far and that perhaps a Mouseketeer roll-call might be in order. Let's refresh our browsers, shall we?

Cast Manager, Donny. Lived with Russ in the Orphanage.

Main characters in the Rocky show at this time: Ron as Brad, Iris as Janet, Mark as Frank, Andrea as Magenta, Sunday as Columbia, Kenny as

Riff Raff, Billy as Rocky, Tony as the Criminologist and Donny as Eddie and Dr. Scott.

Transylvanians: me, Steve, Felicia, Tracey, Jimmy, Cheryl, a few others whose names have been lost in the mists of time, and...Storme.

Storme is best described, I believe, as the female version of Ron, but without all the fucking. She was, without question, the least-inhibited person I had ever known. There was no filter whatsoever between what occurred in her head and what came out of her mouth. If it popped into her cerebral cortex, it shot out of her face. Often, I am sure, simultaneously. The words "shame" and "embarrassment" were, at some point, explained carefully to Storme, but the concepts must have puzzled her greatly because she suffered from neither of these ailments.

This made Storme particularly suited to replace Jackie as the person who wandered out into the audience during the pre-show and asked for money from the patrons. Here's why:

You know that feeling you get when you find yourself in a situation where you have no choice but to approach a complete stranger and ask them for assistance? Your car breaks down or you get lost and have to ask for directions, and you get that little tickle of nervousness or shyness that hits you right before you start speaking to someone you've never met before?

Well, whatever nerve in the body that causes you to feel that way, someone ripped it out of Storme with a pliers. She had absolutely no qualms about walking up to a group of Rocky patrons and blatantly demanding cash from them. It was a gift. An innate talent. And she hardly ever failed in her task. On those rare occasions where someone was able to resist her pitch, they certainly walked away knowing that they had beaten a champion fundraiser.

The trouble with having a truth-teller around all the time, of course, is that it can sometimes get in the way of civil conversation. For example, I remember once seeing my buddy Steve chatting up Cheryl before the show and I'm sure he must have thought he was doing very well, as Cheryl wasn't, you know, *walking away*. Chances are that Steve might have tried to take it to the next level, but it was his bad luck that his overtures had caught Storme's eye as she was passing.

"Wow," she remarked to Cheryl, eyeing Steve up and down, "he really wants to fuck you."

And that was the end of that.

The great thing about Storme was, of course, that you always knew where you stood. She didn't carry a grudge or talk behind your back. She spoke right up, told you to fuck off if you got her mad and never hesitated to speak her mind. She wasn't bitchy about it either. She just didn't seem to understand why people bothered with subtext.

What was the point?

When we got down to the Orphanage that Friday night, the place was already hopping. The post-show cast meeting had been exceedingly brisk, seeing as how we all had somewhere we wanted to be. When the Deerfield cast poured through the front door of the Orphanage to join the party already in progress, the place practically exploded.

Everyone had chipped in for libations and hallucinogenic treats of all sorts, so there was no shortage of ways for people to get seriously messed up or, in my case, just mildly buzzed. Donny's Shotgun Booth opened up for a while and I paid my first visit. Having a 250-pound man who looked capable of scaring the crap out of a platoon of U.S. Marines hunker down and blow smoke directly into my lungs was, to say the least, an unusual experience, but the result was exactly as advertised. I was feeling *fine*.

Also adding to my good mood was the fact that I was hanging out a lot with Tracey that night. We had struck up a close friendship over the past few weeks and I had caught a ride with her down to Hollywood for the party. On the ride down, we talked about our families, how we each had gotten involved with the show and then, feeling that it was safe to confide in each other, we each confessed our secret, never-before-revealed desires to move up the ladder in the cast.

Tracey, unsurprisingly, expressed her aspiration to one day play Janet. I say "unsurprisingly" because she was in every way perfect for the role. She had the look, the attitude and, as far as I could see, the talent to be first-rate in the part.

Following her lead, I blurted out my hope that I would someday wear the Riff Raff tails. She didn't seem any more surprised by my revelation than I was of hers. I was not a Brad-type, I looked nothing like Eddie or Rocky and playing Frank was definitely out of the question. Riff made perfect sense.

After we had made our confessions, we did each other the courtesy of expressing our unwavering belief that each of our respective dreams would come true. We would just have to be patient.

The two of us sort of clung to each other when we arrived at the party, mostly out of a desire not to be swallowed up by the madness swirling around. The music was deafening, the smoke hung in the air like a curtain, and the temperature—that lovely South Florida climate—made the place feel like the inside of a kiln. Lucky for most of the attendees, they weren't wearing much in the way of clothing anyway.

If there was one negative thing I could say about the Orphanage, it would be this: The party *had* to stay indoors. You could open a window or two, sure, and there were a couple of pathetic air conditioners trying to cool the place off, but for the most part, when things got really sweltering, you had to lump it.

Being that close to Federal Highway—one of the busiest thoroughfares in the city—meant that a lot of traffic went by. Seeing as how the absolute last thing this party needed was a visit from a curious cop, we had to keep our heads down. And while no one would be necessarily interested in a house with loud music coming out of it, if a few scantily clad young ladies start standing around the back porch smoking joints, you were bound to attract the wrong element.

To combat the unpleasant conditions indoors, there was plenty of beer to cool everyone down. Indeed, half the folks in the place were so baked, the heat didn't even seem to register.

At some point the music was turned down and an impromptu session of Dungeons and Dragons started up at the front table. Five players took their seats to play and the rest of us hovered around watching. I had never seen the game played before but had heard of it for years, so I was fascinated by the chance to finally see a game in action.

Now, let's pause for station identification for a moment. See, nowadays, D&D is held by many people in the same regard as stewed beets or boy bands. Much despised and highly ridiculed.

But back in the day, Dungeons and Dragons was still in its cult stage and the participants were rabidly enthusiastic about this new role-playing activity. Their games, their characters, their kingdoms, their whole *worlds* took years to create. What's more, the scenarios dreamt up by the Dungeon Master took weeks, even months, to play out to the end. Playing this game, to its true adherents, was a very serious and momentous undertaking.

It soon became clear that this group, the players gathered around this little table, had been at it forever.

Donny, unsurprisingly, served as the D.M. Clockwise around the table from Donny's left were Tony, Tom, Andrea and Kenny. To go into great detail about their game would only confuse matters, but what really struck me about how they played was how perfectly their personalities suited their characters.

Tony played two characters at once: a wizard with astonishing powers to punish or rescue (depending on his mood), who went through life projecting a sage, thoughtful demeanor; and a bad-tempered dwarf fighter with an itchy sword and a razor-sharp tongue. These two characters perfectly mirrored both sides of Tony's mercurial personality.

Tom was a fighter as well, but he didn't seem to do all that much fighting. The other players got on his case because of the number of times Tom's character, faced with danger, would offer to "guard the horses." He could be a little touchy about it but, like Tom himself, there was no doubting his character's loyalty.

Andrea was a no-nonsense elven bitch-thief. Nimble, sharp-witted and crafty. She was usually the second person through the door during a battle, right behind the lead fighter. Death with a bow and arrow. Jesus, even her D&D character was sexy.

Kenny was the best of them all, though. His character was a fighter too but…he was conflicted. Torn between his desire to amass a fantastic treasure with his companions and his compulsion to do the right thing, the poor fellow was a tortured soul. He regretted the sometimes-unavoidable innocent deaths that resulted from his adventures, but still he soldiered on. Because he *had no other choice, dammit.*

I'm here to tell you, they really got into this shit.

And if you think D&D is a messed-up game to begin with, just try watching this sort of thing when you're a little stoned. It'll blow your mind. You find yourself rooting for the characters as if they were real flesh-and-blood beings. It was powerful stuff. I had to get away.

After wandering around a bit, I soon lost steam. I still wasn't used to these all-nighters, and I finally found myself curled up on one of the couches in the main room. I was exhausted and barely awake.

The party swirled around me, fueled by its own momentum, and I imagined myself as being at its epicenter. In my heightened state, I could feel my energy radiating out to the rest of the guests. Every one them was individually connected to me by an invisible silken thread that kept braiding and weaving in and out as people moved from room to room. The music would swell and fade, laughter would rise up in a roar and then subside. The building itself began to seem like a creature and each of us inside of it was an organ of that creature, serving our own essential part in keeping the creature alive. We breathed for it. We hungered on its behalf. We swayed with it and spoke in its voice.

Me? I was its eyes.

I drank it all in. Every movement, every secret glance. The hurt expressions, the gazes of longing, the silly grins of the blissfully content. Nothing escaped my notice until, at last...I was the one who escaped.

By the time I finally faded away and dropped off to sleep on the sofa, the eyes of the party finally closing, no power on earth could have roused me.

I was *gone*.

When I woke up, hours and hours later, I was staring at Ron's dick.

As you can well imagine, this is no way to greet the day. I'm sure my reaction must have been wonderfully comical (at least judging from the others in the room who saw me lurch into consciousness), but it was hardly hilarious from my perspective. See, I'm not at all used to being face to, ahem, face with male genitalia first thing in the morning so it was...a jolt.

"And another one is up!" was Ron's greeting. He grinned wickedly. "I've been *up* for hours..."

I didn't doubt it. Thankfully, Ron wasn't at *attention*, so to speak, but he was indeed pantless and that was disturbing enough. I hardly knew what to say or if, in fact, this display required any comment at all.

And let there be no doubt: I had joined the Rocky cast for many reasons, chief among them being the opportunity to be among people who were not uptight or bound by strict religious codes that stifled their creative energies. So I hardly expected these people to be a gang of prudish schoolmarms who turned up their noses at the first sign of prurience. Far from it.

Still, a guy's dick in your face before coffee was taking things a bit far.

Ron was in his glory. He was intoxicated on his own bravado, gleefully hopping around the place, enjoying himself immensely and taking any and all suggestions that were lobbed his way.

There was, for example, a hole in the wall that was the result of someone having backed the corner of a table into it months earlier. Was Ron, perhaps, interested in fucking the wall?

He was. He did. The crowd went wild.

Some shaving cream was produced. Would Ron be willing to apply it to his member and make it chat with us like some deranged, foam-bearded Muppet?

He would. He obliged. And somewhere out there in the world, Grover shuddered and wondered why.

Ron was working the room, refusing absolutely no request and almost daring the crowd to dream up something too over-the-top for him to comply. He was drunk on his own daring and there was no one who could stop him (nor particularly inclined to do so). The consensus seemed to be that it was best to let him run his course and see where things went. Why kick the wasps' nest? Who would do such a thing?

A voice suddenly sounded from the kitchen doorway:

"Jesus Christ, Ron. What the fuck makes you think anyone wants to look at *that*?"

The room went deadly quiet as Ron slowly turned to face his accuser. Storme stood framed in the doorway, a disapproving scowl upon her face.

This, we thought, should be pretty good. After all, they had never faced off before, Ron and Storme, and a confrontation was well overdue. It was the classic struggle: the immovable object (Ron) versus the irresistible force (Storme). We weren't quite sure how this would turn out, but someone was about to be very, very sorry.

Ron smiled and gazed down at himself. "I see you can't take your eyes off it, Storme."

Storme barely batted an eye. "Well, who could, with you waving it in everyone's face? What's wrong, can't find anyone to put it in so you have to air it out?"

She had landed a blow, you could see it. But Ron wasn't one to wilt under just one punch.

"Honey, I'd have offered it to you," he smiled. "But I don't think you'd know what to do with it."

This was an effective line because, as we all knew, Storme was a virgin. But if the blow landed, Storme never showed it.

Instead, she volleyed back: "What would I *do* with it? I'd probably give it something to eat. The poor thing looks hungry. Don't you feed it?"

The room exploded into laughter.

And that about did it for Ron.

See, Ron's strong suit had never been the witty banter. He was a man of action and when words failed him—as they did at this moment—he used his boundless energy instead. Following Storme's comment, Ron simply marched across the room and, without a word, swept Storme off her feet and into his arms. Storme, for her part, did nothing to resist. She instead looked as if she were interested to see how this scenario might end.

Ron carried her across the room, gently deposited her in a shopping cart, which for some reason was parked in the middle of the living room floor, and then disappeared into the kitchen. Storme seemed unperturbed by this development and didn't even attempt to get out of the cart. Whatever Ron had in mind, she was going to let him play it out.

She was unimpressed. She was unmoved. She was unafraid.

She was also very seriously underestimating Ron's capacity for mischief.

When he returned, Ron had pulled on a pair of shorts and held in his hands a length of rope and a pair of handcuffs. Everyone in the room perked up when these props entered the stage. Things were bound to get interesting now.

Moving with a speed and utility you'd have thought impossible for a teenage boy at that hour of the morning, Ron soon had Storme tied securely into the shopping cart and had neatly secured her wrists with the cuffs. Storme was now clearly, completely and undeniably under his power.

At this point, I would expect that most young ladies in a similar situation would be frantic. Or at the very least, alarmed. Storme looked almost bored. Stoic. It was clear from her expression: If Ron thought he could get under her skin with this pathetic display, he had a great deal to learn.

For Ron's part, he didn't seem in the least bit upset by Storme's lack of emotion. Perhaps because, deep down, he knew that the game was far from over.

"You know," Storme said from the shopping cart, "tying me up doesn't make me want to see your dick any more than I did before. Have other girls given you the impression that it would?"

It was the final dare. And Ron took it.

He flung open the front door of the house, positioned himself behind the cart and trundled her out the door.

Down the sidewalk, down the block, Ron kept pushing. We gathered in the doorway and watched them go. When he got to the corner, he jerked the cart to his right and around the corner. No one at the party seemed inclined to follow them so we simply went back inside, a little stunned by this development.

There was a long pause. I'm sure that each of us was picturing where they could be at this moment, the young half-naked boy pushing the trussed-up girl in the shopping cart down the busy city street.

Finally, I felt compelled to break the silence. "Where will he take her?" I asked, to no one in particular.

Tony replied, "Who knows? Hell, we might never see her again."

This answer seemed to satisfy everyone and we began to talk about breakfast. A few minutes later, Ron returned. He was alone and looked very pleased with himself.

After a very long, very awkward silence, Tracey finally spoke up. "Um... where is she?"

Ron was a Sphinx. He clammed up and gave us nothing. All he wanted was breakfast and brooked no inquiries as to Storme's whereabouts.

It was hours before she finally turned up and we got the whole story.

What had happened was, Ron had wheeled Storme for a few blocks, silently pushing the rattling shopping cart down the sidewalk while she prattled away at him, calling him an asshole and making it clear that she wasn't fazed by his behavior in the least.

Ignoring her, Ron continued piloting the cart down the street, until at last he unexpectedly veered left, crossed the Eastbound lane of the highway and steered the cart into the grassy median. A few lonely trees were placed there for decoration and Ron maneuvered the cart between them, doing what he could to hide Storme among the foliage. Stepping back to admire his handiwork, he pronounced it satisfactory and, without another word, turned on his heel and returned to the house.

And there Storme sat, like a feather in a hat, nestled among the palms, until a concerned citizen noticed her there an hour later and alerted the local law-enforcement officials that a young lady appeared to be tied up in a shopping cart, sitting placidly among the trees in downtown Hollywood. The police had responded and, without gaining very much information from the victim (despite their insistent questioning), released her from her confinement, confiscated the shopping cart *and* the handcuffs and sent the young girl on her way.

Despite this experience, when she finally strolled back through the Orphanage doorway, Storme was unbowed. She leveled her eyes at Ron and pronounced: "I'm still not interested in seeing your dick. Just so you know." It was an impressive recovery but, truth be told, you really had to score this one for Ron.

However, while he might have emerged victorious in this particular battle, their karmic war was far from over.

And You Shall Receive It in Abundance

Holly and I had been going out for at least a month before I finally decided to invite her to the show. She had been dying to see it but I had resisted bringing her for various reasons, all of which seemed…well, reasonable.

For one thing, I wasn't all that crazy about letting her watch me hop about as a lowly Transylvanian. I wanted her to appreciate my work in the show and to think that what I was doing was admirable and worthwhile. Sad to say, there was very little to either admire or deem worthy about Transylvanian work. When you slipped on the black jacket and makeup, you essentially became costumed furniture.

I also wanted her to see me play a real part in the show. It didn't matter which. Something that didn't involve me merely jumping around doing the Time Warp and then disappearing. I was concerned that she would arrive, watch the show and think, "This is how he spends his weekends? Looo-ser."

My reluctance to invite her to tag along with me, however, had gotten to the point where it started to look like I was hiding something.

"C'mon. Why can't I go?" Holly would plead with me.

"You can go. It's a free country and all that. I'm not stopping you."

"You're not *inviting* me either. What is it you don't want me to find out?"

See? Like that.

"Nothing!" I would say. "I don't have anything to hide."

"Uh-huh. Some Rocky girlfriend you're not telling me about probably." She was half-kidding, but the thing about being half-kidding is: you're half-serious, too.

"Honestly, no. I've never even *looked* at another girl in the show." This was not, of course, strictly true, but I hadn't *hit* on any girls in the show either, which amounted to the same thing. Didn't it?

After we'd had variations of this conversation for a few weeks, I finally relented.

"Okay, Friday. How about this Friday?" This was the last weekend in March and I decided I couldn't put it off any longer. It could be months until I actually got a chance to play one of the main characters and my delaying tactics were becoming ridiculous.

But the minute I offered the invitation, I felt like I'd made a terrible mistake. I was upsetting some kind of delicate balance, mixing my real life with my Rocky life.

Daytime Kevin was inviting someone into Nighttime Jack's realm. It was disturbing. A lot like making plans to go hang out with your doppelgänger. I mean, how does Clark Kent invite Lois Lane to share dinner with Superman and pull it off? I didn't *have* super-Krypton speed. Would disaster ensue?

Immediately Holly got all pumped up about it. "Excellent! Friday is great!" A gleam came into her eye. "So...should I dress up or bring stuff to throw or anything?"

Oh, God. It was starting.

"No, no. You don't have to do any of that. You're my guest. It's not like you're just any old person showing up. You actually know someone in the show. So you're...different. I'll tell you what, if you can pick me up and give me a ride over at about quarter to 11, we can go together."

"Great! This is going to be *so* much fun!"

"Oh, and listen..." I wasn't sure how to put this.

"I'm listening."

What the hell? Just tell her. "You should know, they don't call me Kevin there."

"They...they don't?"

"No."

She pondered this. "So what do they call you?"

"They just...call me 'Jack.'"

"Jack."

"Yeah."

Her brow furrowed even more. "Why would they call you Jack?"

118

This should be interesting, I thought. "Well, because...I told them to."

At this, I could see that she was beginning to wonder if this was some kind of joke. Either that or my sanity was becoming questionable.

"You told them to call you Jack."

"Yeah. Why not, right?"

"Because it isn't your name."

"Well, yes I...I know that. I just thought it would be fun. To give myself a new name, you know? A *cool* name." Explaining it, telling her what I had done and trying to make it clear exactly why I had made the decision to re-christen myself, began to sound really, really dumb.

Which, I must emphasize, it wasn't.

"A cool name?"

"Yeah. Jack is cool. Not like 'Kevin.' Jeez."

"What do you mean? Kevin is cool!"

Now, that was nice of her and all but I mean: How could I respond to such lunacy? "Kevin" is a *cool name*? Right. Sure. And "Poindexter" gets the ladies all damp in the drawers, too. Please.

"Well, I thought Jack was cooler. Or something. So when they asked, that's the name I gave them."

She seemed to be getting used to the idea. "Huh. Okay." Then: "So...do you expect *me* to call you 'Jack'?"

It had never occurred to me. What to do?

"No, of course not," I said. "That would...be silly, right?" I mean, would it kill her to do it? "Just...don't call me anything, I guess."

"Don't say your name. Is that the plan?"

Now I officially felt like a complete moron.

"Well, if you can avoid it, yeah. I wouldn't want it to get out."

"Wait a minute," her eyes had narrowed to slits. "You mean to tell me it's not just a nickname? They think your name really *is* Jack?"

"It's...uh." Crap. "Yeah. That's...yeah. That's right."

"I see. Well, okay '*Jack*,'" she said with a grin (for some reason, it didn't sound quite right, her saying it). "We'll give it a shot. Man, this is going to be *fun*."

Yeah, sure. So far it was a *blast*.

119

That Friday, just after 10:30, I heard Holly pull up in her car, a black, two-door Buick Riviera, and shut off the engine. Naturally, she did not simply toot the horn and expect me to come trotting out. No, this was a nice girl and, like most people who met my mother, Holly immediately recognized her innate coolness. So Holly parked, got out, and politely knocked on the door. Like good girls do.

I went to the door and opened it up and...

...she wasn't alone. Jill was with her.

"Uh...hey," I said. (What I thought, but did not say, was: "What the hell is this?")

Jill was Holly's best friend and, like Holly and my brother, was in the sophomore class at our school. And while I was a little disturbed to see her, it wasn't because I didn't like her or anything. In fact, I liked her a hell of a lot.

But this was a pretty big deal for me, bringing my girlfriend to the show. Now I was supposed to bring *both* of them? Jesus.

They were an interesting pair, Jill and Holly. Jill, for her part, was about Holly's size, weight and had roughly the same build. But there the resemblance stopped cold.

In describing Holly, you'd probably say she looked like a very nice, very normal girl. Big, bright eyes. Pretty, with curly hair, an illuminating smile and a shiny disposition. She was curvy, but didn't try to show off her body by wearing revealing or form-fitting outfits. Holly was too demure to be a showboat. She was attractive in a simple, lovely way and was exactly the kind of girl you'd bring home to mother. Which is precisely what I had done.

Jill, on the other hand, looked like sex on a plate. She had dirty-blonde hair that was feathered back in waves. Her eyes were heavy-lidded and when she nailed you with them, she seemed to be saying, "You can't handle this. Move along." She had a large nose, but not so large it would bother you. It made her distinctive. Mysterious. And from the neck down, she was a knockout and didn't bother to hide it. Every stitch of clothing she wore was best described as "clingy," but we would also accept "yowza."

So the question that shoehorned its way into my cranium was: What in the living hell was she doing here?

"Hey," said Holly as if it were nothing. "I invited Jill along. I didn't want to sit alone in the theater, you know?"

I was stunned, but tried not to show it. To cover my discomfort, I simply blurted out, probably a little too loud: "Great! Good idea. Who goes to the movies alone, right? Come on in." I ushered them past me.

And as she walked by, Jill whispered slyly, "How's it going, *Jack*?"

And in that millisecond, I thought maybe I should just die and get it all over with.

My Mom waved the girls over to the kitchen table. She had liked Holly from the first moment they'd met and always enjoyed seeing her when she dropped by.

Come to think of it, most of my friends thought my Mom was incredibly cool. She didn't try to be, but maybe the fact that her favorite ways to occupy the afternoon were smoking, drinking, and listening to rock and roll... perhaps this held a certain charm to my teenage friends. Besides, my mother worked as a barmaid, so connecting with people and getting them to open up to her was a skill she had honed over many years slinging booze.

At the moment, Mom was enjoying a post-shift beverage, having gotten back from work an hour or so earlier.

"So you're finally seeing this thing, huh?" said my mother.

"Yeah," Holly replied. "About time, right? So...what should I expect?"

"Don't ask me. I haven't seen it."

This was true. My mother, who usually showed a great interest in most everything I did, was completely ambivalent about the entire Rocky experience. She hadn't set foot in the Ultravision since I'd started in the show and didn't have plans to go.

This, as you can imagine, didn't bother me one bit. Separation of church and state, and all that. I was better off with her at home, minding the beeswax that was her own. What's more, she seemed to understand that Rocky was something that belonged to me.

Ignoring me completely, Mom said to Holly and Jill: "You'll report back to me if he's doing anything he shouldn't be doing, right?"

Holly smiled. "You'll be the first to know."

Jill liked this, too, and winked at me. "We'll watch his every step."

I could hardly believe this conversation. "Mom, I'm going out to a midnight movie on a Friday night that features transsexuals, scantily clad girls and inappropriate sexual behavior. How much more *shouldn't* I be doing?"

"Uh-huh," was all Mom said. She cocked her head at Holly. "Keep an eye on him."

"Will do."

I rolled my eyes and we took off.

We got to the parking lot of the Ultravision just before 11:15 and the back door was already open. My fellow Transylvanians were hauling in the props and set pieces. I rushed Holly and Jill inside and plopped them down in the auditorium. I was taking a risk letting two girls in without paying, but these were the first guests I'd ever invited. Some of the other cast members had brought their girlfriends a bunch of times and whisked them in the back door, so I felt pretty safe in doing so.

"Be right back," I said to them. "I've got work to do."

"Okay," said Holly. "Bye, *Jack*." They both laughed.

Know why? Because it was *hilarious*.

I got to work.

I ran out to the storage closet and helped finish the load-in with everyone else. Steve saw me and said, "Hey, Jack. Where you been?"

"Sorry. My girlfriend is here tonight. We ran a little late."

"Which one is she?" I pointed her out, making it clear which was which. "Hey, she's cute. Good for you."

"I'll introduce you later."

"Sounds good. And, uh, do me a favor."

"What's that?"

"Introduce me to her friend, too."

"Yeah, yeah."

We finished setting everything up just in time for the audience to start trickling in. Tony grabbed the microphone and started up the pre-show. While he was doing his bit, I introduced Holly and Jill to the cast members who had, by that time, become my friends: Steve, Tracey, Felicia and Jimmy.

It was a little awkward, especially when I heard a cast member say something like, "You've been going out with Jack for a while?" and I'd catch Holly's sidelong glance that said to me, "Jesus, you weren't kidding. You really *are* 'Jack,' aren't you?" But the truth was, I was the most tense person in the room. Everyone else seemed to get along just fine.

Tony eventually put in a call for that evening's virgins and, of course, I ratted out Holly and Jill. The other Transylvanians and I and pulled them up onto the stage and they offered little resistance. Neither one had been expecting this treatment but they were good sports about the whole thing. When the ceremony was over and the previews were about to begin, I sat them back down.

"I've got to get ready. Enjoy!"

"We will!" said Holly, her face lit up with excitement. "See you later!"

As I was walking back to the bathroom to get changed, I felt someone grab my elbow. I turned and found Russ walking along side me and leaning in close. He spoke in a confidential tone.

"Hey, that your girlfriend?"

"Yeah, Russ. That's Holly."

"Uh-huh. Which one?"

"The brunette. The other one is Jill."

"Jill? Great name. You should be going out with her, huh? Jack and Jill." He smiled briefly, but then it disappeared. "But seriously, is she seeing someone?"

I saw where this was going and the alarm bells started ringing. Russ and Jill? Please, let it not be so. My school world and my Rocky world would collide and there would be no going back.

Still, I had to be honest with him:

"Jill? A boyfriend? Not that I know of."

"You don't say." He grinned. "Thanks, Jack. Maybe you can introduce me to her later, huh?"

"No problem."

And he took off to get ready for the show.

I wish I could tell you that the evening turned into some hilarious, crazy night where I was suddenly called upon to perform the role of Frank-N-Furter and the girls were just blown away by my performance, but the truth was it was just a normal night at Rocky. The show went swimmingly, Holly and Jill had a terrific time and everyone in the cast really took a shine to both of my guests.

Afterward, Holly and Jill both made it clear that they completely understood the appeal of being in the Rocky show. Finally, I thought, someone from my "real world" life seemed to get it.

How much did they get it? Here's how much: Russ and Jill were a couple by the end of the night. And while I should have been amazed at how quickly he had moved to secure this young dreamboat, I really wasn't all that shocked. She was gorgeous and he was on the lookout for all things gorgeous. It made perfect sense.

The real surprise didn't arrive until the following weekend. That's when Jill joined the cast and within weeks took over as Floor Show Janet, dancing around in her underwear every weekend night.

I must admit, I didn't see that coming at *all*.

In my defense: The microphone was just *standing* there. And it was driving me *mad*.

Here it was, Friday night, the audience was streaming in, the pre-show was set to start and...no Tony. No announcements. No nothing.

What was to be done? We couldn't very well let these virgins...you know...*stay virgins*, could we? What about the chants, the cheers, the rules? All of these rituals were of supreme import.

And yet the microphone stood unattended. Ignored. Neglected.

No one was stepping up to fill in for the egregiously tardy pre-show announcer and time was ticking by. Pretty soon, the actual previews would begin and for the first time in Deerfield's (admittedly brief) history, there would be no pre-show whatsoever.

This could not stand. Someone would have to tie on the cape and fly to the rescue. It didn't take long for me to decide that that person should be... your humble narrator.

Okay, full disclosure: I had been coveting Tony's pre-show job for months. That was my second big secret, my desire to do the warm-up. Pre-show Guy and Riff. Perform those two jobs before I passed away and I could die a happy man.

So, in truth, Tony's lateness was a blessing in disguise. A gold-plated opportunity to show the folks what I was really made of.

However...actually walking up to the front of the crowd and seizing the microphone without getting prior approval from Donny was one of the most terrifying things I'd ever contemplated. I suppose I could have gone up to him and said something like, "Hey, Donny, you want me to jump up there and get things going?" but it just didn't seem right. Either you had balls or you didn't.

This was go time. So I went.

My heart hammering, my knees benoodled, I approached the microphone. I knew there was a chance I could begin talking to the crowd and immediately get a tap on my shoulder accompanied by a brusque, "Just what the fuck do you think you're doing?" before being escorted off the stage, but goddamn it, chances like this didn't just drop off the tree every day. If they yanked you, they yanked you. Deal with it.

So I stood up, signaled for Tom to hit me with the spotlight and when the beam lit me up, I bellowed into the mike, *"Good evening ladies and gentlemen and welcome to 'The Rocky Horror Picture Show'! Now sit down and shut up, we've got a lot of business to take care of and very little time to do it!"*

And in the hair-raising moments that followed…no one tackled me. No one wrenched the mic from my hand. They just…let me run the pre-show.

I knew the rules by heart, having learned from the best, so I ran through them for the assembled guests. That seemed to go well, so I next directed them to Storme, who had wandered out in search of donations. Again, the money-gathering portion of the evening seemed to go smoothly, so I moved on to cautioning them about being complete and utter girly bitches if they were mistakenly smacked in the head with a piece of toast. I even ran through a Rocky cheer or two. Things were really humming along. And just as I felt I was really hitting my stride…I saw him.

Tony. Standing off to the side, watching me do *his* pre-show.

My blood froze. I couldn't imagine why he had not immediately tapped me out and taken over once he arrived. But no. There he was, just standing there, arms folded, his face a mask.

I couldn't read his expression (or lack thereof) but I assumed that he must have been boiling with rage. Plotting his revenge. I became certain that this pre-show, these few blissful minutes when I was the center of attention, would be my last few moments as a Rocky cast member. The moment I was done, Tony would *end* me. So I decided to enjoy it while it lasted.

I hollered, I kidded with the crowd, I chanted, I bellowed, I cajoled them out of more cash and, at last, de-virginized the chosen first-timers. Finally, I got the signal to wrap things up and said good night, handing things off to the projectionist who dimmed the lights and started the picture. Then I hopped down off the front row of seats, trundled the microphone off stage and started up the aisle to get ready for my first Transylvanian scene. I still hadn't changed into my costume and makeup.

I was pulling on my jacket when I finally got the tap on the shoulder I'd been waiting for. I turned around and there he was, looming in the darkness. Tony. He was looking at me as if he had never seen me before. Like a bug under a microscope. Clearly, he was sizing me up. But for what?

"Nice job," he finally said.

"Thanks. Thanks a lot." After second or so of awkward silence, I finally blurted out: "You know, I wouldn't have done it if you hadn't been running a little…"

He cut me off. "You have fun up there?"

I wasn't sure how to answer. Obviously, I had loved it, but I didn't want him to think I was angling to take over his job. Hell, I couldn't have elbowed him aside even if I wanted to.

"Yeah. It was really great. I can see why you like it."

"Really?" he answered. "Because I hate it. It's yours." He spun around and walked away. After a stunned moment, during which my stomach did a triple gainer, I finally regained my bearings and rushed after him.

"Wait...what? You want me to...?"

"Please. God, I really fucking hate doing it. You like it, Jack? *Vaya con Dios*, man. Save me the trouble."

"You mean it?"

"Yes, I mean it. Now leave me alone. I've got to get ready for the show. I'm late enough as it is." He sounded angry, but he looked relieved and I could have sworn there was a smile dancing around his mouth. I couldn't really tell. I must have lingered, because he finally growled, "Go on, get the fuck away from me. I don't have much time."

Hearing my exit cue, I grabbed my stuff and made for the wings.

And as I padded off to the ladies room to get into costume, I thought to myself: I have a new job. Took me seven weeks to get it, but I got it.

I was Pre-Show Guy.

Onward and upward.

I only had one problem, really. I couldn't find a bald cap.

If you want to play Riff Raff in the Rocky Horror show, it is not actually *imperative* that you find a headpiece that made you look like Richard O'Brien. It isn't easy to come by, for one thing, a wig that features a shaven pate ringed with long, stringy white hair. Given the difficulty involved in obtaining one, you can choose to go *au naturel* if you like and nobody will say, "boo."

But the real hard-core Riff Raffs, they rock their wigs to the *bone*. Kenny, my idol/adversary, had a sweet one, a thick, rubberized cap and this perfect ring of hair that looped around the back in a semi-circle that...well, the goddamn thing was perfect. And for the life of me, I couldn't find one that was nearly as good looking as Ken's.

When Tracey and I had discussed our secret hopes and dreams (and formulated our plans to try to at least become the *understudies* for our chosen characters), we realized that Step One was suiting up. So it was back to the thrift stores.

Based on my ease in locating a black Transylvanian jacket, I thought that locating a tuxedo jacket with long Riff-tails would be a breeze. I was swiftly disabused of this notion. Search as I might, a tailed tux jacket eluded me.

Finally, I got creative and *made* a tuxedo jacket by cutting some material off the front of a regular black jacket and fashioning a homemade pair of tails on the back. It looked...well, let's just say awful, but serviceable. I also dug up an old tatty white vest and a pair of brown gloves, from which I trimmed the fingers to serve as my servant-gloves. I was set. All that remained was to name the gloves themselves.

This is a time-honored Rocky custom, The Naming of the Clothing. The idea isn't simply to give *everything* a name. You didn't name your socks, for example, or your pants. But it was customary to choose your most precious items of clothing (typically a hat or a pair of gloves) and give them a name. Kenny, for example, had a hat named Oscar. Russ's hat was Jake. My cap, worn in my Transylvanian scenes, was named Kilgore, after my favorite Kurt Vonnegut character. Everybody in the cast had a piece of their wardrobe that had been given a moniker at one time or another.

So, when it came time for me to name my own gloves, I decided to follow Kenny's lead. Since gloves are, by definition, a matching pair, Kenny had chosen a world-famous duo and dubbed his gloves Fred and Ginger.

I cast my mind around for an equally famous show-business pair and lighted on what I believed to be an appropriate choice. My new pair of Riff gloves were christened "Amos and Andy." (The thought that this might be the slightest bit insulting or insensitive never occurred to me for a moment. And they were *brown* gloves, okay people? Sixteen-year-olds are idiots.)

Tracey, in her costume search, had much better luck than I had. She hadn't been forced to manufacture anything. The Janet dress she found was spot-on, much better (in my opinion) than the dress Iris wore and hers looked terrific. Tracey's hat was also as close to a perfect copy as could be imagined, and her bra and slip (these are *very* important to a successful Janet) were fantastic.

I thought it might be odd for Tracey to stand in front of me, modeling her brassiere, but in actuality the Rocky experience had made seeing people walk around in their underwear as commonplace as showing off a new pair of shoes. Besides, there was nothing sexual going on with Tracey and me, and the likelihood of that ever happening was slim.

You see, Tracey had become...one of *them.*

There were a number of girls in the cast (not all, but a lot) who were totally and completely enamored with Ron. While they managed not to follow him around like devoted puppies, their willingness to become...*involved* with him could not have been more explicit if they had tattooed "Go Ahead Ron, You Know You Want To" across their foreheads. It was, frankly, a wonder that Ron hadn't just gone through half the female cast members like a hot knife through butter. I surmised that his prior experiences in that regard must have taught him at least a modicum of restraint.

But just a modicum. He was hardly a eunuch.

Tracey, the poor dear, was among the smitten-but-not-yet-conquered. It seemed only a matter of time, though. She was adorable.

So instead of making any moves on each other, she and I became incredibly close friends instead. When I wasn't hanging out with Steve, I was usually in Tracey's company. We would spend all of our off-stage time in the theater on the weekends studying our respective characters, memorizing the moves, the blocking and the choreography. We had large shoes to fill in trying to someday take over from Iris and Kenny, but our thought was:

They can't last forever.

Soon afterward, Tracey and I got married.

It was a beautiful ceremony, but then Rocky weddings always are. It doesn't take much planning, either. You just tell the cast manager you want to get hitched and then, later that night at Denny's, the ceremony is performed and you are forever joined in holy Rocky matrimony.

Rocky weddings are not common, but they are very special. Truth was, I knew of only a few cast members who had been married. Sunday had married Andrea years earlier, Ron and Mark were married and Tony and Tom's union was inevitable if they could just get over the awkwardness of calling each other "husband."

But the minute Tracey and I caught wind of the concept, we locked eyes and knew that we were destined to become a Rocky bride and groom.

There are some ground rules, though, for the affianced couple:

When choosing a Rocky spouse, it is important to pick someone who you love dearly but—very important—who you are *not* sleeping with or even *planning* to sleep with. Rocky marriages are not about sex, petty jealousies or emotional tirades.

In other words, they aren't like *real* marriages.

No, Rocky couples are all about devotion, loyalty, and the promise of a long-term, abiding and lasting friendship. That's what makes them so great and, of course, so rare.

I proposed to Tracey on a Saturday in March. By the following Friday, she was my wife. Russ performed the ceremony as the Denny's waitress delivered the food. He got right down to business quickly so his entrée wouldn't get cold.

"Do you, Jack, take this Transylvanian, Tracey, to be your awful wedded wife?"

"I do."

"Good for you. And do you, Tracey, take this Transylvanian, Jack, to be your awful wedded husband?"

Tracey's grin went out the door of the place, it was so wide. "I do."

"Then, by the power vested in me by the cast of the Wild and Untamed Things of Deerfield Beach, Florida, and 'The Rocky Horror Picture Show,' I now pronounce you husband and wife. Now kiss each other so I can get back to my tuna melt."

We did. He did. Tears were shed. Congratulations were offered. Rice was withheld.

It was inside a Denny's after all. A certain amount of restraint was expected.

Donny walked up to me after the pre-show one Friday night and pulled me aside. "Lemme talk to you a second." He motioned me to the back of the theatre. And my heart about dropped out of my body.

I had only been doing the pre-show for a couple of weeks and I was starting to think I was really getting a handle on it. Storme's monetary intake was pretty good, the virgins seemed to have a fine time and the crowds seemed nice and revved-up by the time I was done.

So as I trotted off to this little private meeting, I was filled with a sense of foreboding. Was the experiment over? Would Donny request that Tony resume his duties as Pre-Show Guy?

I was petrified.

Donny led me out into the lobby as the previews ran inside. He leaned up against the red velvet wall, lit up a cigarette and spoke to me in a low voice.

"Listen," he said, "I've been pulling double duty as Eddie and Dr. Scott since the show opened up here, right?"

"Right. Sure."

"Well, I'm about done with that shit, so lemme talk to you about something: I've been watching you and I think you might be pretty good for what I've got in mind." He took a long drag and continued. "How would you feel about doing Dr. Scott on Friday nights from here on in? Hell, eventually you could do it every night, if you want, but for now we'll start you out on once a week. What do you think? You interested?"

Now, what Donny was so generously offering me was the Rocky equivalent of a double-edged sword.

On the one hand, I would be playing a principal role. Well, sort of. I mean, I'd be playing a major character, but I'd only be doing it once a week. There was no question that this was a step up.

But there was a downside, too. Dr. Scott, in all honesty, is not exactly the most desirable character in the world. You sit in a wheelchair most of the night, you've got one song, you get pelted with toilet tissue and the climax of your evening is when you reveal your sexy, sexy leg clad only in a fishnet stocking. It's not exactly the kind of thing a young Transylvanian sits up nights dreaming about.

The positives? I would have actual lines in the show. I'd sing. I'd roll around a lot (which is kind of like dancing) and I'd have the chance to actually work with Ron and Mark and Iris and the rest of them instead of just being the guy in the background.

In the fleeting second I had before I answered Donny, it also occurred to me that by taking on Dr. Scott, I might be blowing my chances of ever getting to perform Riff Raff. Surely some other young punk in the show would speak up and be selected to be Kenny's back-up while I whiled away my time playing the old German doctor. Saying yes to Donny would definitely be a risk.

Despite all this, the opportunity I was being offered was too huge for me to consider declining. Donny was giving up one of his two roles in the show and the guy he'd chosen to step in for him was...me. It was a vote of confidence from the cast manager himself. Saying no would have been utterly moronic. So, pushing my inward concerns aside, I responded:

"Absolutely. Can't wait. I'll try to be ready in...two weeks? How's that sound?"

"Cool, Jack. Thanks," he drawled. "I think you're gonna like it a lot." He smiled through his scary Eddie makeup at me. "Now let's go watch the opening, huh?"

Sunday and Andrea awaited us. Couldn't miss that.

The first time someone called my house and asked for "Jack," my Mom wrote it off as a wrong number.

The second time, she began to grow suspicious.

And the third time, she was pissed.

Finally, she confronted my brother and me. "Why am I getting calls for someone named 'Jack' at this house?" she asked, a trifle steamed.

My dumbfounded brother looked at me. I had little choice but to confess.

"They're...looking for me."

My mother turned her not-to-be-bullshitted eyes toward me and held me firmly in her gaze.

"And why exactly," she said, "would they be asking for 'Jack'?"

I was standing on the thinnest of ice.

"I told the people at the Rocky show that..." I couldn't look at her as I said it. "I told them my name was Jack."

I tensed, waiting for the coming eruption. It never came.

Rather than explode, my mother got very, very quiet. It was much scarier.

"I see," she practically whispered. "So your name...the name, I hasten to add, that I *gave* you...that's not good enough for you and your friends. You had to ditch it and make one up on your own. Am I understanding this correctly?"

131

Now I ask you, what do you say to that? Do you blurt out, "C'mon, Mom, I'm looking to get laid here. I need a much more impressive name than 'Kevin.' So I chose the most awesome, this-will-get-the-ladies-to-drop-their-trousers name I could think of." Do you think you could really say those words to your own *mother*?

Well I sure as hell couldn't. So instead I mumbled: "I just...thought it sounded...you know..." and this was barely audible, "kinda...cool." The carpet, I should mention, was really fascinating at that moment. I couldn't tear my eyes away. It was really something else.

Mom let the moment sit for what seemed like a week or so before responding. "So 'Jack' is cool. And 'Kevin' is not." She pondered this for another minute or so and then said: "All right. I think we're clear. That's all I needed to know."

She walked away. And that was that.

My relief was inexpressible. I really couldn't believe it. No screaming, no accusations, no confining me to my room. Nothing. She asked me a straight-up question, I gave her a semi-straight-up answer and our business was concluded.

I walked away thinking that I truly did have the coolest mom on the planet.

That weekend, I learned the truth.

"Hey, your mom's really funny," said Steve when I saw him Friday night.

"My Mom?" I answered. "You talked...to my Mom?"

"Yeah. I called your house on Wednesday but you weren't there. Your mother said you were..." and he burst into laughter.

"What?" I was on the verge of panic. What did she say?

"She said..." another paroxysm of laughter. "She said you were in the backyard hanging up the sheets because you wet the bed the night before."

Standing nearby, Tracey caught what Steve had said and about fell down laughing.

"Oh man, that's great!" she cried between hoots of laughter. "Did she really say that?"

"She did!" Steve happily confirmed. They were loving this, the both of them. "She's a riot!"

And that's the way it was from then on. My mother never got mad at me, never asked me to correct my friends or request that they ask for "Kevin" when they called the house. Not once, not ever.

But if she was home and the phone rang and the person on the other end of the line asked for Jack?

Well, Jack was never able to come to the phone. No, I'm sorry. Not at the moment.

So what was "Jack" doing? All sorts of things, I learned.

He was changing his own diaper.

He was taking a long, painful dump in the can.

He was trying to capture his own farts in a bag to set them on fire.

Jack was always just a little too busy doing something absolutely, horrifyingly humiliating and could never be bothered to come to the phone. And, for as long as people called the house and asked for him, Jack would never be available to talk. Not if my mother picked up the receiver. Not *ever*.

Kevin? Sure. He's right here.

Jack? Oh, I'm terribly sorry.

He's got his finger stuck up his ass and can't make it to the phone right now.

Can I take a message?

All the Pieces Seemed to Fit Into Place

Donny, it seemed, had had enough. And none of us was really surprised when he finally announced he was finished.

Not with the cast, of course. He wasn't actually going anywhere. But running the whole show? Oh boy was he done.

To be honest, Donny never really looked all that comfortable in the role of overseer. He had a natural authority, sure, but there was something about being the Big Kahuna that didn't suit him. I guess when you're a rebel, you want to be the one rebelling, not the one in charge.

So that Saturday night, only twenty-four hours after offering me Dr. Scott, Donny announced that he would be retiring as cast manager. He was straightforward about it, as he was about everything, and made it clear that there would be no changing his mind. In terms of naming a successor, he remained mute. It would be up to us.

The baffled cast looked around the room in bewilderment. No one seemed to really want the job. Certainly, Donny left big shoes to fill and not just in the literal sense. We loved Donny and he loved us. Who wants to follow a beloved leader and be judged by the light of his reflected glory? Not too damn many.

But a contender soon emerged: Tony.

Like Donny, Tony brought a certain authoritative charm. We respected him and knew he possessed an iron spirit. He would be tough but, we presumed, fair. And once it appeared that he would not kick up a fuss if he was drafted, he was in. By unanimous consent, Tony was the new cast manager.

We cheered the swift rise of our newly anointed Fearless Leader. Tony's glorious tenure would surely be remembered forever.

135

Because it lasted exactly one night.

The following weekend, the first and only Friday of his reign, Tony stood up to run his first cast meeting. And within minutes, all hell broke loose.

It seemed that Tony was a little fed up with the whole loosey-goosey attitude that had been predominant in the Donny era, particularly when it came to enforcing *rules*. People showing up late had been tolerated. People showing up *stoned* had been tolerated. People ducking out to their cars to get laid during the show had not only been tolerated, but was actually *encouraged*. (It was rumored to "improve morale," or something.)

Well, Tony made it clear right away that the *laissez-faire* attitude of the former regime was now over. The iron fist was swiftly descending. There would be, under the new management, an equally new set of rules to be imposed, starting immediately. The new sheriff was flexing his muscles and he weren't gonna put up with no shenanigans.

Following this brief introduction, Tony started running through the list of policies and procedures to be enforced and by the time he'd gotten to...oh, I'd say number three or so, Andrea was on her feet.

"Just what in the living fuck do you think you're doing?" Her strong, commanding voice rang out and effectively silenced the room.

Tony was not amused. He looked up from his checklist with a cocked eyebrow and said, "Sit down, Andy. You do not have the floor."

Her eyes practically bugged out. "I don't have the *what*? Did you just say I don't have the fucking *floor*? *Seriously*?"

Tony lowered the clipboard and appraised this challenge to his authority. He was clearly in danger of losing control of a meeting he had barely begun. "Look, when I'm finished, you'll be welcome to express your opinion..."

"Oh, *really*?" Her contempt now permeated the room like a fog. "And what if I *don't* wait until you're done? What if I just tell you what my opinion is *right motherfucking now*? What are you going to do then? Huh? Tell me. What are you *going to do*?"

It was at this moment that I learned a little something about authority. Here it is: When you are a leader, you possess *exactly* as much authority over a group of people as they have chosen to *give to you*. If a clear majority of that group of people decides to *withdraw* that authority, lemme tell you buddy, you're shit out of luck. Respect cannot be taken forcibly. It must be earned.

Tony had, unfortunately, attempted to take—nay *command*—respect and this tactic was now backfiring horribly.

So what did he do in the face of this unexpected rebellion? What choice did he make to quell the mutiny?

Tony decided to double down.

He squared his shoulders, looked Andrea dead in the eye, gave his voice a dangerous-sounding growl and said: "I don't answer to you, Andrea, god-damn it. You answer to *me*. Now. Sit. Down."

It was an interesting approach. Suicidal, but interesting.

You see, in attempting to try to assert his absolute power as Emperor (and decimate the Rebel forces), Tony was now performing the argumenta-tive equivalent of pouring gasoline on a fire. He was not, in other words, making things any better.

Andrea, to no one's surprise, hit the ceiling.

"What did you say to me, you fuckin' cocksucker?" she bellowed at him. It must have blown his hair back, it was so explosive. "Did you just tell me to *sit down*, you fucking arrogant piece of shit?"

Perhaps sensing that this wasn't going well, Tony softened his tone. "Andrea, now wait a minute..."

But Andrea smelled weakness and she pressed her advantage. "*Wait a minute*, huh? Just how many of your orders am I supposed to obey tonight? You gonna run my life? You gonna be my mommy now, is that it? Is that what you want? To be my fucking mother? You gonna tell me how to *wipe my ass*, Tony? Are you?"

Tony had finally had about enough. "I don't have to put up with this shit from you, Andrea! You think I wanted this job, huh? I'm doing you a fucking favor runnin' this show. I'm doing *all* of you a favor."

"You want to do me a favor?" Andrea shot back. "Then go *fuck* yourself. That would do me a *big* favor."

"That's it," Tony announced. He took his clipboard with his shiny new rules attached and flung it to the ground. "I'm done with all this bullshit. You can run it yourself, Andrea. Go ahead. It's all yours."

And he walked out. Tom, to no one's surprise, was close behind and looked just about as pissed as Tony was.

Andrea hollered after him, "Fine! Take a walk! See if I care. Just don't tell me when to show up to my own fucking show, Tony! You *asshole!*"

But he was already gone. The reign of terror was over. The Death Star had exploded. And the Ewoks danced.

Following the short and volatile rule of Tony the First, two things of great significance occurred:

1. Russ was swiftly and unanimously elected cast manager.

2. Tony and Andrea started dating the following week.

Now come on. You had to see *that* coming.

All due respect to Donny and all that, but it must be said: Russ was the greatest cast manager any of us had ever seen. He was, put simply, *perfect* for the job.

Personable. Organized. Impossible to bullshit. Crafty. Charismatic. Tough. Whatever quality you wanted in a Team Leader, Russ had it in spades.

Russ was the motivator, the showman, the man behind the curtain pulling all the strings. He made things happen and, when properly motivated, had the ability to charm the pants off of anyone (a talent he employed as often as possible). Better than that, he was approachable. Where Donny, through no fault of his own, had been intimidating simply due to his imposing physical presence, Russ was a walking welcome wagon. His entire persona seemed to say, "What's on your mind?" Russ was always open for a talk or a smoke or a hard-luck story and he had a smile, a sympathetic ear and a hearty handshake for anyone and everyone.

Not that he didn't have his faults. He did. But even his faults were endearing.

For example, of all the people I have ever known, Russ was the most literal. He brooked no sarcasm and had little truck with subtext or obliqueness. Russ said what he meant and, by God, he meant what he said. And he expected the same from you.

Generally speaking, this trait of taking *everything* at face value wasn't much of a problem once you got used to it, but it did prove at times to be an impediment in my exchanges with him. This was due, I'm quite sure, to my deeply entrenched and utterly addictive sarcastic streak.

For instance: Russ was concerned about cast finances one day and announced, to no one in particular, "We've got to figure out a way to come up with more money."

And smartass me said, "Hey, I've got an idea: We could sell the women. That might work."

Russ didn't laugh. Didn't even crack a smile. You could actually see him take in what I had said, contemplate it and then reply, in all seriousness, "White slavery is illegal, Jack. C'mon, we have to think more practically."

And I loved that about him. It wasn't that my suggestion was ludicrous. It just wasn't *practical*. Selling the young ladies in the show, while very likely to raise some much-needed funds, just wasn't a viable option. Sure, we could auction them off to the highest bidder, but at the end of the day, where would we be with no females? Who would play Janet? And Magenta? I just wasn't thinking *long term*.

Good thing we had Russ around to straighten me out.

Another thing that made him a cast manager *par excellence*: When Russ said he was going to do something, it got *done*, by hook or by crook.

One time he decided that the previews just weren't revving up the crowd enough before the show and he was determined to shake things up.

So one night, he arrived at the theater with a devilish look on his face and a huge canvas bag under his arm. We tried to get him to talk but he wouldn't budge.

"You'll see soon enough." And he snuck his secret package up to the projection booth.

That night, after the usual "Animal House" and "Blues Brothers" previews had come and gone, the screen went momentarily black and then, to our utter shock and surprise, there appeared on the screen the beloved visage of Tim Curry, Rocky Horror's legendary Frank-N-Furter, in all his rock-and-roll glory, without his RHPS makeup and singing his fool head off.

Russ had somehow gotten his hands on an actual 35mm *film* of two of Curry's music videos: "Paradise Garage" and "I Do the Rock." He had given it to the projectionist and arranged to have it tacked on to the previews.

From the moment we saw Tim and heard the first few notes, the cast, predictably, went positively and completely bonkers. If you've ever found yourself among a group of people who simultaneously experienced a moment of pure and undiluted joy, you know just what I mean. We danced around, singing along with Tim and almost forgot to get ready for the damned show.

From that night forward, these videos became a staple of the pre-show festivities. The ritual went: previews first, then Tim's videos, then the movie. Russ had hit the Rocky trifecta.

We badgered him to give up his source. "Come *on*," we begged. "Where the hell did you *find* those?"

But Russ was enigmatic. "Don't ask. Enjoy." And that was all we would ever learn about the mysterious provenance of the Curry films.

After Russ took over, extra-curricular cast activities multiplied exponentially. And almost everything we did had our cast manager's fingerprints all over it. Parties, road trips, fundraisers, poker games, cookouts, beach bashes, you name it, there was Russ, toiling away in the shadows.

Gaining the respect of the Rocky cast, which Russ made look effortless, was no easy task. First, we were predisposed not to respect *anybody*. Most of us had joined the cast in a spirit of rebellion, as a rejection of the oppressive real-life world. To then discover ourselves in an actual organization governed by *rules* seemed ironic at best and absurd at worst. But, we discovered, anarchy wasn't going to get the job done. We needed firm guidance, not chaos. Or at least a workable hybrid of the two. Call it "guided chaos." And that's what we got with Russ.

The transition from Donny to Russ (with the brief Tony detour in between) was otherwise as smooth as could be. Russ ran the nightly cast meetings with a blinding efficiency, zipping through the agenda items with a minimum of muss and fuss. Sometimes, as Tony had demonstrated, these meetings could become raucous affairs (especially when someone's feathers got ruffled; not an uncommon occurrence in a cast full of divas like ours).

But Russ would smooth the raised hackles, collect the dues, re-assign roles as needed, plan our events, direct and oversee the building of new props and costumes (or repair the busted ones), and carefully establish new rules and procedures as necessary. On rare occasions, Russ would find himself in the position of having to fire a cast member for some unforgivable offense or other, but this was done in private, to spare them the humiliation of being shown the door in front of everyone.

We took to calling him "Daddy Russ" and he earned the paternal moniker. He was only a couple of years older than most of us, but he was the first guy you went to if you had a problem. Any problem. Or if you needed a place to stay. Or if you just needed someone other than your parents to bail you out of jail. It turned out that when you got in a jam, Russ was the guy you'd reach out to for help.

It wasn't always smooth sailing, running a band of misfits like ours. But Russ was our captain and he guided the show like a pro.

The next week, I performed my first show as Dr. Scott.

Was I nervous? Was I intimidated?

Puh-leeze.

By the time I finally played the role, I had already seen the Rocky show about twenty-two times. Depending on whether you have any familiarity with the Rocky world, that will either seem like a lot or a pitifully insignificant amount. Some Rocky cast members, those who stay with the show for years, will see the show 200, 300, even upwards of 500 times. And if you stop to think that they only went twice a week...well, you do the math. That's a hell of a commitment.

Anyway, when Donny asked me to do it, I wasn't all that worried about *knowing* the part. By then, I knew the lines, the song and the general blocking pretty well. But acting it...that would be something else.

I had some distinct advantages, though. Chief among them was that I was performing a character who is pushed around in his wheelchair most of the night. I didn't really have to decide where to go or when to be there. That was someone else's job. So, blocking-wise, I just had to sit back and (literally) enjoy the ride.

Another plus: Dr. Scott appears late in the film, so I was only on stage for about a half an hour or so. (Not that I wanted to be on stage for this short amount of time. I wanted just the opposite, in fact. But for my first foray into Main Character Land, I needed the least amount of pressure possible.)

In addition, the costuming demands for playing him were minimal. Jacket, shirt and tie, mustache, glasses, fishnet stocking for the end. Nothing to it.

Here is the Dr. Scott track, in a nutshell:

His first appearance comes when Frank, Riff and Brad spot him on the castle's security monitor, hanging out by the castle gate. As they chat about him, wondering how he got there and why, the good Doctor somehow makes his way indoors and is discovered suspiciously eying the remnants of a strange-looking cigarette butt in the "Zen room." Shortly thereafter, he finds himself hurtling through the house, a victim of the super-powerful Triple Contact Electro Magnet, which Frank has activated to summon him forth.

Dr. Scott then meets Frank, is reunited with Brad and almost immediately shares in the stunning discovery of young Janet and Rocky, *in flagrante delicto* in the birth tank.

Magenta breaks the tension with her dinner gong and then it's off to supper. The assembled guests chat a bit more, Dr. Scott sings his little song, Frank does the "big reveal" and the chase is on. Frank pursues Janet out of the room and through the castle, Brad pushes Dr. Scott around the stage for a bit until everyone is frozen to the ground by Frank's activation of the Transducer.

Finally, there's the Floor Show, a nice little monologue, showing off your leg in a sexy stocking, kissing Riff Raff's ass for a few minutes, getting a pardon from Riff and his sister and...that's it. End of show. Head to Denny's.

Piece. Of. Cake.

Okay, true confession time: In the minutes leading up to my first entrance, I was scared out of my mind. Thank God I was in a wheelchair, because my knees were too busy knocking to support me.

Donny had done his best to put me at ease. He checked in with me before the show, gave my costume pieces a thumbs-up and wished me well. But after that, it was all up to me.

I knew just where to start and where to go, but I had not taken the precaution of rehearsing my double-time wheelchair scoot across the floor for my big entrance. Before I knew it, I heard my cue and started zipping across the stage.

Thankfully, there were no blown tires, no patches of ice, and no meteors struck the ground before me. I gracefully slid into place and found myself face to-face-with Mark.

Now, I have mentioned that watching Mark's performance from the audience was a memorable thrill. I have further opined that, standing on the stage in close proximity to him while he played the role was even cooler. But I'm here to tell you: Getting a double-barrel of Frank-N-Furter leveled at you from just a few inches away...that's enough to blow your hair back. I gritted my teeth, settled in and played along.

There was a point during the dinner party, sitting at the table and pretending to eat Eddie's remains, when it suddenly occurred to me that, at long last, I was finally surrounded by...*them.* The heart of the Clique itself. Ron, Iris, Andrea, Sunday, Mark, Billy, Kenny; we were sitting down for the dinner scene and, I was actually a *part* of it.

To the rest of the principals, I'm sure that it was probably just another day at the office. Fun, maybe, but not a big deal. But for me, it was like hitting the lottery. Not the mega-millions lotto or something. Not *that* big. After all, I wasn't playing Riff. Yet. But the euphoria of finally being an integral part of something I had admired for so long was an extraordinary, thrilling experience.

My song went really well, as far as I could tell. At least, no one seemed horrified by my performance. And, up until the dinner scene concluded, there were no unpleasant surprises, either.

But after my number, when Frank pulls the sheet off the dinner table to reveal Eddie's corpse, things very quickly took a strange turn.

See, this moment was the signal for the chase around the castle to commence. (Frank running after Janet, and the rest of us in hot pursuit.) So after Mark and Iris took off running, Ron—as he had done dozens of times before—grabbed the wheelchair by the handles and zipped after them.

Keep in mind, though, that up until this time, Ron had been spending this portion of the show pushing *Donny* around in the wheelchair. Donny, who was about twice my size and not all that easy to maneuver about. *That* Donny.

Ron, as he pushed me away from the table, suddenly realized that he had a much smaller passenger in the wheelchair than ever before and it struck him that he could, if he moved at supersonic speed, potentially make it *all the way around the theater* in time for the next scene. But he would really, really, really have to move.

Without bothering to tell me about this sudden inspiration, Ron rocketed off, pushing me as fast as he could. And this guy could *hustle.*

I am here to positively attest that whatever the previous land-speed record for the quarter-mile wheelchair dash was in early 1982, this record was absolutely *shattered* that Friday evening. There may have been times in my young life when I screamed louder than I did during that terrifying ride, but if I did, windows all over the state must have exploded. Patrons, Transylvanians and theater ushers dove out of the way as we barreled around the circular track and came to a screeching halt back on the stage.

We had made it in time for our cue, but my heart didn't stop racing for another ten minutes.

Ron leaned over to me during the scene. "That was awesome," he whispered. "We'll have to do that every night, huh?" I was incapable of responding. The g-forces had rendered me mute.

The rest of the night was a blur. Soon, I had been turned into a statue. The Floor Show kicked in. I did my speech after Dr. Scott is unfrozen and performed my fishnet-clad-leg reveal bang on time. I even managed to sync up pretty well with my on-screen partner for the big scene with Riff Raff at the end. (Kenny, I should mention, was pretty awesome up close as well, performing right in your face. I could hardly wait to take his job.)

And then...it was over. I had done it. For the first time, I had actually performed a main-character role on the Rocky stage. Transylvanians and principal cast members alike clapped me on the back and congratulated me for not royally fucking it up. Russ made a point of taking me off in private, shaking me warmly by the hand and letting me know he was proud of me.

But Donny's reaction, for some reason, was best of all. And all he said was: "Nice work, Jack." He cracked his sidelong grin. "It's yours now."

I had taken one more step up the Rocky ladder and, looking up, I saw that I had plenty more rungs ahead of me. After this night, I couldn't wait to keep climbing.

Ironically, I had my chance even sooner than I anticipated.

Having performed in a principal role did not, of course, automatically earn me a membership into the "elite" club of Rocky royalty, the Clique itself. I no longer felt the need to genuflect before them but I wasn't exactly issued a membership card, either. Not yet.

Breaking through that glass ceiling and rising to the level of my social betters was going to take a lot of time and work. But I was on my way.

Part of the reason for the exclusivity of the Clique was that the ex-Hollywoodians had gone through so much together before setting up camp at the Ultravision. Years of drama, upheaval, squabbling, recrimination, bitterness, forgiveness and, ultimately, redemption. They were like a family, albeit a wildly diverse, unpredictably volatile family. Maybe they developed these bonds because, for many of them, their own flesh-and-blood relatives were so horrifying. Tough to say.

At any rate, no one in the cast took this bond more seriously than Ron.

Though he never talked much about his life before Rocky, I had picked up on the fact that Ron's childhood hadn't exactly been a carefree, "Leave It to Beaver" existence. As a result, when you bonded with Ron and became a member of his extended family, you *stayed* bonded. His relationships with young ladies might have resembled a carousel (with all the hopping on and hopping off), but if you were family, you were family for life.

Ron had formed one such attachment with Donny. I often heard them refer to each other as brothers and I knew there was a deep trust and affection between them. I never knew exactly where it had originated until one night when Ron was finishing up after the show, peeling off his Brad gear and climbing back into his civvies. As a finishing touch before heading out the door, Ron slipped on a dangly ruby earring and took a moment to admire it in the mirror. Donny spotted him doing this and remarked:

"I can give you another one of those if you like."

Ron grinned and shook his head. "Thanks, brother, but one is enough for now. If I need another, I'll let you know."

Donny shrugged his massive shoulders and continued on his way. "Anytime. Give me a holler."

When he was gone, I couldn't help but ask. "Donny pierced your ear?"

Ron smiled again. "Yeah. About a month or so before we came to the Ultravision. I had mentioned that I wanted to get it done during a cast meeting and Donny jumped at the chance. Said he'd done it dozens of times and it was perfectly safe so I thought, 'Why not?' So one night we're at the Orphanage and Donny walks over to me carrying a bowl of ice cubes and this huge pin. Looked like a fucking knitting needle to me and he says, 'You ready?'

"I don't know if I was or not but I said, 'Sure.' He sits down in front of me and puts a little stud into my hand. 'Once I get the hole poked,' he says, 'put that in and keep it clean. Okay? You don't want an infection.' I say, 'Fine,' and he gets to work. He holds the ice up to my lobe and numbs it down for a while. Then he holds my head steady, grabs the pin and gets this intense look on his face. Before I knew it, I feel this sharp pain, just for a second…and it's done. Donny takes the stud and slips it in, cleans up what little bit of blood there was and that was it.

"Then he leans back with this big smile on his face. 'Not bad, huh?' he says. And I say, 'No, not bad at all. Thanks a lot.' And he goes, 'No need to thank me. I always wanted to do that for someone. Now I have. It was pretty cool.'

"I couldn't believe it. Fucker had never pierced an ear before in his life and decides to experiment on *me*. Son of a bitch," he said fondly. (It isn't easy to say "son of a bitch" fondly, but Ron managed it.) He took another look in the mirror and again admired the little jewel dangling from his lobe. "Nice, though. Isn't it?"

Now, if I had discovered that someone was practicing their lobe-piercing skills on *me* without my full knowledge of their amateur status, I would have lost my marbles. I told this to Ron and he didn't seem surprised by my reaction. Neither, however, did he regret his decision.

"It all worked out. He never would have hurt me. He's my brother. My *morbid* brother, but still."

"What do you mean, 'morbid'?" I asked.

"Well…it kinda goes without saying that Donny has a sort of twisted sense of humor, right? The stuff he finds funny, it isn't what *everyone* would find funny. So this one time, we're driving to the show in Hollywood and Donny sees this…*thing* dead in the road. I don't know what it was. Possum. Kangaroo. Who knows? But it was bizarre and very, very dead. So Donny pulls the car over, gets out and tosses this thing in his trunk."

"He *what*? He put the roadkill in his *car*?"

"Yeah. Decided he wanted to show it off to the cast. Kept it there all night. Showed people after the show. Made 'em guess what it was. It was totally sick. He got rid of it the next day of course, but…" Ron leaned over to me, "not before paying a visit to Mark's house. The night before, see, Mark refused to look in the trunk. Didn't want to see it. So that next day, Donny picks me up and we drive over to Mark's house. Mark is in the backyard, so Donny and I sneak into his bedroom. After a minute or so, we come out on the back porch and tell Mark we left a little something on his bed.

"Mark goes white as a sheet and tear-asses into the house. A couple of seconds later we hear this *screech*." By now Ron is laughing, remembering Mark's reaction. "He comes out of the house…he's screaming like a girl, freaking out." Tears are streaming down Ron's face, he's laughing so hard. "What happened was—Donny bought an old coonskin cap on the way to pick me up and we brought it over to Mark's. Donny puts this thing under Mark's pillow with the tail hanging out…"

Suddenly I can picture it. Mark walking into his room, seeing the tail protruding from under his pillow, imagining the *rest* of this creature.

"We couldn't get him to calm down for about an hour, even after we told him the truth. *Man*, that was great." Ron smiled, recalling the charming little roadkill joke they shared. "Donny's been my morbid brother ever since."

One morning, a week or so afterward, I found myself standing outside of the Orphanage looking up at the Hollywood Bread Building. Ron was sitting on the porch behind me, enjoying the last of an impromptu breakfast he'd conjured up in the kitchen a few minutes earlier, and he seemed to sense that I was in the mood for trouble. Being the Maitre'd of Mischief himself, he was naturally disposed to lend a hand.

"What's on your mind, Jack?"

I wanted to *do* something. Up to this point, I felt as if I'd started to fit in with the cast pretty well. I'd taken over Dr. Scott completely and felt that I was slowly becoming one of the gang. But I hadn't yet done anything *distinctive*.

And I was anxious for that to change.

Right then, looking up at the six stories of the Hollywood Bread Building parking garage across the street, it hit me. The perfect plan.

"I'm thinking," I said very casually, "of walking up the stairs to the top of the parking garage and just tossing all my clothes off. How does that sound?"

I turned to Ron with what I considered to be a wicked grin and hoped to see him with his jaw on the floor, flabbergasted by my audacious idea.

He was singularly unimpressed.

"It's been done," he said, sipping his orange juice.

"What?" I could hardly believe it. My idea of climbing up the stairs of a parking garage in downtown Hollywood and tossing off all my garments... was *unoriginal*?

"Oh yeah. Donny did it about three months ago," he paused, letting that image sink in. "It was pretty memorable."

I was stunned. Deflated. Jesus, was there anything this cast hadn't done?

I turned my attention back to the parking structure. There had to be *something* I could do that was actually unique and memorable. But what?

It was about this time that I noticed something about the structure itself. It was, like most parking garages, made up of slanted ramps that corkscrewed up to the top and back down again. Also, it was open on the sides, with slits in the wall to allow natural sunlight inside (thus, I presume, cutting down on having to light the thing from the inside all day). Finally, there were drainage pipes that ran out of each level, jutting out a foot or so from the building near the bottom of each ramp.

These pipes, it suddenly occurred to me, looked remarkably like handholds.

Before I could even think about reconsidering, I turned to Ron and said, "Oh, yeah? I betcha Donny didn't climb up the *outside* of the building."

At last, I got the reaction from Ron that I had been looking for. His eyes lit up like a little kid's on Christmas morning.

"No," Ron replied. "No he did not."

Without another word, I crossed the street, gazed up at the mountain to be conquered and, getting a good grip on the drainage pipe, started my ascent. Ron, smiling from ear to ear, was right on my heels.

It wasn't really all that difficult, the climb itself. The place was practically *begging* to be scaled. The stucco exterior of the building was a bit of a pain (the white powder came off on your hands and clothes at the merest touch), but the pipes, the slits in the wall and the ledges of the ramps themselves made the place into a virtual ladder.

The only bad thing was that after a flight or two, you quite suddenly found yourself about thirty feet in the air with nothing between you and the ground but your own inflated sense of self.

In other words, the idiocy of this little adventure hit me at about level three.

By that time, though, a small crowd had gathered outside the Orphanage. Word had spread quickly and everyone inside had ventured out, wanting to see the little Spider-Men as we made our climb up Mount Bread Building.

Ron and I never let on to each other that we were in the least bit frightened by what we were doing. Perhaps Ron wasn't scared at all. But by the time we got to the top of level four, I was seriously questioning my own sanity. What I was doing was certainly going to be remembered, but I was hoping that it would be remembered as "Jack and Ron's Amazing Climb" and not "The Day Those Two Fucking Morons Fell to Their Deaths."

The higher we got, the more enthusiastic the crowd below became. I looked down at one point and saw Andrea, Sunday and Tracey gazing up at us with big smiles on their faces and I became inspired. Only twenty feet more to go and we'd be living legends.

Then, all at once, the cheering stopped. It took me a second or two for this to register and for a heart-stopping moment I feared that Ron had fallen. Holding my breath, I turned to look down.

Ron was still clinging to the wall below me, safe and sound. But the crowd of people outside the Orphanage was gone.

It had been replaced by three police cars.

I froze. What to do? Go on? Go back? I had no idea what my next move should be. I had never been in trouble with the police in my life. Could I actually be *arrested* for this? At the moment, it seemed very possible.

I heard a voice, but I couldn't make out what was being said. I looked down again and saw that Ron was looking at me intently.

"Did you say something?" I said.

"*Go in,*" said Ron urgently. I looked in front of me and saw that if I turned my body sideways, I could easily squeeze through the wall of the parking garage. Ron seemed to think this was a good plan and, lacking any other, I complied.

Seconds later, Ron slid through the same opening and we found ourselves inside the parking garage, huddled in the shadows.

"What do we do?" I asked him. His first idea had worked, so I figured he must have more.

Ron whispered, "Come on," and gestured for me to follow him up the ramp toward the exit door. We could easily have gone through it and made our way downstairs, but there seemed to be a very good chance that we would meet a policeman or two on his way *up* the stairs. If that happened... things could get *bad.*

Clearly coming to a decision, Ron turned to me confidently and said, "Okay, here's what I'm going to do. I'm going to go *up* the stairs to the top floor. Then I'm going to cross over to the other side of the building and see if the coast is clear. If so, I'll come back and get you and we'll *both* go up, cross over, slip down the other set of stairs (if there is one) and get the hell out of here. We clear?"

"Got it," I said. Ron pushed open the doorway to the stairwell, listened for a moment and looked back at me.

"I'll be right back," he said. Then disappeared up the stairs.

And that, I'm sorry to say, was the last I saw of *him*.

The minutes began to tick by and still I sat there, waiting for Ron to return. All I could picture was that at any moment the door would burst open and a phalanx of armed SWAT team members would come flying through with their rifles at the ready.

Finally, I couldn't take the pressure anymore. At the risk of being spotted by the cops, I decided to take another look outside. Maybe, I thought, once the two of us had disappeared inside the building, the cops had simply taken off. It was possible. Cautiously, I poked my head out through the side of the building and looked down, praying that I wouldn't see the three patrol cars.

I didn't.

Instead, there were now *five*.

I yanked my head back into the building so fast I smacked the back of my noggin on the concrete sending up a shower of white stucco powder.

Shit! What now? Ron had clearly abandoned me and I was on my own. *Think*, I told myself. *How can you get out of here undetected?*

I pictured the building itself. I was on the west side, near the exit. But there had to be an exit on the east side, didn't there? It was worth a look. So I sprinted across the lot to the other side of the building.

Miraculously, there was a stairwell there as well. My heart leaped. All I had to do was make my way down, exit the building on the east side and I'd be free and clear. I eased open the door and strained to listen with every fiber of my being.

Not a sound.

Cat-like, I slipped down the stairs, making as little noise as possible. I paused at each landing, nerves jangling, listening for the dreaded pounding of police boots. Nothing.

I reached the ground floor. The exit door had a small window, so I peeked out to see if anyone was loitering about, nightstick poised, ready to pounce. The alley was empty. I pushed my way out the door...and I was free. On the opposite side of the building from all the commotion, and back on terra firma. Nothing and no one could possibly trace me back the offending incident or identify me as one of the two idiots hanging off the wall of the building. I had nothing to fear.

Brimming with confidence and secure in the knowledge that I had escaped certain doom, I started north, turned the corner at Hollywood Boulevard and made my way back to the Orphanage.

I was thinking of how perfect it would be. I would simply walk around the next corner, stroll past the policemen sitting in their cars and saunter casually into the Orphanage, presumably to tumultuous applause. The accolades, I thought, would be the icing on the cake. This was gonna be *great*.

But as I turned the corner and found myself facing the crowd of policemen—just at that *exact* moment—a horrible thought struck me:

I was still wearing my Transylvanian outfit from the evening before. I had put it back on after playing Dr. Scott and hadn't taken it off since.

Now...you remember what a Transylvanian wears to work, don't you?

Black jacket. White shirt. Black pants.

Items which, after the climb up the stucco exterior of the building, were *completely covered* in white powder. From head to foot, I was dusted with this crap. I must have looked to these policemen as if I'd been in a food fight in a bakery.

Or, instead, like I had been climbing up the outside of a white stucco parking structure.

I felt the eyes of every cop on the street turn to me. It was as if Tom had turned on his blazing-hot spotlight and hit me with it full in the face. I stood rooted to the spot, unable to take another step. The cops were similarly frozen, looking at me in disbelief.

We stood there like that for what seemed like a month or so. Then a large, burly police officer stepped forward and crooked his finger at me.

"Come here, kid," he said. "I wanna talk to you."

I had no choice but to comply. The option of fleeing never even occurred to me. I was trapped. I slowly made my way toward the policeman as his fellow officers encircled me. I was at the center of a large ring of very displeased law enforcement officials and found myself the sole focus of their displeasure.

The officer who had beckoned me had a nameplate that said "Hardy." He looked it, too.

"And who are you?"

I stammered out my name. It didn't seem to please him (or anyone else

151

in the immediate vicinity) to make my acquaintance.

"You got some ID?"

Now, as we all know, I did not. I was the only kid my age in all of South Florida that didn't have so much as a training permit. I reached into my pocket to see if I had *anything* with my name on it. Turned out I did. I fished out my bank card and handed it to the officer.

He frowned. "This is it?" he said, puzzled.

"Yeah, that's....that's all I've got."

"Let's just take him in," said a voice to my right. I looked over and saw a tall, blonde cop shifting his weight from one foot to the other and nervously fingering the handcuffs hanging off his belt. His nameplate read "Weegman" and, to me, Officer Weegman looked about ready to break out the rubber hose and give me the beating of a lifetime.

Officer Hardy gave him a sour look. "For what? What do I charge him with?"

Weegman looked puzzled for a second or two but then had a brain-wave. "Disturbing the peace. Trespassing. We could charge him with a lot of stuff."

Hardy was unmoved. Turning back to me, he demanded, "Where do you live?"

Hearing that I lived up in Deerfield, he shook his head in disappointment. "What the hell are you doing down here at this hour of the morning?"

And here's the thing: I was brought up to respect authority, give defer-ence to my elders and all that, but...somehow it seemed to me that if I was completely honest with Officer Hardy about why I was here and what I had been up to the night before, there was a good chance that I could wind up in the back of Officer Weegman's patrol car suffering from multiple contu-sions. Rather than simply make up a story out of whole cloth, I punted.

"I'm just down here visiting with some friends. Spent the night."

"Where are these 'friends'?"

Involuntarily, I cast an eye toward the Orphanage and, to my shock, saw that the front window of the house was filled with the concerned faces of my Rocky castmates. I quickly glanced away, lest I should draw attention to the place. God help us if the cops decided to perform an inspection. Be-tween the underage girls, the teenagers reeking of beer and, oh yeah, all the drugs, we could all wind up in the pokey for years to come.

"Actually," I said to the nice police officer, "I was supposed to meet them for breakfast but I got lost."

"Bullshit." This from Weegman, who now looked as if he'd prefer nothing better than to tie me to a chair and give me the third degree. Hell, he might even raise it up to the *fourth* degree if I was uncooperative.

The questioning went on for another minute or two. Hardy would ask me some personal detail, where I went to school, if my mother knew where I was, things like that, then I would answer him as honestly as I could without dragging Rocky Horror into the discussion. I suspected that any mention of my transvestite-movie hobby would be Weegman's cue to suggest to his superior officer that I was a degenerate and, by extension, a thief and a drug dealer and deserved to be hauled down to the station, booked, tagged and bagged.

But, in the end, Hardy's merciful nature won the day. "Here you go," he said, handing me back my bank card, upon which he had inexplicably written my address. "Tell you what—find your friends, have your breakfast and get the hell out of my district. That sound like a plan?"

"Yes sir," I answered, knowing a good deal when I heard it. "Thanks a lot."

"That's okay," he said. And for a second, he looked as if he was just going to simply turn away and get into his squad car.

But instead, looking at me intently, he frowned.

Clearly, there was something that was puzzling him. I couldn't imagine what it could be.

Slowly, Officer Hardy reached towards me. I didn't move, unsure what he was up to. Then, to my great surprise and embarrassment, he stuck his hand into the breast pocket of my shirt. This simple action had happened so unexpectedly that I was completely unable to react. What in the living hell was he doing?

After a moment, and very slowly, Officer Hardy withdrew his hand and revealed what it was he had spotted stuffed into my pocket. The other police officers leaned forward in expectation. Weegman was practically drooling, hoping that Hardy had snagged a bag of heroin and that there would finally be grounds to haul me off to the hoosgow.

Instead, what Officer Hardy unfurled from my pocket, in what seemed like super slow-motion...

...was a long, black, sexy fishnet stocking.

It rustled, slightly, in the morning breeze.

Officer Hardy held it up in front of his face, his mouth agape. The other officers were similarly floored by this unusual development. I was pretty shocked myself.

The moment hung in suspended animation for an eternity. I swear, the birds even stopped singing, unable to tear their eyes away from this spectacle.

Then, excruciatingly, all eyes turned once again to me. Officer Hardy held out the stocking as if he were expecting me to offer up some kind of reasonable explanation. Unfortunately for all of us, I was unable to react in any cogent way.

Finally, Officer Hardy broke the silence:

"This yours?"

What could I say? He had pulled it out of my pocket. I could hardly deny ownership.

"Y-y-y-yes," I stammered. "Yes sir."

His eyes narrowed. He once again looked the stocking up and down and then turned his attention back to me. He chose his words, it appeared, very carefully.

"You...funny?"

We all knew what he was asking me. And to be honest, it was a logical question, given the circumstances. But I was quick to correct his misinterpretation.

"Oh, no. No sir. It's mine, but it doesn't *belong* to me. I mean to say, I don't *wear* it, of course. It's just...mine."

Yeah, that's the best I could do.

Officer Hardy had heard enough. He reached forward and stuffed the stocking back into my shirt pocket. This morning had been odd enough for him already.

"Have a nice day," he said and sauntered, a bit dazed, over to his squad car, got in and took off. The other cops followed suit and pretty soon, after the slamming of doors, the turning of ignitions and the squeal of tires on the asphalt, the police cars had disappeared and I was the only one left standing in the street.

When I was sure they were no longer able to see me, I made my way quickly to the Orphanage. As I approached, the door was flung open, I was dragged inside and immediately swarmed with people, each of whom had a separate series of questions and all of whom wanted their questions answered *first*. Russ rode to the rescue, grabbed me by the collar and hauled me away, finally sealing me off in one of the bedrooms. As he did so, he kindly requested that everyone else, as he put it, "fuck off."

Russ let me catch my breath and allowed my heart rate to return to normal before asking me what had happened. I related the story to him, just as it had transpired. Before I could finish, though, Ron burst into the room.

"Oh *man!*" he said, grinning madly at me. He was panting and pouring sweat, but also as amped up as I'd ever seen him. "That was *awesome.*" He darted across the room and gripped me in a crushing bear hug.

I was hardly ready to let my sudden abandonment be completely forgotten.

"What the hell happened to *you*?" I asked, incredulously. "I *waited* for you. You completely disappeared!"

"I know!" he said without a trace of shame or embarrassment. "It was crazy. I went up another flight or two and then made my way to the other stairwell. I wanted to be sure the coast was clear, so I went all the way to the bottom. I didn't see anyone, but then I thought, 'I can't go back up there! That would be so *stupid!*' So I just...took off."

I was flabbergasted.

"That's it?" I sputtered. "That's your excuse? You left because coming back to get me would be so *stupid for you to do*?"

Ron, either missing my tone of utter outrage or simply ignoring it, continued to revel in our close encounter with the Broward County constabulary. "Did you *see* all those cars?" he said to Russ. "It was in*sane.*" He was practically hopping up and down with excitement. "I was about a block away, watching the cops interrogating Jack, and man, they were just *itching* to take him away. They couldn't *wait* to throw him in some cuffs and toss him in a van!" The two of them burst into uncontrollable laughter. Apparently, I was the only one who found my potential incarceration less than amusing.

"Did you see...?" Russ could barely get the words out. "Did you...did you see...?"

"The *stocking*?" Ron interrupted him and they both collapsed on the floor, screaming with uninhibited hilarity.

I couldn't believe it. They actually thought this was *funny*? "Hey!" I tried to snap them out of it. "I could have been *arrested*, you know." This didn't seem to calm them down in the least. Instead, I think Ron started to piss his own pants.

I was starting to get mad. "They asked me for my ID. You know what I had to give them? My *bank card.*"

Ron couldn't breathe, he was howling so loudly. "Please..." he begged me. "Please stop....you're...you're *killing* me."

And in that moment, at last, the absurdity of the entire situation suddenly hit me. *Bank card*? What the fuck was that?

Involuntarily, I let out a tiny expulsion of laughter. Which evolved into a chuckle. Which then morphed into a gale. Until, at last, the full ridiculousness of the events of that morning finally dawned on me and I joined the two of them, howling with utter abandon on the floor.

When we had recovered and were lying against the wall, wiping the tears from our eyes, Ron turned to me.

"You're my spider-brother now, Jack. I'll never forget it. Ever." He grinned his wolfish smile.

After that, we were thick as thieves, Ron and I.

After that, we were family.

Master, We Have a Visitor

Friday night, late April, I arrive at the theater and immediately pick up on the fact that the mood surrounding the place is *decidedly* different. There is a tension, some kind of bad mojo, making its way around the Deerfield parking lot but I couldn't begin to guess its source. Finally, after watching the eighth or ninth cast member snap at someone over some trivial matter, I pulled Doc aside to get the skinny.

"You didn't hear?" he asked in a hushed tone.

I shook my head. "No. What's up?"

Doc's eyes narrowed and he leaned in close, like he was telling me the secret recipe to KFC chicken. Then he whispered, *"Marshall is coming tonight."* After delivering this piece of news with the requisite dramatic intensity, he stood up straight and spat on the ground to punctuate the sentence.

So...that explained everything. The Big Bad Wolf was finally coming to the Ultravision and the Clique was going to face their old adversary at last. No wonder everybody was jumpy.

After hearing this, I suppose I should've been tense like everybody else. Instead, I was loose as a goose. After all, I didn't know the guy. I had zero history with him. And while all the ex-Hollywood cast members sat meticulously applying their makeup and checking (and re-checking) their costumes as if they were doing the show for the last time, I cruised through my pre-show checklist without a qualm. It was nice to be the relaxed one for a change.

The vets were wound up tighter than a tick's ass. The whole situation would have been funny if they hadn't all looked ready to kill someone. I kept my distance, knowing instinctively that attempting to engage any of them

157

would only result in my head getting chomped off. I got changed as quickly and unobtrusively as I could and prepared to start up the pre-show. Before I took the stage, a thought occurred to me and I paused.

Looking for Russ, I found him pacing around the house.

"What's up, Jack?" he growled impatiently. Like everyone else, he seemed a little juiced. The tension was contagious.

"Well, I was wondering," I said cautiously, "since Marshall is going to be here tonight, do you want Tony to go back to doing the pre-show? I mean... just for this one night? I know you want the show to be the best it can be and everything."

Russ looked outraged. "No. Fucking. Way. Listen to me, Jack: We don't change the show one tiny bit for that fat bastard. We do *our* show, *our* way. He doesn't like it, he can kiss my furry white ass. We clear?" I nodded. "Good. Now get up there."

Okay then. I had my orders. On with the show.

Besides the general air of bitchiness that seemed to pervade the cast, nothing else seemed to be out of the ordinary during the pre-show. The cheers went as planned, the virgins were dealt with according to Hoyle and the crowd—an unusually large one, in fact—was primed and ready for the big event. Truth was, I got so caught up in the preparations for the performance that I completely forgot about the source of all the anxiety.

Until he walked in, of course.

Remember, I had never seen this character in my life so there was no guarantee that I would recognize the infamous Marshall when he finally arrived. All I had to go on were the unflattering descriptions, which were likely exaggerated. From all I'd been told, it would be hard to miss him when he finally waddled into the room. But how was I to know?

When the time came, however, there was no mistaking him. I could hardly believe my eyes or his *size*.

The Ultravision cast, to be clear, was not unfamiliar with big men. Donny, God knows, was pretty huge. Enormous, in fact. But Marshall was big in a much, much more...*disturbing* way.

See, while Donny was undeniably overweight, he carried himself like an athlete. And when his moment came to perform in the show, he was amazingly graceful. Agile. Almost balletic in his movements. His Eddie zipped across the floor, sashayed with Columbia and glided effortlessly through his entire number with an ease that most people would think impossible for a guy his size.

Marshall, however, was a fucking pig. Seriously. He could barely make it into the theater, he was so obscenely huge. And he just kept *arriving*. He didn't seem to fully enter the room for at least a minute. Naturally, when I spotted him, there was no doubt in my mind that our special guest had arrived.

They say that inside every fat man, there is a skinny man just dying to get out. I think that in Marshall's case, he had three of 'em in there.

He found a seat toward the back of the theater and flopped down. It was at this point, once he was fully situated and had a chance to take in his surroundings, that I first saw him goggle at the crowd. He looked around, taking in the mass of people sprawled before him, and his jaw about hit the floor.

And while I knew that my attention was supposed to be fully and completely directed toward the paid attendees whose pre-show I was conducting, when I saw Marshall's stunned reaction, a thought occurred to me. I looked around to locate the nearest Hollywood Twin veteran and caught Iris's attention.

"Hey," I said under my breath, "this guy Marshall. He's seen this place before, right?"

"You mean the Ultravision? Fuck no," Iris shot back. "The little toad probably hasn't been north of Pompano Beach his entire life."

I could hardly believe it. This was the first time that the person actually *responsible* for the formation of the Deerfield cast had ever set foot in this theater? It wasn't possible.

Puzzled, I said to Iris, "Hold on, let me ask you: The Hollywood Twin is about the size of this place, right?"

Iris looked at me as if I had grown another head. "Are you out of your fucking mind? The Twin isn't *half* as big as this place. Jesus, Jack, look around. This crowd wouldn't have fit in that place in a million years." Iris was in no mood to waste time answering my inane questions and so, with that, she whirled away, nervously prepping for the show to begin.

This last bit of news totally knocked me out. I had always assumed that this cast had migrated up to Deerfield from some sort of theatrical Valhalla down in Hollywood. The Twin, in my mind, was the Rocky Horror Mecca of South Florida. Being banished up to the Ultravision was supposed to be a punishment, not a reward. Had they actually...*upgraded* in coming here?

Time for a little detective work.

The only two people I knew from the Rocky show in Hollywood who were *not* directly involved in the whole Marshall fiasco were Tony and Tom. They had been witnesses to the infamous Saturday Night Massacre, but hadn't been a part of Marshall's cast at the time. Coming down off the pre-show, I briefly corralled them as the previews started up.

"Hey, Tony, fill me in for a second," I said. "When Marshall heard about the Ultravision show last year, he didn't just boot everyone out of his cast without investigating this place, did he? I mean, he didn't send them up here without even finding out where they'd be performing, right?"

"Jack," said Tony, sounding almost exasperated at my stupidity, "Marshall just wanted them *gone*. He didn't give a shit where they went. They could have been offered a Broadway contract, for all Marshall cared. He just wanted these people out of his greasy hair. Get it?" His point having been made, he wandered off.

To my surprise, Tom didn't immediately lope after Tony to the dressing room. Instead, he lingered behind and when Tony appeared to be out of earshot, Tom paused to add his two cents: "That's true, Jack. But that's not all there is to it." Tom looked at the floor and his brows became knotted together. Finally, he spoke and with more emotion than I'd expected. "He couldn't handle their bullshit. Know what I mean? This cast, the 'Clique' or whatever, they had this 'we're better than your fucking cast' attitude, right? And he just couldn't deal with it. But what could he do, you know? He was stuck with them."

Tom looked around, lowered his voice and continued: "Finally, this Deerfield show comes up out of nowhere, right? And suddenly he has an opportunity to get rid of these pains in his ass. So, what would you do? He jumped at it. He sent the Clique packing to where he figured they'd do the least amount of harm. Hell, I didn't blame him. I'd have done it myself." He paused, and then added the most insightful comment I'd heard him make the entire time I'd known him: "He won the battle but...he lost the war. Know what I mean? Sure, they were gone. But the real result was..." he swept his hand around the theater, "this. These people are about to show this guy what a real cast is supposed to be like." He grinned. "Well, let's hope so, anyway."

Without another word, Tom wandered off to man the lights. And with that bit of history under my belt, I grabbed my Transylvanian outfit and I headed to the ladies room to get ready.

Suddenly, a lot of things had become clear. For one, Marshall's plan to send the Hollywood troublemakers into exile in a hellish, isolated outpost had obviously been an impulsive, ill-conceived plot. If the lazy bastard had bothered to actually *visit* the Ultravision before sending the Clique to

160

what he thought was the Rocky Horror version of Siberia, things might have turned out a hell of a lot differently than they did.

As it was, he was now getting a glimpse of what his life could have been if he had employed just a little bit of foresight. Judging from the expression on his face as he gazed around, Marshall appeared to finally realize the enormity of his mistake. Spread before him was the Rocky Garden of Eden. And he was on the outside looking in.

I had to walk by his seat on my way to the ladies room and as I passed Marshall in the audience, I took a good, long look. Perhaps due to the stories I'd been told about his obnoxious personality (or more likely due to the fact that I knew about the pain he had caused all my friends), I couldn't help but think:

"Yeah, that's right, pal. This could have been yours. This whole fantastic theater. But it's *ours* now, schmucko. What you gonna do about it?"

This snide, internal aside occurred to me despite the fact that Marshall had done nothing to me at all. He hadn't humiliated me, disrespected me or even so much as *noticed* me. I was antagonistic toward him on behalf of my fellow cast members.

I was a proxy hater.

I had little time to glower at him, though. For now, he was just a regular audience member and I had a job to do. I left the big pile of goo right where I found him and went off to get to work.

Pressure, I've found, is a funny thing.

Some folks, when presented with a situation that is abnormally tense and disconcerting, will react positively, rise to the occasion and prove they have mettle, true grit, balls of steel, that sort of thing. These are those "troopers" that you've heard so much about.

Others, when the moment of truth arrives, have an unfortunate tendency to deflate, become a shell of their former selves, and will disappoint just at the moment they are most needed. This is especially likely if the stakes get too high or the odds seem to be particularly unfavorable. These people, in the parlance of performance anyway, are the infamous "chokers."

On this night, the pressure to do well was practically pushing the theater doors open. The refugees from the Twin were determined to be at their

161

best, believing that tonight's performance would say a lot about whether they deserved their new status as Rocky headliners or if Marshall's judgment of their unworthiness still held water.

It was odd to think that so much could be riding on one show. After all, the Deerfield cast could just as easily have decided that Marshall's presence was irrelevant and that they cared not one whit whether he was blown away by what they had put together.

But for some reason, it mattered to them. They collectively felt they had something to prove to the old bastard and they were gonna do it right there and then. The rules had been set, the players were ready to make their entrances and the game was *on*.

Before I continue, let me take a second to lay in some *bona fides* here, okay?

I have been intimately involved with "The Rocky Horror Picture Show," on and off, for many, many years. I have seen dozens of casts at hundreds of shows in more theaters than I can remember. Some of the casts at these shows have been unspeakably bad, some just north of mediocre and some (very few, but some) have been simply terrific.

So with that out of the way, let's make something clear:

The night Marshall Douglas stopped by the Ultravision for his first and only visit to see the Deerfield cast was undoubtedly the best live Rocky show I've ever seen and is very possibly the best that has ever been done.

Ron and Iris were on fire as Brad and Janet. They had it all: chemistry, timing and a palpable *presence*. Ron played it completely straight (even after getting clocked in the head with a roll of toilet paper) and for two solid hours he perfectly personified Brad's goofy charm. Iris was all flounce and sweetness and goodness and barely restrained sexuality. The both of them just nailed it.

Kenny brought an extra layer of cool to his Riff that night, causing me to once again eat my heart out with envy. Andrea turned the vamp-amp up to eleven and smoldered as Magenta, sashaying about on the stage in her never-sexier maid outfit.

Sunday, in her neon-gold sequins, sparkled brighter than I'd ever seen her before. Columbia is a tough role, at once girly and ferocious, but when

Sunday turned it on full-blast, as she did this night, she nearly set the stage ablaze.

Of course, this was all just a prelude to Mark's entrance. He was our big gun, after all. The fate of any Rocky show, as we all knew, rested primarily on the strength of your Frank.

At the same time, Mark was already considered a known quantity. After all, he had played Frank for months down in Hollywood before eloping with the Deerfield gang, so Marshall couldn't have been expecting much more than he had already seen at the Twin.

But something interesting had happened to Mark since he'd made the move to Deerfield and this change resulted in some very subtle improvements to his performance. Unlike before, he was now with a cast he truly loved and an ensemble that was as tight as could be. Mark was actually *enjoying* himself on stage for the first time. And it showed.

From his first entrance, bounding across the stage in his black satin robes, all the way through the slinky opening number (where he gave each bump and grind a little extra oomph) then continuing through the bedroom scenes, the dinner party and the chorus line Floor Show (which had also never gone better), Mark was a force of nature. Whatever ownership Tim Curry might have had of the role of Frank-N-Furter was relinquished, at least for one night, to our Mark.

For the rest of us, all we needed to do was to hang on and enjoy the ride. We each seemed to sense that we were playing at a new, higher level and it was important for every single one of us to keep the momentum going.

Donny finally made his entrance and his Eddie was electric. His moves were just as solid and punchy as his on-screen twin and he tossed Sunday around as if she were weightless.

I can't say anything about my Dr. Scott except that, if anyone was actually looking at me, they were missing the show. What they *should* have been doing was keeping an eye on the rest of this amazing cast. Chances are they did. The performers were magnetic.

Hell, everything fell into place that night. Billy's Rocky was spot-on, combining the innocence and bestial curiosity that made the role so much fun. Tony's Criminologist was the picture of English pomposity. Even Tom's lighting cues were perfectly timed and crystal clear.

Finally, the gang in the Floor Show, the sexual *creme de la creme* of the Rocky cast, slinked onto the stage. When their number kicked in, they were so steamy hot they'd make your hair curl. Most nights, the regular cast members would skip watching this number, having seen it all before. Tonight we couldn't tear our eyes away.

The audience seemed to sense that this was something different, something special, because when we were done we received, to our shock and delight, a long, sustained and enthusiastic standing ovation. We had received this sort of accolade on previous occasions, but tonight the audience stood and howled all the way through the end of the curtain call and through the credits. In a *movie theater.*

It was, to us, unprecedented.

Post-show, everyone was wired up. The bathroom was jammed with all of us taking off our makeup, packing up our crap and gushing about how well things seemed to have gone. The Transylvanian crew and I finished up quickly and rushed off to stow the gear. Everyone was buzzing.

As we trundled the props to storage, we could see Russ and Marshall standing in the parking lot, deep in conversation. Each of us, I'm sure, wished we could be a fly on Russ's shoulder for just those few minutes. From what we could see, Marshall was shaking his head in disbelief and gesturing back toward the auditorium. Russ didn't betray much emotion, but simply stood there, smoking and listening, occasionally tossing in a remark here or there.

I turned to Doc. "You think he'll come to Denny's?"

Doc shook his head. "He's not invited. Cast only. And he definitely ain't cast." He started to walk away and turned back. "Why? You want to meet him?"

I was a little taken aback. "Me? No! *Hell* no. I don't care."

"Okay then." Doc shrugged and snapped the lock on the storage area. "Let's get going."

One by one, the rest of the cast was making their way out of the theater and heading to their cars. I couldn't help but notice that not a single one of them was stopping by to say hello to Marshall. They just strolled past as if he were invisible (not an easy trick when you're dealing with a guy the size of a cruise ship).

The indifference displayed by the rest of the cast, their "we don't give a shit" attitude toward their former boss, made it all the more surprising when Andrea, stepping out of the lobby after the show, turned and made a beeline for Russ and Marshall.

Under his breath, I heard Doc mutter, "Here we go…"

Nobody knew what was about to happen. Chances are she could pounce on him, strangle him or, perhaps, simply eviscerate him verbally. Anything was possible. All we knew for certain was that it wasn't going to be pretty. As she got closer, we held our collective breath.

Russ saw her before Marshall did and if he thought about waving her off or attempting to intercept her, he soon abandoned the idea. Clearly, she was not about to be stopped. You could see it in her eyes. A woman on a mission.

Andrea marched up to Marshall and stopped, staring up at him. He stood, easily a full-head taller than her.

Their eyes locked. They sized each other up in silence.

Then Andrea broke into a sunny grin.

"Hi, Marshall," she said. "Enjoy the show?"

"Hello, Andrea," he managed, probably watching for the knife thrust that was sure to come. "It was…" he stopped, searching for the right way to describe it. He finally just spat it out: "It was amazing. The best I've ever seen, actually." He had no choice but to admit it, I suppose. Still, it was (if you'll pardon the expression) big of him.

"Yeah," Andrea replied, "it was, wasn't it? And you know what else? It was all thanks to you." She stepped into him so that their noses nearly touched. She looked deeply into his eyes and said, very calmly, "I can't thank you enough. Really."

Then she stepped back, looked him up and down and said, cheerily, "See ya."

And she walked away.

It was the worst thing she could have done to him. He looked as if he'd been punched.

Given the choice between spite and grace, Andrea had chosen the latter and, in doing so, had selected a much more powerful weapon. She had emasculated him with her *charm*.

There was little more to be done or said after that. Russ and Marshall bid each other adieu and we all trooped off to our cast meeting.

Once we were gathered at Denny's, Russ satisfied our curiosity by letting us in on the gist of their conversation. He told us that the Dark Lord had really enjoyed the show, thought everyone was terrific and was hoping, at some point in the near future, to bury the hatchet.

"I think he wants to open up lines of communication between the two casts. Forge a peace, you know?" Russ looked around to see how this sounded to everyone. "He wants to call a truce."

Nobody said a word, waiting for Andrea to say what was clearly on everyone's mind. It didn't take long.

"And you told him to go fuck himself." Andrea was smiling as she said it, but there was danger in those radiant eyes of hers. "Right, Russ?"

Russ knew his cue and didn't miss a beat.

"Of course, Andy," he said, grinning right back at her. "You bet your ass I did."

Andrea looked satisfied. Life went on.

But from that night forward, there was never any question: South Florida had a new champion Rocky show.

And we were it.

The Sword of Damocles

And just like that, Iris was gone.

Well, not *gone*. She would, she said, still show up at the parties and drop by the show every once in a while, but the drive every weekend from her house in South Lauderdale had become a real hassle and, despite the fact that she still loved doing Janet every Friday and Saturday, no one could deny that she had put in her time.

There also seemed to be an unwritten rule at the show: When you were finished with Rocky, you were finished. Begging and cajoling to get someone to stay once they had announced their plans to depart just wasn't done. Cast members, especially long-term cast members, could throw in the towel at any time and they did so with the blessings of the cast.

Iris's exit, though, was not completely free of complications. With her out of the picture (literally), two things immediately became clear. First, we realized that we had somehow gone through two Janets in the space of five months and had no immediate backup. More importantly, it became apparent that both Donny and Russ had been seriously derelict in their duties by not properly training understudies for all of the principal roles.

Iris, of course, hadn't completely abandoned her post. She would do the show for another week before taking off, allowing Russ the time he needed to find a proper replacement. That night, after announcing Iris's planned departure, Russ let it be known that he was looking for a new Janet. Unsurprisingly, it didn't take him long to alight on exactly the right person.

Tracey had been intimating for some time, though very shyly and privately, that she was interested in becoming Iris's heir apparent. Russ, who always had his ear to the ground anyway, seemed well aware of this. The choice was therefore obvious.

But Tracey wasn't the only ambitious person in the cast. In fact, there were quite a number of us who had been making quiet noises about edging up the ladder into some of these understudy positions. The problem Russ faced in tapping someone for such a position was this:

Each of the main roles, Janet, Brad, Frank, et al., were so tightly held by their current owners that the merest hint of a pretender to their thrones was likely to be met with fierce and angry repercussions. The cast members we knew as the Clique were intimidating enough under normal circumstances. To think of what they would be like if you appeared to pose a threat to them...it was unspeakable.

We therefore held our various ambitions pretty close to the chest. Nobody wanted to make trouble.

But Iris's departure decidedly put Russ in a difficult position. He knew, deep down, that he not only needed to move Tracey into her new role...he needed to provide full-time backups for *everybody*. And the more he thought about it, the less he wanted to do it.

Still, Russ was a bite-the-bullet type and after some initial waffling, he tackled his new assignment with gusto. One by one, he corralled each of theTransylvanians into a private confab and got a general sense of the roles we were interested in covering. And he made it very clear: We would be *covering* the roles. Not taking them over. No one was supposed to even hint at the possibility of *replacement*.

Decisions were made quickly: Russ would continue to cover Ron in the role of Brad. Billy would cover Mark as Frank. Tracey would take over Janet as soon as possible and Felicia would immediately become her understudy. Cheryl covered Sunday as Columbia. Storme covered Andrea as Magenta. Steve would cover Tony as the Criminologist. Jimmy would cover Donny's Eddie.

That left me.

Russ had a conference with me late that night at Denny's.

"Okay, Jack. Here's the question: If you had to perform as someone tomorrow night, I mean absolutely, positively *had* to do one of the parts in the show other than Dr. Scott, what would you want to do?"

Naturally, I didn't hesitate. "Riff. I'd want to play Riff Raff."

Russ was unsurprised. "Yeah, I thought so. But you know what you'd be in for, right?"

"What do you mean?"

"Well," Russ was about to light a cigarette but changed his mind. "I mean, you'd have Sunday and Andrea all over you. You know that."

I was a little perplexed. "I have no idea what you're talking about."

Russ leaned in close. "Jack, these girls have been doing the show non-stop with Kenny for over four months. Before that, the three of them were together for over a year and a half down in Hollywood. You think if you stepped into the role one night, out of the blue, they wouldn't bust your balls about it? It would be brutal. They'd eat you alive. You gotta be prepared for that, you take on this job. Understand?"

"Don't they...want me to be good?"

You could practically *hear* his eyes roll. "That has nothing to do with..." He paused, trying to explain it properly. He finally seemed to think of a way to say it. "Look: You think the two of them are protective of their *own* roles? That's nothing. They're even more protective *of each other*. You could get up there and be Richard Fucking O'Brien himself and it wouldn't matter. They'd demand Kenny back in a minute and rip you a new asshole in the bargain. *And* they'd think they were doing the right thing, too. Kenny is now, and forever will be, their Riff Raff. You get it?"

This was, to say the least, devastating news. "So you don't think I should do it." I was ready to walk away, give it all up. Especially if it meant having to go through the Sunday/Andrea meat grinder.

Russ shook his head at me again. Clearly I didn't understand a god-damn thing. "Of course not. I think you should do it. Hell, I think you'd make a great Riff. I'm just saying, if you're going to do it, be ready." He finally lit his cigarette, took a drag and leaned back.

"So," he said, eyeing me carefully, "the question is: Are you ready?"

I thought about it for about a half a second and looked him dead in the eyes.

"I guess we're gonna find out, aren't we?"

Iris left the show the following Saturday night and we had a big blowout at the Orphanage to see her off. She had been with the show—including her stint at Hollywood—for at least two years and figured she had logged, all told, at least 200 viewings of the film. Not an all-time record by any means, but very impressive nonetheless. Since first joining the cast, she had played, at least once, the role of Janet, Columbia, Magenta, Floor Show Janet, Floor

Show Columbia and, once, during a switch night, had even played Brad.

And now, after her long tenure as the go-to Janet, Iris was hanging up her bra forever.

Once at the party, we spent most of the night lining up for Donny's Shotgun Booth and listening to Iris and Mark recount stories from the past: the on-stage miscues and bizarre accidents, some of the more memorable and infamous nights performing in the show down in Hollywood, and more than a few gossipy tales of cast members long gone. Mark was a natural storyteller and Iris woke up domestic animals for miles around as she laughed uproariously through the night.

The party stretched into the wee hours of the morning, as always, but I wasn't able to keep up. I nodded off long before the sun came up and, in doing so, further cemented my reputation as a Grog.

"Grog," I should make clear, was our term for someone who has little or no stamina for staying awake. It is also a verb, referring to the act of falling asleep against your own will.

Example #1: "He's fun to party with, but come 3:00, the guy's a fuckin' Grog."

Example #2: "We were going to drive down to Key West after the movie, but she grogged on me."

You get the idea.

Some people involved with the Rocky show could stay awake for days. Hell, I don't think Ron *ever* slept. Others, like me, would do our best to keep up with everyone else but would eventually (often humorously) "grog" at odd moments during the night. It was a common occurrence to find me grogging on one of the Orphanage couches in the middle of a party, for example. And occasionally someone would catch me in a poolside grog or grogging at the beach. Once I managed to grog sitting cross-legged in the back of Tony's open pickup truck zipping down the I-95 expressway.

What can I say? I was a growing boy. I needed my rest.

Most famously, however, I was known for grogging at Denny's after the show. There I'd be, sitting with the cast, enjoying a late-night snack and chatting away, then...ZAP. It was like turning off a light switch. I was out. And if I grogged *before* my meal arrived, I'd often wake up with an empty plate in front of me and a bill to pay.

Oh, my castmates had their fun at my expense, no question about it.

The night that stands out in my mind, though, was the evening I nodded off at Denny's and Ron and Donny decided that I'd be much more comfortable...*outside*.

They had tried this little trick before, of course. I would fade out and then two of them would swoop in and try to maneuver my chair through the dining room and out of the restaurant, but I'd always ruin their fun by jerking awake and catching them in the act. They never even got as far as the threshold.

Until.

One night they were patient. Oh, so very, very patient.

They watched me power down.

And they waited.

My burger and fries were delivered but I remained unresponsive.

And they waited. To pass the time, they helped themselves to my food.

And still they waited.

Finally, as my breathing deepened and a snore began its steady rhythm, they made their move.

Ron pulled the table away and cleared the area for the grand operation. Donny stationed himself behind me and dropped into a crouch. Then, slowly, millimeter by millimeter, they leaned me back until my head rested on Donny's chest and my feet pointed straight out in front of me.

Ron knelt down with his head between my legs and locked arms with Donny. At a mutually agreed-upon signal, they both stood up...

...and hoisted me into the air, chair and all.

Then they froze. They stood stock still for what I was later told was a solid minute.

Finally, assured that I was truly out, they started for the door. Tables and chairs were cleared for their path. Hell, I think the wait staff might have pitched in. Slowly, they snaked through the restaurant and carefully maneuvered through the door.

At last, they had achieved their goal. I was outside, in the parking lot, still blissfully asleep in my enormous man-cradle.

Clearly, Donny and Ron hadn't considered what to do if their plan actually succeeded. They stood in the lot, my lifeless body slumped between them, clueless as to their next move.

Donny caught Ron's eye. "*Where?*" he mouthed silently.

Ron thought for a moment, then his eyes lit up. "*Follow me.*"

They moved toward Federal Highway, each step a painstaking effort to keep me level. There wasn't a hint of a breeze to ruffle my hair, no drop of rain to shake me from my slumber. I was completely, entirely out.

Arriving at the grassy shoulder of the road, their backs screaming in pain at the effort, Ron whispered a barely audible, "*Now*," and they cautiously lowered me to the ground. Ron stood up first and then, together, they eased me into an upright sitting position.

And there I sat, my head lolling to one side, delicately perched on the dining room chair by the side of the road. Cackling with delight, Ron and Donny made their way back into the restaurant, grabbed a booth by the front window...and waited. The whole operation, taking me from the dining room to the curb, had taken well over a half an hour and their bodies ached as if they had each run a marathon.

If the Denny's staff (or any of the cast members, come to think of it) were concerned for my safety as I sat in oblivious dreamland by the side of the highway, no one was rushing to my rescue. I was under Ron and Donny's watchful eyes, after all, so nothing dangerous was likely to happen.

Perhaps, eventually, a police car would have driven by and, like Storme before me, I would have been scooped up by the local fuzz. Or maybe I would have come to my senses and realized where I was all on my own. We'll never know.

Because what did happen was this: Sitting in my roadside diner chair, I somehow caught the eye of a truck driver piloting his rig out of the Winn-Dixie parking lot next door. A curious sight I must have been. Slumped in the chair, I must have looked either drunk, dead or a combination of both. Curious to know which of these was true, the driver paused momentarily before pulling out of the lot and conducted a test to determine if I was still among the living.

He reached up, grasped the handle of the truck's air horn and *pulled*.

From what I was told later, there was some debate among the viewers in the restaurant over what they found the most hilarious about what followed. For some, the terrified expression on my face when the sound hit me was the hands-down, piss-your-pants moment. But for others, it was the fact that I jumped approximately ten feet into the air and landed in the grass with a hilarious, arms-and-legs-akimbo *splat* that caused them—patrons, waiters and Rockettes alike— to positively lose their minds.

Don't ask me. All I knew was, as I shook the cobwebs out of my brain and realized what had happened, I swore never to eat a late-night meal with these motherfuckers again without ordering some goddamn *coffee* first...

The following Friday, Tracey made her debut as Janet. I checked in with her before the show and she was understandably petrified, but I could tell she wouldn't have traded places with anyone in the world. Besides, she was at last working directly with Ron. That meant getting closer to him and that, in turn, meant...well, God help her after that.

To prepare for her Janet debut, Tracey had been studying Iris (and, of course, Susan Sarandon) the way some people cram for their SATs. Her work paid off spectacularly during that evening's performance. She was simply terrific in the role and her adorableness off stage translated perfectly to her on-stage Janet persona. I was expecting Ron to have to occasionally lead her this way or that, correcting her movements when she veered off course, but she instead sailed through the blocking with a confidence you would have expected from a multi-year veteran. The girl knew her shit.

Naturally her reception, post-performance, was ecstatic. Everyone thought she had risen wonderfully to the occasion and their relief was palpable. After all, we were now the No.1 Rocky show in all of South Florida. We could hardly keep the title with a sub-par female lead.

No worries there. Tracey was aces.

The following weekend, however, Tracey's amazing performance would cease to be the main topic of conversation.

Because Kenny, of all people, was going to teach us all a lesson in stubbornness. And it was going to turn the Ultravision show completely upside down.

The night of Tracey's triumph, Russ saw that spirits were high and took it as an opportunity to announce that he had chosen the understudies for all the major roles and that the current principal performers were supposed to cooperate with their backups as much as possible.

Russ had braced himself for the worst (the worst being, presumably, an explosive diatribe from Andrea or Sunday). But the worst never arrived. The worst, in fact, didn't even phone to say it was coming. It just stayed away entirely. We were worst-free.

Instead, things got *frosty*. No one became angry or incensed by the news. No one screamed or yelled or made derisive comments. Nothing like that. But the temperature in the restaurant dipped about 20 degrees in the moments following Russ's pronouncement and it didn't look like spring was arriving any time soon.

No one could deny that Russ was right. There was no question that we needed full-time coverage for each principal character. That was a fact.

But the Clique, by their silence, made something else clear: They didn't have to like it.

That's when Kenny decided to make his move.

Up until this moment, Kenny had never figured big in all of the political nonsense, the personal rivalries, the sexual escapades and the ridiculous (sometimes childish) craziness that was a hallmark of the cast. He made it clear that he found all of the backstage intrigue to be just so much bullshit. Generally speaking, he rose above it.

So when Kenny picked up on his fellow cast members' reaction to the news about their understudies, their cool, snobbish attitude toward people who, in Kenny's opinion, were guilty of nothing more than offering to back them up, he formulated a plan.

And the following Friday night, only minutes before the show was set to begin:

He quit.

He picked up his shit, flipped the cast the finger and told them all to figure it out for themselves.

And the girls. Went. Bananas.

I got wind of this during the pre-show. Steve came flying up the aisle toward me and pulled me off the front row of seats where I had been whipping up the crowd.

"You'd better get back there," he said, dragging me toward the lobby of the theater. "The shit is hitting the fan."

"What's going on?"

He gave me a dark look and shook his head. "You'll see."

Even before I saw them, I could hear the intermixed sounds of both

Andrea and Sunday losing their minds and the low voice of Russ attempting to calm them down. When I finally stepped through the lobby door, I could see the group of them spread out before me like chess pieces. Kenny was standing near the exit door wearing his regular clothes. His costume and all the rest of his Riff stuff was stuffed into a bag. He looked ready to leave.

I froze. The show was going to start in just a few minutes. He should have been ready a half an hour earlier. What the hell was going on?

In front of him stood Andrea and Sunday, who were cursing and shouting at both Kenny and Russ. They alternated back and forth, not seeming to care who caught most of the shrapnel. They were in their full costumes, Andrea in her Magenta outfit and Sunday decked out as Columbia. Something about the fact that they were dressed in character and screaming at a clearly unmoved and dispassionate Kenny in civilian garb made the scene all that much more disconcerting.

For his part, Russ was standing opposite Kenny, on the other side of the shrieking women, holding up his hands in a placating gesture. The gesture, I should mention, was placating diddly-squat.

Beyond this group, and just to Russ's right, Donny stood with his back against the red velvet wall of the lobby, his Eddie costume making him look like a warrior from some future, dystopian nightmare world. A cigarette dangled from his lips and he seemed not the least bit interested in the drama playing out before him. He simply watched and smoked, betraying not a hint of emotion.

What had happened to lead up to this scene, I later discovered, was this:

Kenny arrived early at the theater and waited for the girls in the ladies room, knowing that Sunday and Andrea were always among the first to arrive. Their makeup (especially Sunday's) took forever and they were too particular to ever arrive late and have to rush the creative process. Everything had to look perfect.

Knowing their habits, Kenny rolled in at about 11 o'clock, propped his long legs up upon the makeup table, opened up a Sci-Fi magazine and waited. Sure enough, the girls arrived right on cue.

Kenny ignored them for a bit, waiting for them to get settled in, start on their makeup and engage in their usual pre-show babble. Finally, during a lull in their conversation, he sensed his moment arrived, closed his magazine and tossed the first bit of red meat to the two tigresses.

"Hey, how about Russ last week, huh?"

The girls' eyes narrowed as they turned to him.

"You mean that understudy bullshit?" said Sunday, carefully dabbing some rouge on her whitened cheek. "He can do what he wants. But it'll be a cold day in hell before they get anywhere near that stage, I can tell you that."

Andrea nodded in agreement. "It's the message that pisses me off. Like we're gonna miss a fuckin' show. Please."

"I'd have to be missing an *arm*, I swear to God," said Sunday. "Seriously, a truck would have to come by and rip my goddamn *arm off* before I'd miss a show. But Russ, he's got to have these people waiting in the wings, breathing down our necks, just dying to get on stage. It's all such a load of crap."

This continued for a while, both of the girls sneering at Russ's attempts to shoehorn them out of the way and immensely enjoying the fact that they, in actuality, held all the cards. Kenny didn't say anything, just bobbed his head up and down agreeably.

"It's unfair to *them*, if you think about it," Andrea continued. "To make them think that they're ready, that they can just jump up there at any time and do what we're doing. Shit, I've been doing this for two years. It isn't as easy as it looks."

"Fuck no," said Sunday, putting the final touches on her eyes. "But whatever. Let the baby have his bottle, that's what I say. Russ wants to pretend he's in charge, let him."

Andrea, by this time, must have noticed that while Kenny had been drinking all of this in he had not, during the entire time they'd been talking, made a single move to get ready for the show himself. And the top of the show was rapidly approaching.

"Hey," she said, appraising him. "Shouldn't you be getting dressed?"

Smiling amiably at the two of them, Kenny stood up.

"Nah. I don't think so." He picked up his bag full of stuff and headed for the exit, pausing in the doorway. "I think you should do the show without me for once. Have fun."

And he walked out.

The girls took one look at each other and came flying off their chairs, screaming after Kenny. He'd only gotten a few steps into the lobby before they were in his face, demanding an explanation.

Kenny demurred. "I don't have to explain a thing. I don't want to do the show, I'm not doing it." He tried to walk past the girls but they weren't having it.

"You can't just walk out of here, goddamn it!" Sunday blared as she blocked his path. "The show starts in like two *minutes!*"

"Sure I can. Watch me."

Andrea, just as incensed as Sunday, seemed to sense that something more was going on. "Look, if you're pissed off about something or you're trying to make some kind of fucking *point*, make it after the show. We don't have time for this bullshit now, Kenny. Get your costume on, asshole."

"Mmmmm. I don't think so. See ya." Again he tried to leave and once again they flanked him. It was dangerously close to getting physical.

Very quickly, word got to Russ and Donny that something had gone radically wrong in the lobby. By the time the two of them arrived, the situation had escalated beyond anyone's control.

Kenny had deposited his bag by the door and was leaning nonchalantly against the wall. Andrea and Sunday were imploring, nay, demanding that he pick up his gear and get into his costume *immediately*, and it was clear from their colorful use of language that they weren't taking no for an answer.

Russ and Donny's entrance into this spontaneous soap opera did little to quell the storm. If anything, it just gave Andrea and Sunday a new target for their considerable wrath.

"I'll tell you this," said Andrea, her voice getting dangerously low, "if he doesn't do the show, neither do I. You can put on two understudies for all I care. I won't fucking do it."

"Hold on," said Russ. He looked as if he were standing knee-deep in the Atlantic Ocean trying to hold back a tidal wave with a tennis racket. "I just got here. What the hell is going on?"

Kenny piped up cheerfully from the corner. "I'm not doing the show, Russ. That's all. No big deal. I don't know what they're so freaked out about."

"Stop saying that you fuckin' asshole!" Sunday shot at him. "You *are* doing the show and it's about time you knocked this shit off and got ready."

Donny took in the entire scene without a word, drifting back against the wall and lighting up a smoke.

It was about this time that I arrived.

Andrea was ratcheting up the pressure in an effort to get Kenny to snap out of whatever spell had a hold of him. "Kenny, there is *no show* without you." She spotted me and spat out, "Who's gonna do it? *Him?*" She dismissively waved her hand at me. "He doesn't know which way is fucking *up*."

Kenny saw me and bounced off the wall. "Hey, there he is!" He grinned expansively. "I don't know, Andy. Jack looks ready to go to me. Okay. We all set? Great. I'm just going to hit the road now that my understudy is here." He turned to Russ. "We all cool?"

Russ took a deep, calming breath. "Ken, what the fuck is this about?" There was a vein popping out of Russ's forehead that I'd never seen before and it looked about ready to explode. "*Why* aren't you doing the show?"

Kenny, who had again taken a step toward the door, now paused. He turned slowly to Russ and we could see that, for the first time during this exchange, he was deadly serious. A moment earlier, he looked like he was really enjoying himself. Having the time of his life. The madder the girls got, the more he seemed to get off on the whole thing. But now, as he approached Russ, his voice became thick with emotion and all pretense at having taken any pleasure in the last few minutes disappeared completely.

"Why?" he said. "Why am I leaving? Why won't I do this show tonight? Here's why." Kenny leaned close to Russ, towering over him. Russ practically had to lean back to stare up at him. "*I'm not going to turn into Robby, Russ.*" His expression was intense, penetrating. Russ looked as shocked as I'd ever seen him.

"I won't be like him," Kenny said simply. He snatched up his bag and headed for the exit. "Not ever." He banged through the door and it slammed behind him.

And with that enigmatic pronouncement, he was gone.

Don't Dream It, Be It

Nobody said anything for about ten seconds. Then, finally, Donny spoke for the first time:

"Well," he said, barely containing a laugh. "That shut you up, didn't it?"

And very slowly, all eyes in the room turned...

...to me.

Russ moved in my direction, approaching cautiously, as if he was afraid he would spook me off if he moved too quickly.

"Jack," he said in a soothing voice. "It looks like you're it. You sure you can do this?"

Andrea was still refocusing after Kenny's dramatic exit, but she managed to say, "Does he have a costume is the real question."

I found that I had lost the capacity for speech.

Russ tried to prompt me. "You have a costume, Jack?"

I was paralyzed. Was this English? Was this gibberish directed at me?

Still standing in the doorway of the theater, Steve spoke up for me. "Yeah, he's got one," he offered. "The jacket and vest are in his bag. No wig though."

I had expected everyone to be disappointed, or at least show some mild disapproval. Nobody blinked.

"Okay," said Russ to Steve. "Grab his stuff and bring it to the dressing room." Russ turned to Donny. "You've got Dr. Scott tonight, right?"

"Sure," said Donny casually. "No problem."

"Great." Russ again turned to me. "You," he said, clapping his hand on my shoulder, "this way." He led me into the ladies room to get ready and I trotted obediently after.

It didn't take long to outfit me properly. Besides the wig, all anyone needs to play Riff are the deep-set eyes, the emaciated cheekbones, the suit, the vest and the gloves. I suited up in the clothes, tried Amos n' Andy on for size and then situated myself in front of the makeup mirror. Methodically, as if he had done it a thousand times before, Russ began applying the appropriate Riff blush and liner to my face. As he did so, Andrea appeared and hovered over his shoulder. I hazarded a glance at her and found I couldn't look away. She had locked eyes with me and was looking deep, apparently searching for some kind of reassurance.

"Be honest with me," she said low, almost whispering. "Are you ready for this?"

I was a deer in the headlights of an oncoming ballistic missile. But I managed to squeak out, "I'm pretty sure."

Andrea hissed to Russ, "He's not ready."

"He'll be ready," Russ barked. "Just give him a minute, will ya?"

Outside, I could hear that the previews had begun. Russ ordered the girls out. "Go do your song. We'll be here when you get back."

Andrea and Sunday were due on stage in a couple of minutes for the opening number. I wouldn't be needed until Brad and Janet were actually approaching the castle, so I had time. The girls took one last, baleful look at me and headed off. Russ continued his work, doing his best to make a 16-year-old kid look like a middle-aged, humpbacked, balding manservant.

He had his work cut out for him.

As Russ worked, I tried to clear my mind and think ahead to what I had to do in the show. It was hopeless. The only thing in my head was the question of why Kenny would do what he had done and, more specifically, why he would choose tonight of all nights to pull this stunt?

Finally, I couldn't take it anymore. As Russ checked my face in the mirror, I blurted to him, "Okay, who the hell is *Robby*?"

Russ wasn't in the mood for chit-chat.

"No time. Tell you later," he said, adding the finishing touches. "Now... let's take a look at you."

I stood for my inspection. Russ looked...not disappointed.

"Not too shabby." He squinted at me. "Yeah. I can see it." He nodded and stood. "Okay. Let's go."

I had passed muster. Now it was time to head to the stage.

By the time we got to the lobby, Sunday and Andrea had completed the opening song and met us entering the auditorium. They stopped and examined me.

"Okay," Sunday said after a moment. "Not great. But not bad." She turned to make her way back into the ladies room to apply her own final touches but she suddenly thought better of it and grabbed my arm. It was time for my pep talk.

"Hey, Jack," she said, pulling me close. "Try not to fuck it up, okay?" Then she *winked*. Jesus. How do you respond to that?

"Okay," I said. She let go of me and headed off to get ready. I started to make my way into the theater...

...and found Andrea standing in my path.

She didn't speak for a moment or two, looking me up and down as well. Then she locked eyes with me again.

"You've probably been waiting for this a long time," she said quietly. I nodded. "Okay. Here's your chance."

Russ spoke up. "He's gonna be fine."

Andrea didn't even look at him. Her gaze was still riveted on mine. "I know he will," she responded. Her eyes appeared to soften momentarily and she almost smiled. "After all," she said, "he'll be with me."

A second more of eye contact and she broke it off, walking past me and toward the ladies' room. Russ grabbed my arm and led me into the theater to gather my props.

It was showtime.

Naturally, you don't pine for a character and spend week after week hoping and wishing for the regular performer do *exactly* what Kenny had just done without at least doing the basic preparations.

I had studied Kenny, studied O'Brien, studied the soundtrack over and over and (for good measure) over again. I had reviewed the blocking, the gestures, the timing, the dance moves...everything that made Riff Raff the cool, enigmatic character that he was, I had it down.

I hoped.

Russ walked me down to the front of the theater, calmly giving me a

181

pre-show pep talk. "Stick with Andrea and keep your eye on the screen when you can. Don't freak out. We all know what we're doing and we'll keep a lookout for you, don't worry."

By the time I got to the stage, Ron and Tracey were just finishing up their first Brad and Janet number and Tony, as the Criminologist, was taking over the narration. In the brief second or two she had between "Dammit Janet" and the car scene, Tracey ran over and grabbed me by the arm.

"You're doing it? Really?"

I must have been shaking like a frightened puppy. "Looks that way, yeah."

She threw her arms around me.

"You're gonna be fuckin' *great*," she whispered to me and then rushed off to get into Brad and Janet's rainy car.

Russ led me to where my first entrance would be and leaned in close. "I'm gonna follow you as long as you need me. You get turned around, you give me a signal or something, okay?"

"Okay," I managed.

"But if you really need help: *Keep a lookout for Andy*. Nobody knows the show like her. Got that?"

"Got it."

He looked at me closely, perhaps trying to see if I was getting ready to bolt out the door. "How you feeling?"

"Good," I lied. "Great. Can't wait."

"Okay," he looked unconvinced, but mollified. Just before he left me on my own in the dark, he offered me a toothy smile and said, "Knock 'em dead, Jack."

And with that, Russ faded back into the shadows. Moments later, the opening strains of "Over at the Frankenstein Place" began.

Now, here's what's *supposed* to happen:

On screen, Brad and Janet get out of the car, Janet puts a newspaper over her head and the two of them walk to the castle, singing. This is when the audience members whip out their newspapers, pull out their squirt guns and create an actual rainstorm in the theater.

Meanwhile on stage, the actors playing Janet and Brad shadow their on-screen avatars, singing the first verse and then, as they approach the castle, the first chorus. Tom, working the spotlight, would keep his beam tightly trained on these two actors, the light slicing through the water squirting up from the patrons.

Then, after the first chorus, the camera zooms in on the castle and finds Riff peeking out of an upstairs window. After a moment, Riff joins the song, singing his brief verse before disappearing once more. Naturally, when the on-screen view switches to Riff in the castle, Tom would swivel his light up to the lower corner of the movie screen where the actor playing Riff is discovered, ready to go.

And then, at that moment, something magical occurs. Every night.

It was a little something called: entrance applause.

See, the audience (most of it, anyway) is well aware that the actor they are now seeing on the screen is the one-and-only creator of all things Rocky. They know that the odd-looking fellow in the butler suit is none other than Mr. Richard O'Brien, author of the play, the music, the works. He is, therefore, the true hero of the piece. Thus, as a tribute to him, when O'Brien's character makes his first appearance, the crowd shows their appreciation by erupting into a chorus of enthusiastic and ecstatic applause.

Every. Night.

And the lucky performer standing in for Mr. O'Brien that evening (up until now Kenny alone) would have the pleasure of drinking in all that love as it washed up, in waves, onto the stage.

To be honest: I was kinda looking forward to that. Had been for quite a while.

But it's one thing to spend a few months eagerly anticipating, even dreaming about a moment like this. It is *something else entirely* to find yourself smack-dab in the middle of your fantasy with little to no time to mentally prepare yourself for it. What's more, it is absolutely gut-wrenching to discover, as I did now, that everything suddenly looks *very* different from your new perspective than what you had anticipated.

Standing there in the dark, awaiting my big moment, it quite suddenly occurred to me that, instead of what was supposed to happen, the following scenario would, in fact, take place:

Tom would dutifully aim his orange beam up to where I was supposed to be standing, poised as Riff Raff. But the audience would not erupt into an enthusiastic round of cacophonous applause at the appearance of their hero, Mr. O'Brien. Oh, no. Instead, the crowd would explode into a chorus of disappointed and terrified shrieks as, to everyone's horror, the spotlight illuminated the crumpled form of a young performer who had fainted dead away of sheer fright.

I swear to you, it almost happened exactly like that. Just before my big moment arrived, I stood in the utter darkness of the theater knowing that in a few seconds the light would swing my way and make me the sole focus of the show. This realization sent a thrill up my spine that I thought might cause my head to explode in a shower of brain matter and hyperbole.

This came *close* to happening, but I am happy to report that it in fact did not. Instead, some...*feeling* rose up from the depths of my being...sheer will, let's call it...that seized control of my entire person, straightened my spine and denied me the right to check out of the Consciousness Hotel. This sudden surge of power triggered some heretofore hidden inner strength, allowing me to pull myself together, strike the appropriate pose and prepare for the oncoming, all-important beam of light.

So when my moment came, Tom hit me full-on with the spot and just like that...

...I was Riff.

My ear was tuned for the sound I'd been waiting for but, for one horrifying moment, I thought it wouldn't be there. In that instant, I believed that the audience would choose this one night to forgo their nightly tribute to Rocky's creator.

But then, sure enough, there it was. Low at first, but then rising up in a mighty wave. In the few seconds between the time that the camera focused on Riff Raff and the actual singing began...it hit me full on. That spontaneous, joyful, wonderful sound of Richard O'Brien's entrance applause.

As the only Riff Raff actually present at the time, I was happy to accept this offering on his behalf. Actually, "happy" doesn't quite describe the feeling. The cow had nothing on me. I was over the moon.

And after drinking in their approval, I then set about trying to earn it.

The lyric is very simple: "*The darkness must flow down the river of night's dreaming. Flow morphia slow, let the sun and light come streaming into my life. Into my life.*"

Riff, at the end of this brief contribution to the number, then shrinks down and out of sight in the window. On our stage (lacking said window), all you had to do was slowly drop to your knees, at which point Tom would fade the light on you and shift it back to Janet and Brad.

After which, of course, the *exit* applause would occur.

Every night.

Playing Riff was, needless to say, an embarrassment of riches.

And it really would have sucked if I had fainted instead.

Things move pretty quickly after that, but I knew just where to go. Without the benefit of illumination, I gracefully loped down the ramp and readied myself for the entrance-to-the-castle scene. I had watched Kenny do the blocking dozens of times. I had practiced it, alone, in my bedroom at home. And with my first entrance behind me, my nerves were no longer jangled and raw. I suddenly had confidence and possessed the certainty that I could pull this whole thing off without a hitch.

I was ready. I was sure of it.

The next scene began outside the castle. The light hit Janet (Tracey) and Brad (Ron). They chat for a moment, ring the bell and then...the door creaks open and Riff leans out.

And the crowd yells: "Say hello, Riff!"

I creaked the imaginary door open. I leaned out. The crowd yelled their line. And in perfect sync with Riff on the screen, I greeted the new guests: "Hello."

More cheers. Riff knows how to please a crowd.

Brad and Janet make their introductions. Riff shows little interest. Brad mentions his desire to use the phone, at which point Riff feels the need to point out to them that they are wet. A bit confused by this response (they have been walking through a rainstorm, after all), Brad and Janet simply agree with his assessment. What more can they do?

Then a flash of lightning reveals a number of motorcycles parked at the entrance to the castle, something Riff clearly didn't want them to see. He quickly invites the guests indoors. They agree.

Ron and Tracey "entered" the castle and the beam of light followed them.

Now, at the Ultravision, we had a cool little moment here. See, in the film, Brad and Janet have a little private conversation, which Riff interrupts by banging the front door shut. On our stage, Kenny would meander over to the big EXIT door of the theater, push it slightly open and then, along with Riff, bang it shut, causing every audience member in the first few rows of seats to leap right out of their skin.

I sidled over to the door and eased it open. I waited patiently a few seconds and then, when my cue arrived, I jerked the door shut with a resounding boom. The first three rows of patrons jumped a mile. Excellent.

Squeezing between them, I beckoned Ron and Tracey to follow me.

We were now mere seconds away from the Time Warp. And things could not be going better.

Janet, hearing noises coming from the next room, asks Riff if they're having a party. This stops Riff in his tracks. He turns to her slowly and announces that they have arrived on a very special night. It is, he informs them, one of the master's affairs. She tries to be polite. "Lucky him," she says.

Then, out of nowhere, Magenta appears in all her maidenly glory. She cries out, to Janet's apparent discomfort, "You're lucky! He's lucky! I'm lucky! We're all lucky!"

Bang on cue, as she had so many times before, Andrea appeared from out of nowhere and delivered the line exactly as Patricia Quinn served it up in the film.

And at this point, I am sorry to relate, things began to go just a tiny bit haywire.

But just the tiniest, tiniest bit.

First, it is important you know that Magenta, being a maid, is carrying a feather duster at this point in the film (not one of those short, typical dusters—the long, thin ones that look like giant pipe cleaners). And when she is done with her initial jack-in-the-box line, she tosses the aforesaid feather duster to Riff Raff who snatches it out of the air.

As the opening strains of "The Time Warp" begin, Riff approaches an upright coffin and flicks the feather duster over it (presumably "dusting" it) as he sings the first few lines of the song.

Simple enough, right?

So Andrea, as she is supposed to do, flipped me the feather duster. Never having practiced catching it, I reached out nervously and was stunned to find that I had actually plucked it out of the air, exactly the way Riff did in the movie. Hey! Not too shabby!

I walked over to the coffin, my new prop in hand, and I "dusted" it in perfect unison with my on-screen partner. And I started to sing the beloved anthem of Rocky lovers everywhere.

There I was, at last. I was singing "The Time Warp." On stage. At the Rocky Horror show. And the entire experience was full to the brim with awesomeness.

That, friends, was the good news.

The bad news: I had no freakin' idea what to do with the goddamn feather duster.

I knew, deep down, that Riff drops it at some point. But I didn't know when. And I didn't know where. And I didn't know how. So, for reasons that have been forever lost in the mists of time...I kept it in my hand.

For what seemed like *forever*.

In my defense: When I had practiced the damn number at home, I never had any props. I never had any *scene partners*. I never had any *guidance*. It was just *me*.

Me without, let me make clear:

A fucking *feather* fucking *duster*.

And it just *wouldn't go away*. It seemed stuck to my hand. Like it was stapled on. I couldn't drop it. Impossible. I couldn't get *rid* of it. How could I? It had, in just a few seconds, become a part of me, an appendage, an extension of myself. It was like a prosthetic hand that could...you know...*dust* things.

At first, Andrea didn't notice it at all. After all, I was doing the rest of the blocking just fine. And the crazed look of panic in my eyes must have been pretty well hidden. Her lack of alarm allowed me to briefly believe that I might actually pull this off and that later, when things quieted down, I would figure out a way to ditch the stupid thing.

And that plan might have worked. However:

There is a second, a moment, just before Riff and Magenta burst into the room full of Transylvanians, when the two of them engage in a little bit of stage business that we in the Rocky business call...

...Elbow Sex.

To the uninitiated, this is doubtless an odd expression. Allow me to explain:

In the film, on a number of occasions, Riff Raff and Magenta square off (sometimes very quickly, sometimes with wonderfully agonizing sexual slowness) and perform a peculiar ritual. They face each other, splay their hands flat in the air at chest level and move their fingers toward their respective partner. When the fingers touch, the hands curve upwards, so that each part of the arm—the hand, the wrist, the forearm, all the way up to the elbow—touch briefly and release.

The fact that Riff and Magenta are brother and sister adds an element of undeniable creepiness to the whole thing, but who are we to judge?

The first of these Elbow Sex rituals happens very early in "The Time Warp" and zips by very quickly, just as Riff and Magenta sing the line, "And the void would be calling." They run at each other, enjoy a very brief bout of

187

Elbow Sex, then bang open the doors to reveal the Transylvanian partygoers, all set to dance.

I knew my cue, I moved toward Andrea, I delivered the line and I engaged in my first-ever, on-stage Elbow Sex.

And to my indescribable shock and horror, I soundly batted Andrea in the head with the feather duster.

Maybe no one else heard it. But I did. It made a sound like this:

THWOCK.

Do you know it what feels like to hear a THWOCK in the pitch-blackness of a movie theater and know, with a gathering sickness, that you just inadvertently clocked your new scene partner in the head with a prop that you never in a million years should have been holding in the first place?

In case you don't, here's what it feels like: It feels like instant death.

Your heart stops, your skin goes cold and you freeze stock-still, as if in the grips of rigor mortis. You are, for that brief second or two, stone-cold dead.

And then, horribly, life goes on and you have to face what you did.

In the millisecond after I gave Andrea a good old-fashioned thwocking, I fully anticipated that her reaction would be to whip around, reach into my chest, pull out my still-beating heart and show it to me just to teach me a good lesson.

Or perhaps she would snatch the feather duster out of my hand and return the favor, neatly cleaving my head from my shoulders with a thwock of her own.

I didn't know what was going to happen. I only knew it was going to be *bad*.

"*What the fuck was that?*" she managed in a low voice, shaking her rattled noggin.

"*I'm sorry,*" I whispered back urgently. "*It was the feather duster. I didn't know when to drop it and I...*"

"*Get rid of it!*"

"*What?*"

"*Get. Rid. Of. It.*"

"*Where?*"

Out of the dark, I felt her iron grip on my arm as she found my hand, located the offending household cleaning implement, wrenched it out of my grip and flung it behind her.

The horrible thing was finally gone. I was free.

This entire exchange took place in the time it takes for the Transylvanians to sing. "Let's do the Time Warp again!" twice and for the Criminologist to begin his recounting of the Time Warp's dance steps by intoning, "It's just a jump to the left."

By that time, especially if you're playing Riff and Magenta, you better be goddamn good and ready to jump to the motherfucking left.

And now that Andrea had thankfully and efficiently jettisoned the unholy and unspeakable object...

...we were.

It's an odd sensation, actually performing in the Rocky show. This is true for many reasons, but the primary cause of this uneasy feeling is the constant awareness of so many different bits of stimuli that are vying all at once for your concentration and attention.

First, of course, there is the movie screen and your character's movements upon it. It goes without saying that your primary duty is to mimic your counterpart as closely as possible. Fair enough.

But apart from that, there is the actual blocking of the show within the movie theater itself. The space where you are performing is obviously not going to be the same shape and size as Frank-N-Furter's on-screen castle, so it is incumbent on the cast members, the cast manager and, when you have one, the cast director to decide where the different scenes will be placed within the theater and where certain actions can or cannot be performed.

Frank's entrance, for example, has to be predetermined as being on one side of the theater or the other long before the show begins. After all, Brad and Janet need to approach this area walking *backward* so it is essential that this spot be known specifically to all parties involved. Once agreed upon, Frank must *never* be placed anywhere else in the theater for his entrance unless specifically agreed upon.

In a similar vein, the Criminologist *must* pop up for his scenes from the same, exact spot (down in front, just to the right of center) every single time. No exceptions. And when Riff Raff appears on the monitor, interrupting Brad's blow job in the bedroom scene, he needs to be placed not eleven, not nine, but *ten seats* from the aisle. This is *imperative*.

Once these movements and placements are agreed upon, it becomes the job of the actors playing those roles to remember exactly where the hell to be and arrive there *precisely* at their scheduled times. Otherwise, Tom up in the lighting area won't know where to point his spotlight, and then where will you be?

Out of the goddamn spotlight. That's where you'll be, dummy.

So, in addition to the character mimicry, there is also a great deal of very precise blocking to commit to memory and to follow religiously. That, you would think, should be enough to keep you occupied.

But that's not nearly all. There is the also the movement of the rest of the cast to keep in mind so that you don't bulldoze over a Translyvanian or another principal while moving this way or that. That is no small task, given that half of your performance is delivered in the bright, blinding whiteness of the spotlight and the rest of the time you are plunged into utter, equally blinding darkness.

Next, there is the placement and use of the props and set pieces. These must be either pre-set by you or graciously delivered to you by a helpful assistant. So it is crucial to know where your props are. Because if you find yourself in need of a laser-beam-shooting pitchfork-gun and you forget where you put it, well...you're shit out of luck, pal.

Then there are the costume changes, some of which are lickety-split and can be complicated as hell. Most of the changes you can probably perform without assistance but even these changes are illuminated only by the dim, reflected light of the theater screen.

And, finally, there is the audience. You forget about the audience *at your peril*. After all, they're the ones with all the rice, toast, cards and toilet paper to lob at you. Ignore or neglect them, they will remind you of their presence in a red-hot minute and when you least expect it.

That's the long way of saying: Performing the Rocky show successfully means staying on your toes at all times and never losing your cool.

I was off to a *fine* start, wouldn't you say?

After the feather-duster incident, I entertained the notion that the rest of my evening as Riff Raff might devolve into an unintentionally hilarious series of Inspector Clouseau-like mishaps and I was determined, with all my heart and soul, that this should not be the case.

We continued through the Time Warp and my senses were sharper than I'd ever known them to be. I was riffling through my mental Rolodex for all of Kenny's moves and, step by step, did my best to mimic what he had done the previous week. This was done in conjunction with my attempts to keep the on-screen Riff Raff well within my peripheral vision.

The rest of the Time Warp moves, as I went through them, went a little something like this:

Getting ready to cross to Columbia? Great, don't forget: arms down, then up, then down, then up, repeat three times, face off with Magenta and take a beat and...thrust hands forward, back, forward, back once again for sixteen beats then *down* on the floor. Hold, hold, wait for the dance, wander over here, three steps, then stop. Then beat, beat, wait for the line then jump to the left. Then step to the right. Then hands on the hips. Now knees in tight. Now dance with Magenta while they pelvic thrust. Then move to Columbia nice and slow, hold by the juke, it's tap dance time. Watch while Columbia jumps about. Falls on her face then...one more time: Jump to the left, step to the right, hands on the hips, knees in tight. Pelvic thrust (we're almost done): Let's do the Time Warp again (one arm and kick this time) let's do the Time Warp agaaaaaain (once more then collapse on the floor).

Breathe.

Enjoy.

First Time Warp under your belt, I was thinking. But still a hell of a lot to get done.

And that's the way the rest of the night progressed. It became a series of milestones reached, plateaus achieved and new heights to conquer.

Time Warp? Check.

Sweet Transvestite? Done. (The pose by the throne being my favorite moment.)

Next up: elevator scene, the trick to which is to time the gulp of champagne, the bottle drop and the door sequence just right.

Lab sequence. Mostly fun for the big dance number in Rocky's song, sandwiched between Columbia and Magenta, kicking up your heels.

Eddie. The "wedding." Then a break.

All this time, I'm following Andrea like a hawk, all pistons firing. After rattling her brains in the first scene, she was understandably a bit wary of me, but after a while she began to realize that I had actually prepared for the role and wasn't just making wild guesses as to what the blocking might be.

191

When I got the kick routine down during "The Sword of Damocles" (no easy piece of choreography, let me tell you) Andrea might actually have looked (though I wouldn't swear to it) *slightly impressed.*

The next scene, though, was the one I had been both dreaming about, and dreading, ever since I first set my cap to take on the role of Riff. It is the famous candelabra scene and it is noteworthy, not only because it involves a tricky series of blocking moves (waking up and torturing the post-coital Rocky and driving him from the castle), but it concludes with the most highly charged *actual* sexual moment in the entire show.

Once Riff has finally chased Rocky down the elevator shaft, he is approached by his sister Magenta. Finally alone, Riff performs an excruciatingly slow bit of elbow sex with her, after which he unexpectedly swoops in to bite her on the neck, vampire-style, as she rapturously throws back her head and moans with carnal pleasure.

Now my turn had come. I was suddenly facing a situation where, in just a few minutes, it would become my actual *job* to slowly move in, cozy up to Andrea and give her the granddaddy of all hickeys. I was at once intimidated beyond measure and excited beyond reason.

The scene began with Magenta's mopping the floor of the lab. (The audience, at this point, would begin singing, "I'm so glad we had this time together..." If you don't get the joke, I'm not going to explain it to you.) Riff, finishing up his own cleaning job, catches Magenta's eye and they both look off into the bedchamber where Rocky is resting from his wedding night with Frank.

Magenta seems to be reading Riff's mind. She cocks her head in Rocky's direction as if to say, "Go for it." Riff discards his cleaning rag and moves off in Rocky's direction. Entering the bedchamber, he stares down at Rocky, who is facing away from him and sleeping on his stomach. (The audience: "Servants enter from the rear!")

Riff looks around for a weapon and spies the candelabra in the corner. He picks it up, moves slowly toward Rocky and then taps him with the base, rousing him. Rocky turns in horror (Fire bad!) and Riff cruelly thrusts the flames into his face. Rocky attempts to move out of the way but...oh no!... Frank has chained him to the bed with manacles around his ankles. Try as he might to move to safety around the bed, Riff appears at every turn, driving him into a frenzy.

Finally, in a superhuman lunge of desperation, Rocky breaks his chain and flees in terror down the elevator shaft. Riff is close behind and malevolently hurls a candle down the shaft after him.

All of this, on our stage, seemed to go beautifully. Billy, as Rocky, was suitably terror-stricken as I chased him about. I lunged and thrust and he dodged and weaved. Then he finally disappeared down the shaft, I threw an imaginary "candle" after him for good measure and then...

...I turned.

And there was Andrea, in all her Magenta glory, looking at me adoringly. (I know she is required to do that, but I let it go for the moment.) I gazed deeply into her eyes, brought my hands forward and moved slowly into our first (non-THWOCK-enfused) bout of Elbow Sex. Up, then down. Smooth, sensual and uneventful.

That having gone *very* well, she bared her neck to me and I moved in.

Swear to God, I can still smell her neck to this day. The sweet ambrosia of her hair is a memory I can conjure up at a moment's notice.

I didn't actually bite her, of course (I'm not an idiot), but I did plant a kiss on her neck as big as the great outdoors. I heard her moan in ecstasy and silently prayed that this moment would never end.

This is a long moment in the film. I savored every bit of it.

Sadly, eventually, the spotlight turned off and we broke apart in the darkness. I don't know how long our embrace had lasted. It might have been three seconds, it might have been an hour. I have no idea.

Time meant nothing. Never would again.

After the show, in Denny's, I was getting thumped on the back a lot and showered with accolades. It was great to finally get some feedback from the rest of the cast, as no one had spoken a word to me during the show. I thought, at the time, that it was because I was sucking so terribly hard that they couldn't bear to look at me, but it turned out that their treatment of me was more related to baseball than anything else.

See, when a pitcher gets about five or six innings into a no-hitter, it is an unwritten rule that the rest of the players are not supposed to say anything about it to him lest, by doing so, they mess with his mojo. In fact, the players will pretty much treat the pitcher as a pariah during the course of the game in order to preserve his luck. This, apparently, was how the cast had perceived my performance. It was considered, from what I was hearing afterward, the Rocky Horror version of a no-hitter. They thought I was perfect.

193

I, of course, knew better. Right out of the box, I had given up what I considered to be a grand slam (if I can possibly keep this metaphor alive any longer), by actually clocking my scene partner in the cranium with a fuzzy stick. Sure, things had gone smoothly after that. Maybe even better than smoothly. Maybe really, really great. But a no-hitter? Hardly.

Something else was weighing on my mind, though, and the moment I could get him alone, I cornered Donny and asked him the question that had been nagging at me all night:

"Okay, I'm dying to know: Who the hell is Robby?"

Donny smiled and lit up a smoke. "You caught that, huh?"

"How could I miss it? Kenny dropped his name like a hissing snake. One minute Andrea and Sunday were howling at him to get on stage and the next minute they were speechless. So who is this guy?"

As he often did before launching into a story he knew was going to be good, Donny leaned back, took a long drag of his cigarette and stared momentarily up at the ceiling. Then he looked over and began:

"Robby was the Hollywood Twin Riff Raff, Jack. Kenny was his understudy. And I guess if you really want to know the whole story about how the shit hit the fan down there last year, you couldn't find a better example than Robby.

"Russ told you about the way Marshall ran his show, right? If you were playing a main character, you owned the role. Period. Forget about if you were wrong for it or if someone better came along or if you just sleepwalked through the show. So what if you didn't give a shit about your performance? It didn't matter. Marshall had your back and you were never in any danger of being replaced. I think Marshall saw it as being loyal, somehow. Even if did result in the show sucking flaming donkey dick.

"Anyway, Marshall eventually realized that he needed to have formal understudies for each of his main characters and by process of elimination he wound up choosing most of the members of this cast. Everyone here, all of us, we were the second string. The junior varsity. And, over the weeks and months we were there, each of us got to go on and play the roles. Me, Russ, Andrea, Iris, Sunday...all of us. And most of the time, not to exaggerate, we were head-and-shoulders better than the people who played the roles down there on a regular basis. But that didn't matter. Marshall had his rules.

"And then there was Robby. Robby was unlike anyone else at the Hollywood Twin in one regard. Know what it was? Robby *never* missed a show. Ever. Week in, week out, Robby showed up, played Riff, went home. And I'm here to tell you, Jack: He was fucking horrible.

194

"His timing was always off. And not just a little. It was like he was shadowing the movie in the next theater. Even when he tried, his movements were wooden and robotic. It was like watching a mannequin get pushed around the stage. And his face. Jesus. I mean, you just played the part earlier tonight. You know how cool O'Brien is in the movie. He shoots Magenta these sly looks all the time. He grins when he thinks nobody is looking. And then, at the end? He just *loses* it. '*He didn't like me! He never liked me!*' You know what I'm talking about. He's *awesome*.

"Robby? There was nothing going on at all. No expression. No change in his facial features, no matter what scene it was. Happy? Sad? Pissed? It was all the same to him.

"You remember that mask the guy wears in *Halloween*? Mike Meyers?" I nodded. "That was Robby. A big nothing. Just awful."

Donny paused, remembering. "This went on for months. Every other understudy had been on, some of us three or four times. But not Ken. He just sat there. On the sidelines. On the bench. Waiting to get in the game.

"Finally I talked to Marshall myself. 'You've gotta give him a chance,' I told him. 'He's put in his time. Let him have a show.' Marshall wouldn't budge. 'It's Robby's part. When he decides to take a night off, Skinny Kenny gets Riff.' And that was it. End of discussion.

"Well, eventually it was bound to happen. Robby wasn't Lou Gehrig, you know? He couldn't do it forever. And sure enough, one night, Robby didn't show. The cast waited around and, finally, at about fifteen minutes to showtime, someone called his house and got word that Robby was in the hospital. Burst appendix. Emergency surgery. Robby would survive, but he'd be out for at least a couple of weeks.

"This was it. Kenny's turn at the plate. He went on that night for the first time."

Donny shook his head and smiled. "Man, I'll never forget it. Ken was just on *fire*, you know? It was like...watching a starving man *eat*. He was just loving the shit out of it. Every song, every scene. He was tearing it up.

"And we're all looking at Marshall like, 'See? That's how you play the fucking part, man. That's Riff. Not that bullshit that Robby was bringing.' But come the cast meeting, Marshall doesn't say a thing about Ken. He just says, 'Let's all send our good thoughts out to Robby,' and...that was that.

"Kenny played Riff for three weeks total. Every night he got better and better. By the third week, he was impeccable. I mean dead-on great. Nobody had ever seen anything like it.

"And the week after that...Robby returned. He took over the role again.

195

And he sucked worse than ever. And Marshall never said a word."

Donny was shaking his head in disbelief at the injustice of it. I didn't bother to comment. I couldn't believe it myself.

"And you know what else?" Donny leaned forward and almost whispered to me, "Kenny never played Riff again. Until he got here. Four months later. *Four months*. Can you believe that shit?"

Donny leaned back again, took a sip of coffee and looked across the room at the cast gathered around the big table. From where I was sitting, I could see that Andrea and Sunday were in an urgent conference with Russ. And they all looked deadly serious.

"You know what I think, Jack? I think Kenny scared the crap out of those girls tonight. I really think he did."

I was looking over at the Sunday and Andrea. They were both listening to Russ and nodding their heads.

"How?" I asked.

Donny smiled. "He showed them what they were turning into. He demonstrated, pretty dramatically I'd say, that they were turning into little fucking diva versions of Robby." He snubbed out his smoke. "Not a very flattering thing to call someone. You know?"

Moments later, Russ convened the cast meeting. As usual, he got right down to business.

"First, let's hear it for Jack and his kickass Riff Raff tonight."

The table erupted in cheers. I must have turned bright pink.

Russ waited for the noise to abate and continued. "I think if tonight taught us anything, it's that we need our understudies to be ready."

A chill wind blew through the restaurant. Things were about to get icy again.

"So I've made a decision." Russ raised his voice and announced: "Every understudy in the show, every single one, will go on and perform their character at least once a month, every month, whether the regular cast member is available or not."

Every eye in the room swiveled to Andrea and Sunday, waiting for the inevitable explosion.

But they didn't move. They didn't blink. They stared up at Russ as if they thought he was making all the sense in the world.

Russ continued, "Storme and Jimmy, you're up next Friday as Magenta and Eddie. Billy and Cheryl, you're Frank and Columbia the Friday after that..." He went on, assigning a separate Friday night for each understudy to perform a role every month, rain or shine.

And the girls just sat there and took it. The miracle of the loaves and fishes had nothing on this. I couldn't figure it out.

Until I did. All of a sudden, I knew:

It was their idea. The whole understudies-go-on-every-month plan. Sunday and Andrea had proposed it to Russ. Probably *insisted* on it. It was the only explanation.

But you'd never guess it to look at them. They just sat there.

A couple of goddamn Sphinxes, they were. Unbelievable.

About ten minutes later, the restaurant door banged open and Kenny strolled in. He had a big smile on his face and sauntered casually up to the table. Every muscle in the room simultaneously tensed up. This could not end well.

"So," he grinned. "How'd it go?"

He looked completely relaxed, as if he didn't have a care in the world, which was surprising since practically everyone seated around the table assumed that these would be his last few moments of life.

After what seemed like about ten hours, Andrea looked across at me and caught my eye. She smiled, but just barely. It was there for a millisecond and then it was gone. She then turned to stare back at Kenny. Finally, she said:

"He was a hell of a lot better than your sorry ass. Pack your shit, asshole. You're done."

There was a momentary pause, and then the table exploded in laughter. Kenny didn't seem to mind at all. He, like the rest of us, knew that despite the stunt he had pulled, he would resume his Riff duties the following week. But he also knew that before things returned to normal he would have to endure a spanking from the ladies he had so unceremoniously abandoned. Taking his punishment like a man, Kenny nodded his head approvingly and slid his eyes over to where I, his new understudy, was sitting looking up at him, grinning like an idiot.

As happy as I was, I swear: I think Kenny was even happier.

Hot Patootie

Summertime in Florida is like a new morning in Hell every damn day. And yes, I know it's called the Sunshine Goddamn State. And yes, I know that the big draw is supposed to be the sunny beaches, warm climes, tanned ladies and all that. <u>I know</u>. But Jesus Tap-Dancing Christ it gets way too fucking *hot* down there and that's the honest truth.

I mentioned earlier that almost everyone in Florida has either a pool in the backyard or at least some sort of access to watery relief, right? The reason for this is because, honestly, there was just no surviving without it. The air was like soup, the temperature was not unlike the inside of a roaring kiln and the sun made it feel as if someone threw a red-hot blanket over you every time you stepped outside.

The air conditioning, refreshing as it was, couldn't be everywhere. Besides, my mother didn't make the kind of money that allowed us to keep the A/C on all day anyway. So we endured the heat and cursed our fate.

This meant that we were dripping with sweat about five seconds after getting out of the shower. You could get a sunburn walking to the store and back (those of us who actually walked, that is). But the worst was when you got into a vehicle that had been sitting in direct sunlight with the windows up for more than ten minutes. In those circumstances, it was like stepping into a car parked just outside the fifth ring of freakin' Hades.

Needless to say, when summertime rolled around in Florida, finding activities that kept you cool was a high priority. And nobody, but nobody, knew cool like Russ.

By June, the Rocky cast at Deerfield was no longer simply confining our mutual activities to the weekends alone. We had begun to crave each other's company on the weeknights, too. And once school let out and we no longer had to get up early for class...it was Friday night *every* night.

We needed ideas for exciting and interesting things to do and Russ, God love him, was the emcee of frivolity. The wizard of merriment. The ringleader of good, clean fun.

Who arranged for the mass trip to the local water park every month that summer? Daddy Russ.

The pool party at Storme's house? Russ's idea.

Even when we did something that involved moving about in the great outdoors and sweating (like the Great Softball Tournament of 1982, for example), it was Russ who showed up with a cooler brimming with tasty beverages to ward off the worst of the heat stroke.

And while we're on the subject of that softball game…

We had long since washed our hands of Marshall and the rest of the Hollywood cast, rebuffing their offer to join forces and create a mighty Rocky army. By doing so, we had (unofficially at least) declared war.

With a war on, it was inevitable that we would have battles. So, I ask you: What better place to hold a battle than a battlefield?

I want to say it was Marshall who proposed the big game, but it surely must have been one of us. (If it *had* been Marshall who conceived of the idea, Andrea would have refused to participate on general principle.) However it came about, we somehow agreed to play a game of softball against each other. We issued official challenges, accepted same, fixed upon a date, lined up equipment (gloves, bats, etc.), reserved a field for the big day and rehearsed the demeaning catcalls to be bandied back and forth between the rival casts.

Clearly, a lot of preparation goes into these grudge matches.

With our Transylvanian pride on the line, we were all itching to trounce the Hollywoodians and forever seal our reputation as the Best at Virtually Everything. Our zeal was such that we actually managed to organize a practice session the week before the game.

Even more surprising—we actually showed up for practice. Yes, we acted like good little girls and boys, turned in early the night before and arrived bright-eyed on the field the following day, all ready to give it a go. We had considered just showing up on the day of the Battle Royale and winging it, but we didn't want to ruin the perfect chance to humiliate Marshall and his cohorts. To avoid looking like complete idiots, at least one practice session was deemed necessary so...off we went.

It's a good thing, too. Because inside of five minutes, the horrifying truth came out:

We were fucking awful.

It was like the Bad News Bears, if the Bears had been retarded and slightly drunk.

The problem wasn't our hitting. We could hit just fine. Hell, some of us (especially Donny) could send the ball a mile. That wasn't the issue at all.

It was our fielding. Dear lord. In our attempts to perform the simple task of capturing a batted ball in an oversized leather glove, we were simply atrocious. *Spectacularly* bad.

We couldn't field ground balls. We couldn't snag pop-ups. We couldn't catch a friggin' cold. What made it worse, when the ball finally stopped rolling (after bouncing off our mitts and sending our hapless players scurrying after it) it turned out that most of us couldn't *throw* either.

Russ immediately attempted to make adjustments. Those of us who had actually played Little League (I was in this group) were given infielder positions. The truly abysmal players were relegated to the outfield. I suppose the strategy was to put his strongest defensive players up front and if it got by us...oh well.

Everyone rotated in and out of various positions until Russ finally agreed on a starting lineup. My sweet wife Tracey was kicked out into right field, poor dear. Sunday was in center. Felicia stood out in left. Andrea, one of our strongest players, actually, wound up at first. Russ got the hot corner at third, Ron played second and I took my place at shortstop. Donny was behind the plate, Tony took the mound and the rest were the reserves.

Despite this shuffling, we were still pretty horrifying. Balls regularly squeaked their way through the infield's defenses and the ensuing chaos in the outfield would have been supremely comical if it hadn't been so pitifully heartbreaking. It was *sad*.

Nobody seemed to know the rules, either. Players didn't call for pop-ups and so would either run into each other trying to snag one or, in the alternative, would slam on the brakes *before* the collision only to watch the ball drop pathetically to the ground between them. The concept of the "squeeze play" was lost on virtually everyone who hadn't seen a professional game and this included the majority of our team. Half the players didn't even seem to grasp the idea that it wasn't cool to spark up a cigarette *while you were playing.*

After a while, Russ called for a break. We all slumped back to the dug-out, much wiser than we had been when we arrived, but depressed as hell about the type of wisdom we had each received. Hollywood, if they were any good at all, was going to kick our sorry asses.

We dug into Russ's cooler for refreshments and sat in silence for a bit.

Finally, to break the tension, someone suggested bringing in a ringer.

"No ringers," Russ immediately shot back. "I thought Marshall might pull something like that himself so..."

"So?" said Ron.

"So we traded cast lists. Nobody who isn't on the list plays. Only full-time cast members."

Once again, we all fell mute. There seemed no way out of this disaster. We were doomed.

As we sat there, wallowing in our own sense of foreboding, a familiar scent began wafting its way down the dugout, causing eyes to snap open and nostrils to flare with considerable interest.

Russ caught it right away.

"Goddamn it, who's getting high?"

There was a moment of guilty silence, then:

"Why the hell not?" This from Sunday. "As long as we're going to play like shit, we might as well enjoy it."

This sentiment seemed to be shared among most of the assembled play-ers. The joint, produced from who knows where by God knows who, was passed among the interested cast members. I took a pass. I followed Russ, who had wandered away from the dugout dejectedly.

He was standing near the mound, staring in the direction of the out-field. In his dark glasses, I couldn't tell if he was focusing on anything in particular but his expression was dour. After a moment or two, I tried to lighten the mood.

"Hey, who knows? Maybe they suck worse than we do."

Russ wasn't biting. "No way, Jack. Back in the day, we used to split the cast in two and play at a field down in Hollywood." He turned and looked me square in the eyes. "They can play."

I had no response. Russ stared off for a few more minutes and then turned, plodded back to the dugout and called out to the cast.

"Okay, two more innings and we'll call it a day. Let's go."

Needless to say, getting everyone back out onto the field wasn't the easiest thing in the world to do now that they had self-medicated. But eventually we managed to get nine of us in position and Russ took up a bat, squaring off at the plate.

He tried not to sound defeated, but it was hard not to detect the note of tragedy in his voice.

"Okay, the play is to first."

He lofted the ball in the air and sent it skittering toward third, where Cheryl had stepped in as his replacement. I was standing immediately to Cheryl's left, at shortstop, and was fully prepared to back her up when she muffed the play.

Miraculously, however, Cheryl somehow managed to scoop up the ball cleanly, digging the grounder out of the dust. She paused momentarily, looking slightly surprised. Then she pivoted, planted her foot and rocketed the ball to first. Andrea caught it clean.

One out.

The silence was deafening. None of us could quite believe that it had happened. Cheryl had executed a perfect play, perhaps the first of the day.

In the moments afterward, despite this display of unexpected athleticism, there was no congratulatory praise heaped on Cheryl, nor did she seem to expect any. Andrea simply dug the ball out of her glove and heaved it into home where Donny caught it without a word, turned and casually flipped it to Russ.

Russ held the ball and looked out at Cheryl, somewhat stupefied. Not seemingly inclined to call attention to her defensive gem, he simply called out, "That's one," tossed the ball into the air and sent it sailing into the outfield.

Tracey, who had spent most of the morning standing in right looking bereaved and out of her element, was suddenly moving gracefully through the grass, tracking the fly ball. All at once, she planted herself and the ball fell into her glove. Plop. Ron had stepped forward as her cutoff man for the play at second but...there was no play at second. She had made the out.

Two down.

Again, the moment hung suspended. We were frozen, dazzled by the unexpectedness of this development.

And at this moment, we were all consciously aware that we faced a choice. We could either call attention to these astonishing occurrences (and risk jinxing the whole thing), or we could play it cool and act like what had happened was perfectly normal.

We opted for the latter choice. Tracey threw Ron the ball, he sent it home to Donny and we played on in silence.

For the next half hour or so, the defensive abilities of the cast improved exponentially with each play. Andrea caught a ball in foul territory that she had no business being able to get a glove on. Sunday ran in to snag a blooper that should easily have fallen for a base hit. And Ron and I, to our amazement more than anyone else's, actually managed to turn a double play.

The whole time this was occurring, Russ never said a word that wasn't related to the defensive play at hand. He'd call out, "Man at second, one out. Play is to first if hit to the right, to third if hit to the left." And he'd swat the ball out to us and watch us do our thing.

After we had notched fifteen or so outs, Russ announced that we were done. We all trotted in and gathered in the dugout.

No one said anything. What had happened was beyond words, so we didn't even bother trying. We waited for Coach Russ to weigh in on the proceedings.

"Well," he finally said. "I think we've got our strategy for next week."

He looked around at us and then shook his head disbelievingly.

"If we're going to have any chance of kicking Marshall's ass on Sunday," he finally said. "You're all gonna have to get baked out of your *minds* before the game."

As inspirational speeches go, lemme tell ya: It was a beauty.

We arrived at the ball field early the following week. Not to limber up. Not to chuck the old pill around. Not even to take a few drives off the fungo bat.

No sir. We came to get *knee-walking stoned*. And then we aimed to play some quality softball.

Marshall and his gang showed up about a half hour before game time looking fresh and ready. By then, our team looked like a collection of Jeff Spicoli impersonators. Red-eyed and barely coherent, we staggered into the dugout.

The Hollywood cast had proposed a bet: They should be allowed to play the Ultravision if we lost. We had declined this offer. The Ultravision was our shrine and we didn't want it defiled. Instead, we made the wager more personal:

The losing team's players would wash the car belonging to the winning team's cast manager. And everyone on the losing team had to participate, no exceptions.

Knowing that the outcome of this game could potentially mean Andrea and Sunday polishing Marshall's back bumper gave us all the added inspiration we needed.

It was game on.

Until that day, I had never laid eyes on the Hollywooders (Hollywoodians?) that I heard so much about but, all of a sudden, there they were. Tony ticked off each of their names to me as they stepped onto the field. There was Robby, the Twin's legendarily selfish Riff. Becky, their notoriously slutty Columbia. Fred, Lee, Alphonse...all names I had heard thrown about with disgust at various cast gatherings, and here they were at last, in the flesh.

And then, I saw her: Shelly.

There was no mistaking her. Besides Marshall, Shelly was the most talked-about member of the Twin cast. She was also the one and only member of the Hollywood group who was spoken of with anything but contempt. Shelly, I had heard many times, was a knockout. And now that I'd laid eyes on her, I could see what all the fuss was about.

She had blonde hair that she wore to the shoulder and it hovered around her face like an aura. It wasn't feathered, in the fashion of the day, but curly and lush, like the girls on the magazine covers. Farrah Fawcett would have knifed a nun for this hair.

Shelly was slim, but curvy. Short, but not tiny. And had skin so smooth and lustrous that it looked as if she were glowing with an inner...

...ahem.

Yeah, okay. I was a little smitten. So sue me. The girl was gorgeous.

And cut me a break. I was kinda high at the time.

Doc had been chosen to be the umpire, as it was universally acknowledged that he would be fair to both teams. He motioned for the coaches and both Marshall and Russ stepped forward ceremoniously. They met at home plate, shook hands and tossed a coin to start things off. Marshall won the toss and the Hollywood cast took the field.

According to the rules Marshall and Russ had established, we wouldn't be playing for nine innings. For one thing, this was softball, not baseball and, for another, it was hotter than an afternoon spent picnicking on the sun. After some debate, they decided on six innings of play. That was about all they figured we would tolerate before our enthusiasm waned.

Also, while there would be nine players on the field playing defense, everyone in both casts would get a chance to bat. So instead of batting ninth, for example, there was a chance that you batted eighteenth. What was important was to know the person who came up before you. In our current condition, the Deerfield cast members would be lucky to remember that the gloves didn't go on our *feet*.

Ron batted lead-off, which was perfect since he had a deep familiarity with our rivals and could match their taunts with his own patented brand of smartassery. They immediately tried to get under his skin, calling him a traitor for turning his back on them and suggesting that the day would arrive when he would come crawling back.

Ron was unfazed. "What, you didn't hear?" He unleashed his patented ladykiller smile. "You guys are over. Done. We're the best cast in Florida, motherfuckers. And don't you forget it."

And to fully make his point, Ron spanked a double into right field. Just like that.

Tony was up next, followed by the heart of our order: Tom, Donny and Billy. Each of them managed to get a hit, completely stunning the Hollywood team. By the time I came to bat (I was up eighth), the score was six to nothing and Andrea was standing on second base, having smacked a double in the previous at-bat and scoring two runs.

I'm sorry to report that I got the first out of the inning, but I did manage to move Andrea along to third. Russ, batting behind me, also hit into a groundout, but brought her home. By the time Felicia struck out, two batters later, the score was already seven to zip.

It was Hollywood's turn at the plate. And our theory (that bong hits + softball = victory) was about to be put to the test.

The Hollywood lead-off batter was a wiry-looking Transylvanian-type named Carl. I had never heard of him before but he looked fast. He came up to the plate and faced off against Tony who stood glaring at him from the mound.

Carl stepped into the batter's box cocky and sure-footed, looking as if he invented the game, his confident attitude making us hate him all the more. He propped his bat on his shoulder and didn't even square off against Tony for the first pitch, allowing it to drop in for a strike without seeming to care. He was taunting Tony and, in my opinion, that didn't seem like a bright thing to do.

Tony's next pitch was a brush-back and Carl had to jump out of the way to avoid it. It was called a ball and Carl clearly got the message: Stop fucking around. He finally choked up on the bat and leaned in, ready to tee off on the next pitch.

Tony delivered and Carl let 'er rip.

I won't speculate about how hard he hit the ball. All I can tell you is that, in the moment after it smacked into my glove, I would not have been surprised to look down and see my arm flopping about helplessly about on the ground like a dying fish. He had lined it right at me and, under normal conditions, I might have had the reflexes to leap out of the way in an instinctive move of self-preservation. Dulled as my senses were, however, I only had time to open up my mitt and snag the line drive as it zipped toward me, nailing down the first defensive out for the team.

The Ultravision cast cheered and Carl's eyes shot daggers at me as he trudged back to the bench. We had drawn first blood. But the game was still young.

The Hollywood cast was no less interested than we were in bringing defeat crashing down upon their enemies and they gave as good as they got. Unfortunately for them, our team...

...well, we were under the thrall of that badass Mary Jane and, for reasons we could not begin to explain, it had somehow transformed us into The Bingo Long Traveling All-Stars and Motor Kings. (Look it up.)

That's not to say they didn't get their licks in. They surely did. In the first inning, they managed to push across three runs before we retired the side. But they were both thoroughly disconcerted by their comparative lack of offense and *completely* shocked by our level of defensive play. On the latter point, they weren't the only ones.

At the end of one, the score stood Deerfield 7, Hollywood 3.

We did not fare nearly as well in the second inning as we had in the first and only pushed across two more runs before they sat us down. Unfortunately for Hollywood, the bottom of their batting order was due up in the second and we had the top of ours coming up in the third.

They needed a big inning. We refused to give it to them. They only scored one run in their next round of at-bats and our defense sparkled even more brightly. Russ snapped up a hot bouncing ball to third and nailed the runner at first by ten feet. Felicia made a running catch in left that sent a chorus of "Oooohs!" through even the Hollywood bench. And Andrea was rock-solid at first, snagging anything that came near her.

Things began to unravel in the third inning, though. Despite the heavy hitters coming to the plate for Deerfield, the Hollywood team somehow blanked us. Ron, Tony and Tom all smacked the ball, but the Hollywood outfielders appeared to have been tipped off in advance as to where the balls would drop. One, two, three, we were done.

Still, there was a healthy five-run lead heading into the bottom of the third. All we had to do was hold them.

It didn't take long for us to realize that our magic softball fairy dust was, to our rising horror, wearing off.

The leadoff man for Hollywood made it to first on an error by Ron. A routine grounder to Russ got mishandled and when I scooped it up, I dropped the throw to second, putting two men on. With three unforced errors in a row, our confidence level dipped for the first time and, as we all know, paranoia and pot do not mix. Once we began to think that we were unable to play stellar defense, our self-fulfilling prophecies began to come true.

One after another, the Hollywood batters punched line drives through our infield. Runner after runner crossed the plate. Tony finally managed to strike out one of the Hollywooders and Andrea snagged a foul ball for the second out, but we were still in a lot of trouble. By the time Robby hit a hopper to Tony, who flipped it to Andrea to end the inning, the tables had turned.

The score, heading into the fourth inning, was Hollywood 14, Deerfield 10.

We huddled together in the dugout, looking to Russ for inspiration.

"Stay here," he said. "Don't grab a bat. Don't do anything. I'll be right back."

He whipped around and strode purposefully toward the Hollywood dugout, waving over Doc as he went. The two coaches and the umpire met together on the field.

"We want a halftime," said Russ.

Doc and Marshall exchanged incredulous looks.

"This isn't football, Russ," said Marshall. "There's no 'halftime' in softball."

Doc nodded his head. It sounded right to him.

"No, I know," said Russ casually. "But it's a hot day, we're halfway through the game. I thought we could take a beer break or something. Nothing wrong with that, right?"

At this suggestion, Doc's eyes widened a bit. He had been on the field for three full innings and a beer sounded awfully good to him. He turned to Marshall.

"Any objection?"

Marshall shrugged. "Fine by me."

Doc grinned. "Okay then," he said, and called out to everyone, "Halftime! We start the fourth inning in ten minutes." Russ walked Doc back to the Deerfield dugout, tossed him a beer and motioned for the rest of the cast to follow him.

We all trudged out to the parking lot and gathered by the parked cars. "Time for a pick-me-up. Smoke 'em if you got 'em." He got out a lighter and slipped into his own car.

The entire cast quickly followed suit. Within seconds, five different vehicles in the parking lot looked as if they had caught fire.

Minutes later, we were back on the field and there wasn't a white pair of eyes in the bunch.

"Let's do this," said Ron, looking ready for action.

And so we did.

By the time the dust settled three innings later, the Hollywood cast was toast. We scored runs in each of the last three innings and culminated our offensive attack with a spectacular seven-run sixth. In the meantime, we had regained our defensive flair and not only held them to two runs in the fourth, but somehow managed to keep them from scoring a single run in the last two innings.

The final score was: Deerfield 24, Hollywood 16.

We had trounced the hated Hollywood Rocky cast and we had done it (and this is being generous), with about fifteen functioning brain cells between us.

Marshall, Robby, Shelly and the rest of the Twinkies (as we dubbed them) were all gracious in their defeat (certainly more gracious than we would have been, had the tables been turned). In a rare moment of detente, we all gathered on the field afterward to toast the first coming together of the two casts.

Fresh from our victory, the Deerfield cast members were in magnanimous moods and none of the rancor toward our Hollywood rivals was present, at least for this brief cease-fire. (Some of this uncharacteristic magnanimity could well be attributed to our current state of narcotic stimulation, but I'd also like to give the ex-Hollywooders some credit for their generosity of spirit.)

Introductions were made, stories were told, hatchets were buried.

It was decided that a party at the Orphanage was in order so we all piled into our cars and took off. All those vehicles exiting the parking lot at once caused a minor traffic jam on the narrow road that led away from the ball field, and at one point we all found ourselves in a long convoy headed toward I-95.

I don't know exactly what happened (something darted out into the road, perhaps), but whatever it was caused the lead car to very suddenly apply their brakes, leading to a chain reaction of quick, jerky stops like a row of dominos tumbling. There were, thankfully, no fender-benders and, with only one exception, nobody was hurt.

Unfortunately, the somebody who got hurt...was Ron. He had been riding in Cheryl's car without a seat belt and when she slammed on her brakes, Ron went flying into her windshield. Cheryl threw the car into park and called out for help. We all rushed to see what had happened.

Ron had a thin trickle of blood seeping down his face but insisted that he was fine. The shattered windshield on Cheryl's car appeared to suggest otherwise, but after we got back to the Orphanage, a bandage seemed to patch him up just fine.

It was strange. This had been the second time Ron's face and a car windshield had been on adversarial terms in less than a year. It crossed my mind that he seemed to be some kind of accident magnet.

Turned out, I could not have been more tragically right.

Give Yourself Over To Absolute Pleasure

I've spent an awful lot of time in these pages ragging on the '80s and on South Florida in general so, in the interest of fairness, I'd like to give the early '80s just a tiny bit of credit: If there was one thing this particular era got absolutely right, it was the development of one of the greatest fashion trends of all time. You see, if it wasn't for the early 1980s, we wouldn't have that miracle fabric:

Spandex.

True, Spandex has developed a bad reputation over the years due primarily to the manufacturer's attempt to (literally) broaden their customer base by making the pants in larger and larger sizes (triggering gag reflexes all over this great land of ours).

But back when Spandex was first released, and young girls started painting these leggings onto their shapely young thighs and buttocks, well...it was as if the fashion gods had looked down on every teenage boy in America and decided, "You know what? Let's have Christmas early this year."

It was *fan-damn-tastic*.

In the Rocky world, of course, Spandex was even more prevalent, ever since school administrators created strict rules prohibiting young girls from wearing these outfits on campus. This, in turn, provoked the girls into wearing them whenever they *weren't* at school, just to snub their noses at the school officials.

You want to make something popular? Ban it.

This development suited me and every other guy my age just fine and dandy, thank you very much.

It was win-win no matter how you sliced it. At the Rocky show, girls

211

would arrive at the theater in Spandex pants and clingy shirts. They would then take *off* these outfits and put on tube tops, maid outfits and fishnet stockings and parade around for two hours in tarty makeup. After that, they would strip off the lingerie and slip *back* into the Spandex.

Yeah. It was horrible.

And in case you were wondering, the answer is yes: The parking lot of the Ultravision was occasionally the setting for some pretty serious pre-show and post-show monkey business, no question about it. Some cast members seemed to be under the impression that they couldn't bring their A-game to the show without a *full release* before things got under way.

We even had a term for it: scromping.

If you felt the need to get your rocks off prior to the movie, you nipped off and had a scromp. Nothing wrong with that. It was as natural as can be.

But once you got in the theater, it was all business. There was no messing about once the show was in full swing.

Well...that was the rule, anyway. But there was that one little incident...

Tom called in sick one night in July. As a result, someone was needed up on the lighting deck to run the spotlight. Russ, perhaps because he knew the show better than anyone else, volunteered to take over for the evening and just as the pre-show began he took his position.

The thing about the lighting deck was this: Unless you had a ladder to get up to it, the deck itself was completely inaccessible. It was located just underneath the projection booth at the back of the theater and just above the entranceway. It was a tiny, rectangular area about nine feet off the ground with nothing more up there than a chair and an enormous spotlight. (I suspect Tom also kept a cooler full of beverages on hand, too, but that was only a rumor.)

The pre-show kicked off and Russ hit me with the light, just as Tom had done for months. I did my thing, getting the crowd nice and revved up. When I was finished, Russ snapped off the spotlight and the theater lights dimmed for the previews. This would be Russ's official break, as it was the only time in the next couple of hours where the spotlight would be unnecessary. He could take a time-out until Andrea and Sunday started up "Science Fiction" at the top of the movie.

As I made my way out of the theater and into the ladies room to change into my full Transylvanian outfit (Kenny was pulling Riff duty this night), I happened to spot Jill making her cautious way up the ladder to the lighting deck. I didn't really think much of it, really, as (a) Jill was Russ's girlfriend and (b) she wouldn't be needed on stage until the end of the night when she went on as Floor Show Janet. Still, seeing a scantily clad bombshell dangling high above you in nothing but a black teddy and a pair of garters is the kind of thing that grabs your attention so, naturally, I noticed.

I also noticed, on my way back to the theater, that the ladder leading up to the deck...had disappeared.

Clearly, Russ and Jill were desirous of some privacy up there and, after all, who was I to deny them their rendezvous?

I will go out on a limb and say that if there was anyone who could have timed a scromp to coincide exactly with the necessary lighting needs of the Rocky show, Russ was the man for the job. He knew the movie backward and, should he choose to be derelict in his duties for the requisite time it would take him to attend to business, there is no doubt that he would choose wisely.

This he did.

Russ, thinking quickly (and perhaps not *entirely* with his brain), chose the perfect spot to leave his light unattended: the driving scene with Janet and Brad. For those few minutes, the spotlight just sits there, trained on the two youngsters in the vehicle. Soon afterward, of course, they are up, moving around and singing "Over at the Frankenstein Place." But if you time it right and can do what you need to do very, very quickly, you could conceivably pull off whatever you need to pull off and no one would be the wiser.

Russ, needless to say, did not time it right. Not one little bit, in fact.

As Brad offered to leave the car and head back to the castle, Ron did the same on stage. Tracey, as Janet, offered to go with him. Brad/Ron protested that there was little sense in the both of them getting wet, but Janet/Tracey insisted, saying: "Besides, darling, the owner of that phone might be a beautiful woman and you might never come back again." Brad/Ron laughed, they got out of the car, the tire got kicked and the song began.

In a perfect world, the beam of light is supposed to follow Brad and Janet as they approach the castle singing their song.

Theoretically.

Instead, Tracey and Ron got out of the "car" and made their way toward the castle in utter and complete blackness.

And the spotlight stayed on the car.

The song continued. Tracey and Ron sang on, doing the blocking they had been performing for months and making their way across the stage as the squirt guns filled the air with water.

The spotlight, however, stayed on the car.

It wasn't until Riff's entrance was approaching that Steve, in his Transylvanian attire, arrived in the hallway under the lighting deck and started calling frantically up to Russ.

"*Russ!*" he tried to both yell and whisper at the same time. "*Russ! Are you up there?*"

Nothing from the deck.

The spotlight stayed, inexplicably, on the car.

Seeing Steve under the deck as I re-entered the theatre, I stopped to ask him what was going on.

"*The light!*" Steve hissed. "*It isn't moving!*"

He turned his attention to the lighting deck again.

"*RUSS!*" Steve called up. "*ARE YOU THERE?*"

Cheryl and Felicia, by this time, had joined Steve and I, both girls wide-eyed as the spotlight remained frozen in place.

"*Is he there?*" Felicia demanded.

"*I don't know!*" Steve replied, looking scared to death. "*I've been calling up to him but he hasn't said anything!*"

"*Do you think he's okay? Should we get help?*" Cheryl sounded panicked.

"*Let me try to climb up there, see if he's all right. Maybe he...hit his head or something! I don't know!*"

Steve attempted to scale the wall, but there were no handholds, nothing to step on and nothing to use as leverage. It was a completely smooth nine-foot wall and there was simply no way he was going to climb it.

The girls and I attempted to hoist him up, but after he fell once, we decided against trying again.

By the way, the spotlight, in case you were wondering, remained fixed on the car.

The crowd under the lighting deck by this time was becoming a regular mob and the tension was getting thick. Also, all pretense of trying to keep their voices down had been discarded. Finally, Tony strolled up and surveyed the situation.

"Hold on a minute," Tony called out to the crowd, silencing them. "Let's find out what the fuck is going on." He looked up at the deck. "RUSS!!" Tony hollered. "Goddamn it, Russ, answer me! Are you all right up there?"

In the moment after Tony called out, there was an audible moan from up above. It was not, however, a moan of distress. It was, instead, a very clear moan of pleasure. One might also describe it as a moan of...utter satisfaction. Hearing this sound (and believe me, everyone in Broward County heard it), we all knew precisely why the spotlight had never strayed from the car.

Tony, sharing in our moment of clarity, was extremely displeased.

"Jesus *Christ*, Russ," he called up. "Will you fucking pull out and start running the lights, goddamn it? We've got a show to do!"

Seconds later, the spotlight jumped to life and caught Riff and Magenta just about to start the Time Warp. A voice drifted down from above:

"Everything's under control." Russ called down in a very, very relaxed voice. "You can get back to work now. I'm all good."

At this, all of the Transylvanians darted for the stage in order to be in place for their big number. Tony stalked away disgustedly.

"Boy, you try to run a professional show," he mumbled. "And this bullshit happens."

A couple of minutes later, the ladder once again snaked its way down the wall and Jill, looking a trifle sheepish about the whole business, made her way shakily down the rungs.

Forever afterward, guests were forbidden from setting foot on the lighting deck. It was, of course, a good and necessary rule. But to be honest, it was a little like shutting the barn door after the horse has been delightfully laid, if you ask me.

When you're dealing with a show like Rocky, involving late-night ribaldry, girls in skimpy clothes and an auditorium open to the public, you're bound to have your occasional troublemaker or two show up and make trouble. It could hardly be avoided.

When these ugly moments occurred, we had a crack team that sprang into action:

First, we'd send the girls. Generally speaking, a group of drunken louts could be handled easily by Storme and one or two of the other young Transylvanians. All they wanted was attention, so we doled out a tiny bit to tide them over and it usually sufficed.

Sometimes, however, they were not satisfied with our female offering and would either demand a bit *more* attention or, in some cases, would ask for something inappropriate from one of our young ladies.

At this point, the second wave would move in, usually Russ (who was Mr. Reasonable) or sometimes the theater management, to explain very patiently to the loudmouths that as long as they were willing to behave, they were welcome to stay, but if they insisted on raising the temperature in the room, they would be escorted out.

Ninety-nine times out of a hundred, that would do it. Most people are fairly respectful of authority, especially when those in power are being respectful themselves.

There were, however, the very rare cases where we would be forced to take more drastic measures and go to the bullpen. In these instances, we would send for Donny.

Now, I don't care how drunk and disorderly you are. When a 300-pound biker dude strolls up to your seat in a movie theater and pointedly asks just what the fuck is going on, you sober up pretty quick. If you do not show due deference, however, this man will lean down *really* close to your face and, his voice resonating deep in his chest, he will ask you just how much you value your present existence and suggest, in an *extremely* believable tone, that your continued enjoyment of that existence was very suddenly in real jeopardy. After that, you can pretty much bet that whatever trouble had previously presented itself would disappear *immediately*.

I loved these moments, watching Donny completely dominate whatever asshole decided to try to piss in our litter box. Seeing douchebags get properly schooled is a rare occurrence and makes for some delightful entertainment.

One night, after Donny had dealt with a pair of teenagers who had clearly dipped into daddy and mommy's liquor cabinet and thought it would be funny to mess with the "Rocky fags," I turned to share my amusement with Tony.

"You know what kills me about this?" I said as the teenagers slipped out the side door, their tails between their legs. "If they had any clue what a total cream puff Donny is, they'd never fall for his act. I mean, this is the nicest guy I've ever *met*. He wouldn't lay a finger on them."

Tony turned and smiled. "You only say that because you never saw Donny the Destroyer, Jack."

I must not have heard that properly, I thought. "Donny the...the *what*?"

"The Destroyer," Tony replied. "I was there. I saw it. He was a fuckin' animal."

I was a little stunned. Donny? An *animal*? I mean, sure, he *looked* like his professional wrestling name should have been "Soulcrusher Jones," but I'd spent a lot of time with this guy over the past six months and he'd never so much as raised his *voice*. What the hell was Tony talking about?

"What the hell are you talking about?" I asked Tony.

Tony was getting ready for the show and didn't have time for my bullshit questions at the moment. "I'll tell you after," he promised. "It'll be worth the wait."

At Denny's later, Tony settled in with a cup of coffee and related the Legend of Donny the Destroyer.

"It was down in Hollywood, Jack. Halloween, last year. Normally a nice, cool time of year but, '81 was an Indian summer, you remember? Not cool at all. One of those really hot nights when everyone's temper is at its boiling point, you know?

"And Donny and his girlfriend at the time...I forget her name...let's say Julie, okay? Donny and Julie show up at the show in costume. Halloween and all that, naturally. And Donny has this toga on. I think he's trying to be Caesar or Cassiopeia or some shit and Julie, she's done up like a '20s flapper. Really slutty, but really, really cute.

"Anyway, they're hanging out in the theater before the show and Donny leaves Julie alone for a minute or two, maybe he's grabbing a smoke, maybe he's checking his props, who knows? But while he's gone, these three big guys in the audience get a good look at Julie and start talking shit to her. 'Hey, baby. You want a piece of this?' The usual crap. No big deal.

"Julie, naturally, can handle herself. Most Rocky chicks can. And she's telling these guys to fuck off, go jerk one in the parking lot, that kind of thing. And these guys get kinda riled up, hearing this, and they move in.

"Now, they're not necessarily getting out of line, but they are definitely trying to intimidate this girl and she's not liking it one bit. And the second she raises her voice to these assholes, Donny's ears shoot up like a fucking

Doberman and he's across the theater quick as a shot.

"Donny steps between Julie and the fellas, probably just to calm things down. He's not looking for trouble. But I guess one of the guys didn't really see who they were dealing with (maybe because the toga hid how big Donny really is) and the guy says something to Donny like, 'Is this your bitch, dude?' or some other bright comment like that.

"Without thinking, Donny reaches out and kinda gives this guy what he considers to be a little marshmallow smack on the chin, right? Except Donny isn't capable of throwing marshmallows. He throws manhole covers, okay? This jab hits the guy full on the face and opens up a gash in the side of his mouth that sprays blood all over the front of the theater. And the guy crumples like a sack of potatoes. BAM. Just like that.

"Now, his friends, they must figure Donny hit the guy with a hammer or something. I mean, these aren't little dudes. They don't go down that easy, normally. And they're not about to let their friend get smacked around like that, either. So they look at each other for a second and then decide to return the favor and smack *Donny* around.

"So Don sees the first one coming and he kinda gives the guy a shove in the chest. Just to get him to back away, you know? And the force of this blow sends the guy backwards over three rows of seats. I mean it was like he was shot out of a cannon. Ka-POW. And suddenly guy number two isn't moving much either.

"So here's the third guy. He's looking at Donny and Donny isn't even out of breath. His two friends are *out* and Donny's standing there, blood all over his toga, looking at the guy like, 'Well, whudda *you* got?' And the guy takes a second or two, realizes that the blood sprayed on the toga isn't *Donny's* blood and, just like that, he thinks better of making a big deal about the whole thing. He holds up his hands in front of him and just says, 'Hey, man. We don't want any trouble.'

"Don isn't sure quite how to respond to that, so Julie does it for him. 'You don't, huh?' she says. 'Then get your friends the *fuck* out of here unless you want *your* ass pounded, too.' And the guy slowly gets his buddies to their feet and the three of them limp out of the theater, never to return.

"And Jack, I'll tell ya: I had never seen Donny raise his fist in anger until that night and I've never seen it since. He's one of the kindest, sweetest dudes I've ever met in my life. But, sorry to say, the legend of Donny the Destroyer was born that night and no matter what he does, the legend will never die."

Tony finished off his coffee and left me to ponder the deeper meaning of the Donny myth that was created that Halloween night. For my part, I could do nothing more than stare in amazement at my friend Donny who, until that night, I had been sure I knew.

Mr. Nice Guy. The Teddy Bear. The Cream Puff.

He was all those things. I knew it firsthand.

But he was also, apparently, the Most Dangerous Man in Florida.

Sins of the Flesh

Around the time that Holly and I hit the four-month mark, we both decided (mutually and painlessly) that our relationship had run its course and we should probably shake hands and call it a day.

We liked each other, we enjoyed putting our hands all over each other when we could and she got along splendidly with all of my wet, wild and wonderful Rocky friends. That was all fine. But that elusive *spark* just didn't seem to be there for us and, thankfully, we both seemed to realize and acknowledge it in plenty of time before we made any kind of long-term commitment or far-reaching mistake. Yes, we had...crossed the threshold, so to speak, and were neither of us sexual neophytes anymore, but beyond the physical attraction, we both knew: We were kaput.

So, Holly went on her merry way. And I embarked on an entirely new kind of adventure: the post-virgin Rocky Horror experience.

I figured I was ready.

I had no clue what I was in for.

I will freely admit that from the time I broke up with Holly in late-June of 1982 until I started dating Alice that winter, I went a *little* over the top when it came to pursuing young females—*any* young female—who were willing to take off their clothes in my bedroom.

Or their bedrooms.

Or their back seats.

Or their parents' living room floors.

Or, once or twice, the bathroom at whatever party we happened to be attending.

No place was safe. If it was possible for me to get a girl to remove her panties there, I was game. And the Rocky show, as you well could imagine, provided a veritable smorgasbord of young, sexually curious teenage girls with, let's say, *flexible* curfews.

And while you might think that the first group of potential partners I would approach would be my fellow cast members, you'd be dead wrong. In fact, you should be ashamed of yourself for even thinking it. The girls in the Rocky cast—Andrea, Sunday, Tracey, Felicia and the rest—were, for obvious reasons, off limits.

This philosophy was based on the famous Latin phrase: *Non excremento in loco edendi.* Roughly translated, it means either "Don't shit where you eat" or "Pooping on the restaurant floor is something you should reconsider."

So I stayed completely away from any girl directly involved with Rocky, due entirely to my deeply held feelings of devotion and cast unity.

Well, that and the fact that none of them was in the least bit interested in me.

But more to the point, I very soon discovered that there was an embarrassingly large number of Rocky groupies who showed up to see the show almost every weekend and who appeared, at various times, to be ready to make time with what they considered to be "important" members of the Rocky cast.

Luckily, this definition appeared to include "guys who did the pre-show" and "guys who performed the role of Riff Raff once a month." Knowing that I miraculously fit into *both* categories, there was a temptation to simply wade into the midst of this nubile bunch and hope never to return. Thankfully, I received sage advice on this subject from, of all people, Ron.

Yes, the King of Rocky Horror Backseat Bliss, my Spider-Brother, had a thing or two to impart to me about the womenfolk. And when the guy who was getting more ass than a toilet seat the morning after "Questionable Burrito Night" wanted to chat with you about the local action, you listened.

I'm assuming he saw me during the pre-show, paying inordinate attention to the more physically gifted members of the audience, because when I was finished up with the virgin initiation one Friday, very soon after the Holly breakup, he pulled me aside and spoke to me as seriously as he had ever done before.

"So...you're looking to get a little something out in the house, am I right?"

"Out in the...?" I wasn't prepared for this insightful comment and, as truthful as it was, his ability to see through to my hidden agenda took me aback. I finally stammered out, "What do you mean?"

"C'mon, Jack. Be straight with me. You're looking to pick a little something off the Rocky-audience tree, am I right?" His eyes flashed and he seemed to project an aura of trustworthiness and confidentiality. "You can tell me."

"Well...yeah," I conceded. "I've seen some...interesting prospects."

"Exactly." Ron grinned wickedly. "Of course you have. They're out there, aren't they?"

He was gazing out at the house, so I joined him.

And there they were. Or seemed to be. The eager, upturned faces in the audience appeared as a sea of young, precocious, impatient young ladies just waiting to be approached, won over and conquered. The possibilities seemed endless.

"They sure are," I said admiringly.

"Well, I gotta tell you, Jack," Ron said, "you're a whole lot fucking dumber than you look."

It was as if he'd punched me in the face. I could hardly believe what I was hearing. "I'm...*what*?"

Ron turned to face me again and all trace of humor, camaraderie and impishness had vanished. "What's the matter with you? Do you have any *idea* what is out there? Do you?"

I felt pretty sure that I did, so I said so. "Well, *girls*, for one thing."

"Congratulations. You figured that one out. Yeah. Girls. And you're sure that's what you want, huh? Absolutely positive about that?"

I had no idea what he was driving at and I wasn't in the mood to be lectured. And certainly not by *this* guy. After all, who the hell was he to give advice? Ron had legendarily boned every under-25 girl in Broward *and* Dade counties. And he was going to give me tips on self-control and moderation?

"Look, I think I know what I'm doing," I said confidently. This confidence, I should mention, arose from the fact that I had, until recently, been having daily sexual dalliances with not three, not two, but *one* girl for the past five months and it had gone really, really, moderately well, I thought. Bordering on not bad.

223

Ron was nodding his head with what I perceived to be a patronizing air. "Okay. You know what you're doing. Fine." I started to move away, but he stopped me. "Hold on a second. Before you go, let me point something out to you, okay?"

I magnanimously paused, waiting for the "big lesson."

"Sure," I said. "What is it?"

Ron took my shoulders and turned me in the direction of the cast. They were, most of them, gathered in the first few rows, putting together their costumes, props and belongings and waiting for the show to begin.

"Lemme ask you something," said Ron. "Take a close look. Do you see any *girls* here?"

This was clearly a joke. And it wasn't particularly funny.

"Yes, Ron. At least seven or eight. What's your point?"

"No, Jack," he said patiently. "I'm not talking about *females*. I know we have a lot of *females* in the cast. That's not what I'm asking. What I'm asking is: Do you see any *girls*?"

And quicker than it takes to write it down, I understood.

There were, I could clearly see, no girls in the cast. Not one. They were women, each and every one. *Young* women, yes. Most of them still in their teens, granted. But *girls*?

Nope. Girls were immature, not-so-bright, sweet little young things that had no clue about who they were or what they wanted. And those kinds of girls (for the most part) did not sign up to do the Rocky show. It took guts and a fairly strong sense of self to do what we did. Girls just couldn't cut it.

But while I might have understood what Ron was getting at with this little display, and as illuminating as this revelation might have been, I was hardly in the mood to start making concessions. His insight had done little to change my libidinous intentions. After all, what was wrong with going after a *girl*? Hell, I was only 17 years old myself.

"Look, I gotta get ready," I said, pulling away.

Ron didn't resist. "Absolutely. Have a good show." And without another word, he wandered away as if he had better things to do.

I prepared for the show, quietly pondering the lesson that Ron had taken such care to try to impart to me.

And then, because I could, I promptly dismissed it.

Luckily, I was spared the worst. But a lot of other people were not.

How do you define "the worst"? Depends on how you look at it, I suppose.

Accidental pregnancies? Those happened on occasion. And they were pretty awful.

Ill-advised marriages? Oh, yeah. I saw a few too many of those.

Venereal diseases? I'm sure they cropped up occasionally, but it wasn't the kind of thing you talked about. That sort of outbreak was taken care of on the sly and not discussed. Too embarrassing and, frankly, too disgusting to admit.

Somehow I avoided it all. I never, thank goodness, experienced the worst. Or anything close to it. But...things certainly did get interesting.

There was Nancy, the girl who couldn't stop talking. And when I say that, I mean this girl simply *could not* stop herself from giving voice to her every thought. She had this incredible body, but her mouth was in constant motion, offering a stream of observations on the most trivial, boring and downright-shallow bullshit imaginable. I think I had sex with her partly just to get her to make sounds that I actually wanted to *hear*.

Trisha was another, but this mini-relationship was over before I knew it had begun. Apparently, Trisha was a Rocky groupie who was attempting to bone her way through the entire roster of male cast members, and once she had checked me off the list, we were done.

One afternoon down at the Orphanage, I added Randy to my list (or I was added to hers). Randy wasn't a cast member, but she rented a room from Russ after her folks kicked her out of their house. I only knew her from one of the Orphanage parties I'd attended and maybe a couple of times she had dropped by the show at the Ultravision.

I had driven down to Hollywood one Saturday with Steve to see if anyone was up for a party and Randy turned out to be the only person at the Orphanage. I hadn't been in the place for ten minutes before Randy had me in her room doing things I had never experienced before and a few I haven't had the nerve to try since. I was lucky to escape without a fractured pelvis.

This sort of thing seemed to happen every week. And the talent pool (if you can call it that) was inexhaustible. The girls who approached Rocky cast members like me for sex apparently thought that all we wanted was dirty, anonymous coupling and then a quick, emotionless parting.

And for a while, I completely agreed with them. From July through November of that year, I gained a reputation in the cast as the guy who didn't say "no" to very much at all.

Then I met Dorothy.

Cast/audience hookups could happen in a lot of different ways. You'd get introduced to another castmate's friend or the friend of a friend. Sometimes a girl or two would tag along with the cast over to Denny's and when the cast meeting was over, you'd meander past their booth to see if there was anyone willing to make it a late night. Or there would be an Orphanage party and at some point, usually around 3:30 or so in the morning, everyone's standards would begin to decline, lowering exponentially as morning approached. At these moments, girls had a time-honored tendency to do things they thought better of in hindsight. Lord knows I did.

I should also mention that, by this time, word had gotten around the cast that my real name wasn't "Jack." (This was doubtless a direct result of my mother's nefarious, behind-the-scenes plotting.) As they learned my birth name, the cast members' reactions varied from "Who cares?" to "What kind of idiot would do a thing like that?" to "Kevin? Seriously? That's the dorkiest name I ever heard. I don't blame you." But there was another side effect:

As I made my determined way through the various Rocky fans who came to the show aiming to copulate with one of the players (and I was pretty determined, no question), a strange thing started to occur. The minute we finished up one of our trysts, each of the girls would immediately and absolutely refuse to call me "Jack" from that moment forward. I don't know if calling me by my real name made them feel closer to me or if it made them feel less trashy, but it was as if they had all made some secret pact that the use of my Rocky name was *verboten* once we had knocked boots.

Pretty soon, news of *that* development had also spread through the cast and Sunday, in particular, took careful notice. She would pretend to become incensed every time a new girl showed up calling me "Kevin." Rolling her eyes in disgust, she would turn to me and say, "Jesus, Jack. You nailed *another* one? Give it a fuckin' rest before it falls off."

I was not inclined to give it a rest. By any means. Which brings me back to Dorothy.

Dorothy was an interesting case, to say the least. She had no subtlety and didn't play coy, girly games. So what made her so memorable? Well, it wasn't that she was more mature or grown-up than the other Rockettes. No way. She was clearly as shallow as a puddle on a pool deck. But I'll say this for her:

The girl knew what she wanted.

The particular evening I'm talking about, which was around Thanksgiving of 1982, what she wanted was: me.

We had finished up the show and were hunkered down at Denny's, taking part in our usual post-show confab. Dorothy, I noticed, had planted herself in a booth across from the cast table with three or four of her friends. She was making no secret of the fact that she was appraising me the way a hungry lion eyes a limping gazelle.

She was a tiny little thing, a good six inches shorter than I was, with dark-brown hair cropped short. You'd look at her and think, "gymnast." Or, rather, "slutty gymnast." She wore a black choker around her neck that looked remarkably like a dog collar, and offset her freckled, youthful face by encircling her eyes with enough liner to alarm a raccoon.

Those eyes kept flashing over to me and that was all the signal I needed.

When the evening finally wound down, I stood up to go talk to her, but she and her friends were already walking out the door. I didn't pursue them and, to be honest, I almost wrote her off, thinking she was just a tease or, worse, that she was somehow intimidated by me.

I flatter myself with this assumption. I was, I knew, about as intimidating as a sleepy kitten.

So I was surprised to hear a sharp knock on the restaurant window, looked up and found her standing outside the front window of the Denny's, one hand cocked on her hip, looking impatient and motioning for me to come outside.

I was out the door like a shot.

She looked a little pissed as I trotted up to her.

"I thought you were gonna follow me out," she said. "What happened?"

I wasn't sure how to answer. "Well, you...you looked like you were leaving, so..." And that's about all I had.

"You always give up so easily?"

"No!" I said, defensively. "I really don't. I just..."

She cut me off. "So you want my number or not?" She had a real gift for getting to the point.

"Sure!" I said, maybe a little too enthusiastically. "That'd be great."

"Okay." She waited a second or two and then frowned a bit. "You planning to get a pencil or something?"

"Oh, right," I said, and then realized I had nothing of the kind on my person.

Seeing that I was clearly incapable of anything so complicated as actually *writing something down*, she whipped open her purse and plunged in her hand. Rooting around for a moment or two, she pulled out a tube of something and turned back to me.

"Give me your arm."

"My...my what?"

"Your *arm*. Give it to me."

Reluctantly, I offered her my right arm. She pushed up my shirtsleeve and, pressing the tube to my forearm, started to write.

It was at this moment that the smell hit me and I realized what she was using as a pen.

Somehow or other, in lieu of putting her hands on an actual writing implement, this young lady had instead fished out of her bag a tube of cherry-flavored sex cream (complete with glitter!) and was using it to jot her name and number on my outstretched forearm.

And I, to my utter bafflement, was letting her.

She finished up and looked with a critical eye at her handiwork.

"Can you read that?"

Scrawled up my arm in glittery translucent goo was the name "DORO-THY" and a ten-digit phone number. I was pretty sure I could make it out.

"Yeah, I've got it."

"Good." She grinned. "Don't lose it."

Then she reached out, grabbed me by the back of the head and pulled me down to her face. Our lips met briefly and she jammed her tongue so far down my throat that there's a good chance it poked out the other end.

Then, before I could say, "What does my lower intestine taste like?" she was gone.

I staggered back inside, a little unfocused from the experience. Finding my mental balance, I quickly borrowed a pen from one of the waitresses and transferred the phone number from my arm to a napkin, all the time wondering if calling this crazy tramp would be a good idea.

Steve, who had seen me follow her out into the parking lot, sidled up to me.

"So, how did that go?" he asked, clearly hoping for a good story.

I wasn't sure how to answer.

"I don't know," I said at last. "I guess we'll see."

I'm not big on the psychological games involved in courting rituals. You know what I mean. Variations of the "Don't call her for two-and-a-half days and then only after 2:00 in the afternoon, and when you do, act like you're really bored and then leave her alone for a week." Not much point to it, I figure. So, to get things rolling fast, I called her just a few minutes after I woke up that Sunday (which was around noon). To my great surprise, she answered almost immediately.

"Yeah?"

"Um...is this Dorothy?"

"That's me. Who's this?"

"This is Jack? We met last night? At the Rocky show?" I don't know why I was talking in questions. It was just happening.

"Oh right. You were the wheelchair guy in the show, right?" I had played Dr. Scott the previous evening, so she was right about that. I was, indeed, "the wheelchair guy."

"Right." There was a pause. And then there was another one. I decided to break the awkward silence with another, "Right." I was really dazzling her here with my verbal acuity.

"So," she said after about a half hour or so. "You want me to come over?"

That was the problem with my home phone. It was always making the oddest noises.

"I'm sorry...what?"

"Well, you called. I figured you might want me to drop by. You interested?"

I guess the phone was working fine.

"Uh...sure. Absolutely."

"Sweet." Another silence. Then she said, "You want to tell me where you live?"

"Oh, of course. Sure." I rattled off the address.

"See you soon."

"Wait!" I hollered before she could hang up. "Listen, can it be around 7 or so? My..." I couldn't say "mother." "My *roommate* goes to work then. Is that...cool?"

"Okay. See you then."

I started to hang up, but then I heard her say, "Oh, hey!"

"Yeah?"

"What's the name again?"

"Jack. I'm Jack."

"Jack. Right. Okay, I'll see you later."

I spent the rest of the afternoon getting ready. I wasn't sure what for, exactly, but I wanted to be prepared for anything. The first order of business was to get rid of my brother so I could have the house to myself, but he had plans anyway (there was a big smokeout party at the house of a stoner friend of his) so that was no problem. My mother would leave for work at about 5:00 and I'd have a couple of hours to contemplate the possibilities.

The key would be: Assume nothing. Maybe she was looking to come over and mess around. Maybe she wanted to get to know me, watch some TV, go swimming in the pool. It could be anything. Don't count on this being anything more than what it was: a visit. That's all.

David left. My mother left. I was left to myself, with nothing better to do than anticipate my visitor.

After an hour or so, I realized that the time seemed to be crawling by, so I turned on the television to keep myself distracted. As a result, I didn't hear the car pull up at 7 and about jumped out of my skin when Dorothy knocked on the door.

I would have preferred answering the door *without* my heart leaping out of my chest, but it was not to be.

"Hey," I said as I stuck my head out. "You made it."

She had changed her look, opting to switch from Teen Slut to a very convincing Pat Benatar impersonation, which was all the more compelling given her small stature. She had dabbled some white base on her face and slashed it with some dark-red blush, but also tinted her hair, which looked even shorter than I remembered it.

As she had made clear the evening before, she was all business.

"Of course I did," she said. Then, after a pause: "You planning to invite me in?"

"Sure, sure," I said, stepping aside and ushering her into the living room. She looked around, but didn't seem to take in anything. The surroundings were, it appeared, beside the point.

"Can I get you something?" She turned and looked at me with an odd expression on her face. "We've got...soda. Beer, even, if you want one." My mother drank this awful, low-cost beer. Dorothy might opt for one, but I suspected that she wouldn't be all that thrilled if she did.

"I'm good," she said. And again she looked around. "Which way's the bedroom?"

"The...?" It wasn't possible she'd said "bedroom" less than one minute in the door, so I assumed she hadn't.

"Bed. Room," she repeated carefully, as if to a dimwit. "Which way?" There was a very slight edge of impatience in her tone, which was disconcerting.

I leaped into action.

"Right...um...right this way." I started down the hallway to my room and she followed closely. I walked into my room and sort of vaguely gestured around. "This is it."

"Nice," she said in a tone that indicated that she thought it was anything but. "You mind if we keep the light off?"

"It doesn't...bother me, no." She reached over and flicked the wall switch and the room was plunged into darkness.

I sensed, but didn't see, that she had taken a step toward me so I did the same. I put up my right hand and found her shoulder and the moment I did so, I felt her hands slip around my neck and pull my face down again.

Our lips met and she started kissing me. And I know it should have been great. Wonderful, even. I mean, this was instant sex. How cool was that?

Instead it was...mechanical. Passionless, really. I had never been with a hooker, but I couldn't help but think that this is what sex must be like when you're doing it with someone you were paying for the privilege. It was as if kissing me was her *job* and she wasn't all that thrilled to be punching in for her shift.

After a few seconds of this, she abruptly jerked her tongue out of my mouth, stepped back and—in one fluid motion—yanked off her top. Just like that, *fwip*, and I could tell that she was standing in front of me in the darkness without her shirt. Not wanting to make her feel uncomfortable, I followed suit.

Without waiting for me to reach out for her again, she decided to jump ahead a few steps. I distinctly heard, but again could not see, as she went through the various motions of removing her bra, pants and underwear. After she had disrobed, she made her way over to my bed and lay down, waiting for me.

If it was a race to get naked, I was falling way behind and it took me a while to catch up. I stripped off my jeans, pulled off my underwear and fumbled my way over to the bed. She was reaching up for me when I arrived.

I tried to kiss her again, but apparently that part of the opening ceremony had come to a close and wasn't to be revisited. Instead, she put her hands on my hips and guided me to the proper position over her as she lay back on my pillow. Then, sliding her hand down my stomach, she grabbed my full attention and made sure I had the proper aim.

A moment or two later, I was inside her and she was busy reaching around, getting a good grip on my ass and pulling me as far inside her as she could manage.

It was a land-speed record, at least in my experience. Front door to carnal intercourse in less than five minutes. Bing. Bam. Boom.

The actual act lasted longer than it should have, simply because it was so devoid of...anything. Here I was, a 17-year-old boy with a pretty, young girl lying naked on my bed, practically forcing me to hump her repeatedly and I felt...zip-a-dee-doo-dah. In fact, I realized in that moment that I would rather have been almost anywhere else than deep inside that young lady.

"So," I thought. "This is fucking." And it was. I had heard the term my whole life, but never really knew what it meant. Now I knew. "Fucking" was the act of inserting yourself into a person *for whom* you have no affection, *with whom* you have no connection, and *from whom* you are receiving no exchange of emotions whatsoever.

Dorothy and I were fucking. And, frankly, I couldn't wait for it to end.

Eventually, mercifully, it did. We both made the appropriate sounds of pleasure and fell back on the bed, pretending to be completely satisfied by the experience.

We didn't talk. We didn't even touch. We just lay there.

Less than a minute later, she was on her feet again, feeling about on the floor for her clothes. I thought I should do likewise and joined her, pawing about for my shirt and underwear. It could have gone a lot faster if we'd turned on the light, but I don't think either one of us was much in the mood to look at each other.

Finally, we were dressed and we made our way back to the living room. Dorothy didn't pause, she headed straight for the door. Opening it, she turned to me briefly and, for just a second, her brain signaled the muscles in her face to turn up the edges of her mouth into what is generally considered to be a smile and she said, with no inflection at all: "That was fun."

"Yeah, it was," I lied to this girl. This girl who I had fucked. "It was really nice."

She nodded as if our business had been concluded in a proper and professional manner. "See ya," she said. And she started for her car.

"Yeah," I called after her. "See ya."

I watched her get in the car. I saw her light up a cigarette. I heard her start the engine. I watched her drive off.

I never saw her again.

Rose Tint My World

That fall, I started my senior year of high school.

This was an exciting time, obviously, but not for the usual reasons one would associate with entering one's final year of school. Like a lot of seniors, I was both looking forward to and dreading my graduation day. But my reluctance to head off into the wild blue yonder had less to do with leaving the comforting confines of school and embarking on life in the great unknown. My trepidation was based in something far more selfish than that: I simply didn't want this Rocky experiment to come to an end. I was having way, way too much fun.

But I knew: Once I graduated and went off to college, that would be it. My Fridays and Saturdays would quite suddenly be sadly, tragically, horribly...

...free.

Theoretically, of course, I could have avoided this eventuality by applying to colleges in South Florida. If I chose to go to, say, the University of Miami or Florida Atlantic University, I could have enrolled in college *and* continued doing the Rocky show.

This solution, however, was never on the table. Not for a minute.

I had grown up with the fixed goal in life of finding the exit out of this place. Ever since I was a kid, I had looked forward with great eagerness to my last sweltering day in the Swamp and had dreamed of little else than escaping this tropical maximum-security prison. I was, therefore, not going to spend a single second longer than necessary in this godforsaken rathole. I was going to get the hell out.

How serious was I? Here's a clue: The only colleges where I applied were in New York. Nowhere else, just New York State. In this way, I guaranteed that when I went to college, it sure as hell wasn't going to be FAU. And you could bet your ass I wasn't going to be a Hurricanes fan.

No. Fucking. Way.

But this choice, this completely intractable choice, meant that at some point in the next twelve months, I was going to bid this Rocky world goodbye forever. It would, I imagined, be the only thing I would miss about life in the Swamp.

To be absolutely clear, at this point in my life I had almost no serious connection, emotionally or otherwise, to my high school. School was nothing more to me than the place where I spent my non-Rocky hours. That was it. "School spirit" was a concept I grasped only in the abstract.

By that fall, the only friend I had in the entire school was Dean. Everyone else might as well have been crash test dummies for all I cared. And despite the fact that Dean and I had been close buddies for years (and remained so until 3:00 every afternoon), we almost never saw each other after school hours and I had never, not once, invited him to see Rocky.

So if you want to know the reason *why* I would have chosen to throw my hat in the ring and run for Student Council President, I really couldn't tell you. Certainly, if you'd have asked me when I was a junior if I would have considered running for student government the following year, I'd have laughed in your face. (Or maybe I would have been polite about it and simply said, "No, I never really thought about it." Who can really say what I would have done?)

In any case, for reasons that remain murky to this day, about three weeks after I went back to school that fall, I found myself picking up the nominating petition and scrawling my name under "President." Maybe this unusual move was the result of spending nine months or so with the Ultravision gang. I was becoming, to my great surprise and for the very first time in my life, impulsive.

My rival for the position of Student Council President was a girl named Rose. I knew her really well because, as I may have let slip, my graduating class was not exactly something that you would classify as huge. But the entire high school was electing us, not just the senior class, which meant that Rose and I would have to address the student body—all of them—at an assembly the day before the election to try to persuade them to vote for us. These speeches would determine everything.

Rose, thankfully, went first. And she gave a very nice, understated and completely commendable address on why she was a good choice to pilot the student government in the coming months. She made a number of excellent points. She was extremely clear and very informative. All in all, she did a really fine job.

Then I got up there and mopped the floor with her.

I stood before the assembled students of Zion Lutheran Christian School and pretended to look at a handful of note cards that I had brought with me up onto the stage. Then I dramatically tossed the cards into the air as if I was abandoning my prepared remarks and wanted simply to talk directly to the students as equals.

It was unbelievably contrived. Theatrical. Overdone. Ridiculous.

And, naturally, it worked.

I leaned over the podium, looked them in their collective eyes and promised them the best year of their lives. I wasn't going to get them better grades or make sure that everyone got dates to the school dances, but by God I was going to make sure that the 1982-83 school year was the best in history.

The first step:

Homecoming.

I laid it on the line: Elect me and you'll have the best homecoming any school has ever seen. It will blow your doors off. Guaranteed.

The crowd went wild. I walked off the stage in a blaze of glory.

Poor Rose. She never knew what hit her. It was a landslide.

Traditionally, the homecoming dance had been held in some lame, off-school-property dance hall or Shriner's club that regularly hosted this type of event. The school itself budgeted a couple thousand dollars to rent the place, put up decorations and hire a band. The way it worked was: The date was set, tickets were sold and the students showed up. Lousy music was played, the attendees had a crappy time, they went home. That was that. The formula could not have been simpler to follow.

I decided to change things up a bit. I went to the principal and proposed that we hold the dance on school grounds. In fact, I suggested, we could hold it outside. In the quad. The space, I argued, was perfect: a big open area with a raised stage at one end and plenty of room in the middle of the grounds for the dancers to congregate. The weather wasn't really an issue. It was Florida, after all, and it didn't rain often enough to pose a serious threat.

My thought was that we could take the money we usually spent renting the hall and use it to hire a really *good* band, rent some tables and chairs and cater the living *shit* out of it.

The principal had no objection to my master plan (he had better things to worry about) so he signed off on it without a second look.

After that, I took the homecoming budget and started moving money around. And the line item slated to get the biggest boost in cash would be… the band. For God's sake, we needed a good band.

I had absolutely no idea, until I started holding auditions, that there were so many tiny little four-piece bands in the world simply *begging* to perform at high school events. If you, in your naiveté, ever dare to announce that you are scheduling a school dance and are in the market for a musical act, prepare to be inundated with the most diverse group of…well, I can't say "performers" because half of the groups I saw had no business attempting to play organized music to begin with. A few of these combos sounded as if they'd met in the hallway and decided to stroll inside and play "Don't Fear the Reaper" in whatever key happened to strike their mood.

In the midst of this audition fiasco, a completely unexpected group of musicians came in the door to try out. It was my friend Dean, followed by a group of three or four other students who had, like everyone else in the state that week, formed their own band and wanted a chance to perform at the homecoming dance.

My heart immediately dropped through the floor. This was truly a nightmare come to life. I was now faced with not only having to endure their audition performance, but then, once they had erupted in pure suckiness all over the room, I would be forced to turn them down flat, thus alienating my best friend in school *and* his friends.

And I ran for this position for *what* reason exactly? Oh, right. *Impulsive*. Great.

They got up on stage and plugged in their instruments. And I gritted my teeth, anticipating the worst.

I know what you're expecting me to say here. You're expecting me to say, "But, through some miracle, they were wonderful! They began to play and the clouds parted, and the Lord Jesus himself appeared and accompanied them on rhythm guitar."

Sorry. Didn't happen. They sucked. I wish I could report otherwise, but there you are.

The good news was, they sucked the *least* of anyone else who had showed up that afternoon, so they got the job. So, happy ending after all.

However, before I extended the offer to them to play at the dance, I had one tiny request. Just a minor requirement, really. I placed my little caveat before them and awaited their response. The band members looked at each other, shrugged their shoulders and appeared to come to an agreement.

"Okay," said Dean. "Sounds good to us."

"Great," I said, smiling. "You're hired."

Four weeks later, homecoming night and I was dateless. I didn't really mind. I was the designated emcee, after all. I didn't really have time for date-related pleasantries. Or so I told myself.

The quad was awash in decorations: crepe paper, streamers, balloons, the works. It looked like a million bucks. Okay, five hundred bucks. But still.

Even better news: The weather forecast was unbelievable. Not too hot, not too cold, no rain, no wind. I would have been happy with "mildly sweltering." But this kind of mild, pleasant weather was nothing short of astonishing down in the Swamp.

Ticket sales had been brisk. We were sold out and anticipated a standing-room-only crowd. The tables and chairs had been delivered on time. The caterer had shown up when he said he would and, to my great relief, the food actually looked edible.

Finally, everything was in place. The band had performed their soundcheck. The chaperones were readying their nightsticks. And the crowd started to arrive.

Naturally, I knew everyone in attendance and most of their dates as well. Some students were dating other students, but a lot of them showed up with dates from other high schools. And two students, Holly and Jill, showed up with dates who weren't in high school at all.

Jill walked into the dance with Russ. I had known he was coming and had been looking forward to seeing him at this dance for a month. The minute he arrived, I knew that he was going to live up to all my expectations.

I didn't know that they still made velvet suit coats, but Russ had put his hands on one, along with a ruffled shirt, bow tie and, naturally, his hat Jake perched on top of his head. He looked terrific, but it was hard to keep your eye on him because of the young lady attached to his elbow.

Jill was sporting a strapless, light-blue dress that went from just below her shoulders straight down to her knees and didn't stop to ask for directions on the way. It was clingy in the way that all things should be and in none of the ways they shouldn't.

Holly was close on their heels and I had to admit that she looked amazing herself, having pulled her hair up for a change and shoehorned herself into a burgundy number that really...well, let's say it brought out her eyes and leave it at that.

These two girls had set the bar atmospherically high, as far as the hotness factor was concerned, and it was going to be tough for anyone to match them.

Yet, despite the molten-lava-level hotness of these two fine young specimens, there was another guest at this evening's dance who appeared, to me at least, to be the most interesting to observe. And he stood, in a bespoke dark suit and tie, looking dapper and out-of-place, on Holly's arm. It was, of all people, Skinny Kenny himself. Our own Riff Raff. At homecoming.

Now, I'd like to say it had been my idea for the girls to invite a pair of RHPS dates to the school dance, but the idea had actually originated with Jill. Jill and Holly never went anywhere the one without the other, and since Jill was going with Russ anyway, she convinced Holly that they would have a lot more fun if she brought along a date from the Rocky show instead of one of the school schlubs.

Holly agreed and took a look around the cast for a prospective date. She had some difficulty deciding, but since she had met Kenny through me months earlier while we had been dating and had deemed him the most fun (and safe) person to invite, he got the nod. Any one of the other cast members might have taken her invitation as a romantic overture and tried to press the advantage. Kenny, a perfect gentleman (this evening, anyway), knew he was there to function as arm candy and was behaving himself.

I greeted them at the door (this was my party, after all) and made them feel welcome. Jill and Holly couldn't wait to hit the dance floor. Kenny and Russ seemed less inclined to be the first to jump up in front of the entire school, but once a few others trickled out onto the floor, they grudgingly obliged.

The band was now warmed up and the crowd began to swell. Within minutes of the food being brought out for their inspection, the student body swarmed the food tables like a pack of locusts and, deeming the fare acceptable, cleaned us out.

Within an hour, the quad was jammed with the biggest homecoming crowd the school had ever seen. The punch flowed, the assembled guests swayed and the party hopped.

About halfway through the proceedings, the Homecoming King and Queen were announced. Jill and Holly, though easily the best-looking dates in attendance, were not eligible, as they were juniors. Thus, the anointed royalty paled in comparison. Still, Russ and Kenny—well aware they had the best-looking companions in the joint—did nothing to disabuse the King of his belief that he had the sweetest arm-candy in the place.

After the homecoming crowning ceremony and honorary dance was completed, Dean and his bandmates took a break. Seeing that the moment was right, I detached myself from Russ, Kenny and the girls and made my way to the back of the stage.

Dean and the rest of the band were pretty charged up. Dance bands are, for the most part, loathed on general principle, but these guys had obviously done a lot of rehearsing since the audition and the crowd really seemed to love them.

I sidled up to Dean and made sure I had his attention.

"Now," I said.

Dean's eyebrows shot up. "Now? Really?"

"Well, after your break," I conceded. "But yeah. Next song."

"You got it," he said. I faded back into the crowd and found my way back to Jill and Holly. They were relaxed, cool and loving every minute of this evening.

They had no idea.

A few minutes later, the band stepped back onto the stage and J.R., the lead singer, grabbed the microphone.

"Hey everybody! How you doin'?" he called out. It is a well-known Law of Rock that when a lead singer asks how you are doing, you scream with enthusiasm. Even if your dog just got hit by a car, you are required to yell, "Whoooooo!" at the top of your lungs. So the crowd obliged.

"Good to hear it!" he called back. "Now, listen, we've got a little something we'd like to do for you."

241

The moment had arrived. All of my plans for this evening were about to be fully realized.

"This," said J.R., "is by request. Hit it!"

I truly wish I could properly describe the looks on Russ and Kenny's faces when they heard the opening chords of the Time Warp coming from the lead guitarist at our homecoming dance. There was some shock, mixed with complete dumbfoundedness, rounded off with a dash of utter confusion.

Their heads whipped around to look at me and I hit them with a high-wattage smile just before I leaped to my feet and legged it for the dance floor. Both they and their dates were, naturally, close behind.

Happily, the five of us up on the stage were not the only people at homecoming who were familiar with the Time Warp. By the time we actually got to the part where you needed to jump, step and thrust, there were easily twenty people joining in. The faculty, of course, had not been privy to this musical selection, but by this time, even if they were inclined to object, there seemed little point in trying to put a stop to it.

So for that one evening, homecoming night, 1982, Rocky Horror took over the Zion Lutheran Christian School dance.

Nobody seemed to mind one little bit.

Well…until they played "Sweet Transvestite."

The Charles Atlas Seal of Approval

The next Friday, the cast meeting was winding to a close when Russ announced that he would be distributing ballots for the upcoming "Wild and Untamed Things 1st Annual Awards Show Spectacular," which was scheduled to take place at Iris's house the following Saturday.

I was completely knocked out. Awards? There were actual Rocky *awards*? Who came up with that?

Before I could ask, Russ got busy. He handed out the official ballots and instructed us to fill them out and get them back into his hot little hands by the following night so he'd have time to tally up the votes, identify the winners and prepare the actual award certificates in time for the ceremony.

I got my copy and started to look it over. Almost immediately, I realized that the Rocky awards ballot was…unique.

At first, the categories seemed pretty straightforward for this sort of thing: Cast Member of the Year, Best Actor, Best Actress, Best Supporting Actor, that sort of thing. All your traditional awards categories. But then, as you got past the first part of the list, things began to get a bit…strange.

"The Sleeping Beauty Award for Best Grog." "The Domino's Award for Best Pizza Face." "The Leprechaun Award for Most Charming." "The 'Oscar' for Best Hat" (after Kenny's eponymous chapeau). There was even the "Edith Bunker Award for Worst Singer." All told, there were over a *hundred* awards to be distributed and each category (Fight of the Year, Most Likely to Be Late) was odder than the last.

Asking around, I soon learned that ever since they were first presented, back in the old Hollywood days, these awards had been highly coveted (most of them) and the actual voting process was closely guarded and very secretive. Chatting amongst yourselves regarding your voting plans was strongly discouraged. Friendships, I learned, had been put at risk by voting for (or against) each other for particular categories.

This was a blood sport and we were, each of us, unwilling combatants. Two men enter. One man leaves. That sort of thing.

Also, there weren't any rounds of voting. The first round was the last. No list of nominees, no whittling down of names. This was it. Vote, count, present the award. Quick and dirty. That's the way they liked it.

So, with that in mind, we each took our ballots home and began the soul-searching process of voting for the person most deserving in each category.

In some cases, it was easy.

Best Actor? Had to be Mark.

Best Actress? For me, Andrea. Piece of cake.

Best Supporting Actor? Being honest, I voted for Kenny, but I burned with secret envy in doing so, not only because he held the role I loved so dearly, but because he was so goddamn good at it.

Best Hat? My own Kilgore got the vote, naturally.

The voting was going pretty smoothly. But then:

Cast Member of the Year. Boy, that was tough. Donny? Russ? Impossible to choose. Donny had led us all to glory, but Russ had taken up the flag when Donny could no longer shoulder it and had borne it ever since.

I finally pulled the lever for Donny, since he was the one who had brought me aboard and given me my first break. Still, if Russ won, no one would be upset.

After that, the choices got a bit tougher:

Best Pizza Face? A horrifying category. How do you vote for someone to receive an award for their horrendous acne and not feel like shit? I could hardly contemplate the humiliation involved in "winning" this cruelly conceived trophy, much less consider voting for someone to receive it, deserving or no.

However, I also feared that I might actually win it myself if I *didn't* vote, so in an act of self-preservation, I finally put down Kenny's name. After all, he had it almost as bad as I did. But I wasn't exactly proud of my behavior in throwing Kenny to the wolves.

It didn't get much better after that. "The B.O. Award" for stinkiest cast member. "Boston Bean Award" for the fartiest cast member. And then, at the bottom: Worst Actor. Worst Actress. These were *awards*?

I hardly knew what to do, so I just filled in the first names that came into my head and handed in my ballot the next night.

There were a few awards that I stood a chance to win. But I didn't covet very many of them.

In fact, a few of them scared the shit out of me.

Awards night arrived the following week and we all gathered early for the pre-show activities. It was a new venue for us, Iris's house, and we were admonished not to mess up the joint. Fair enough. We weren't animals.

The presentations would be made by Mr. Entertainment himself: Russ. The tension was thick. The votes had been tallied. This was it.

Finally, the big moment arrived and we all took our seats. In the scramble to get a good view, I somehow wound up (to both my amazement and delight), on a couch in the first row directly in front of where Russ would be making his announcements, with Andrea sitting behind me, her legs snaked around my waist and my back pressed up against her. She was actually resting her chin on my shoulder.

Do not ask me how this occurred. It is an ungrateful lottery winner who questions why the numbers went his way.

Russ got right to work. The routine, established back in the Twin days, appeared to be that the presenter (in this case, Russ) would read each category, describe what the award meant (if necessary) and then announce the winner. There were no acceptance speeches. You simply took your award, smiled if you could and then sat the fuck down.

As awards ceremonies go, it zipped along quickly. (Given the number of categories, speed was an essential component to the hosting duties.) We roared our approval or dismay as the winners were announced and shouted down those who felt they were undeserving of a particular slight or insulting "win." I soon realized that the "bad" categories were to be taken in the spirit in which they were given and that no harm was meant (though I was thrilled when Kenny did wind up winning the Pizza Face award. I was a hell of a lot more sensitive about my blooming complexion than Kenny seemed to be.)

To no one's surprise, including my own, I won the Grog award and I'm quite sure I clobbered the competition. But as happy as I was to receive even a single award, there was only one that I truly wanted. This particular honor was scheduled to be bestowed toward the end of the ceremony, so I had some time to wait. I ran into Tracey in the kitchen during intermission when I went to get a beer and I could see she was as excited as I was.

"I voted for you," she said, reading my mind.

"I voted for you, too," I said. "It's the least a husband can do."

She laughed and we took our seats, waiting for the second half to begin. Finally, after a few more minor awards, Russ quieted the room with a wave of his arm.

"Okay, lads and ladies, here we go. The Rookie Award for Most Promising New Cast Member, Female, goes to..." He paused dramatically. "...Tracey!"

I looked over and Tracey's face had turned bright red. The room exploded into applause. Eleven months earlier, she had been an anonymous nobody in a Transylvanian coat. Now she was the Principal Janet, kicking ass every weekend. She richly deserved the acclaim she was receiving.

"Okay, okay," Russ called out after handing Tracey her award. "Shut the fuck up and let's get on with it. The Rookie Award for Most Promising New Cast Member, Male."

I felt Andrea squeeze me ever so lightly with her knees as if she knew what was about to happen.

"And this year's winner is..." Russ again paused for effect. Then he smiled. "Get on up here, Jack!" Russ called out.

I would be falsely modest if I said I was *completely* surprised. After all, I had been working like an Iditarod sled dog ever since I came aboard—doing pre-show, performing Dr. Scott and covering for Riff Raff—and I had been hoping that my efforts would be recognized. Ever since the moment I had spied the category on the ballot, this was the one moment that I had wished would come. And somehow it had.

I practically floated up off the couch and reached out for the award, which Russ was brandishing like a diploma. The entire cast was cheering enthusiastically and I turned to them and smiled, waving the paper in silent thanks to all of them. I saw Tracey in the back, howling her wifely approval. Sunday, Tony, Andrea, Kenny, Donny, Ron...all of them were whooping and cheering.

Then I did what I was supposed to do. The award safely in hand, I sat the fuck down.

The night rolled on and we finally got down to the most coveted awards. Mark won Best Actor in a walk. Iris won Best Actress, nudging out some stiff competition. Andrea won Best Supporting Actress and, fittingly, Kenny picked up the Supporting Actor trophy.

The big question hanging over the proceedings was the winner of Cast Member of the Year, but we were all pleased to see that Russ got to bestow the award on…himself. Nobody seemed more happy than Donny, who responded to the announcement by pounding the floor with his beefy legs and applauding uproariously.

Later that night, after the awards ceremony had concluded, we were all handed a bit of sobering news: Mark announced that he was quitting the show. This seemed a pretty shocking development at first but, upon reflection, it made sense. He had been performing Frank for more than two and a half years and that's just about long enough for anyone. Besides, his best friend, Iris, had left the cast months earlier, so the show didn't have the same thrill for him that it once did.

In true Rocky fashion, no one attempted to argue with him. When you hung up your bustier, you were done and that was that.

The question was: Who did we have who could fill those silver, high-heeled shoes?

When the answer came, we discovered that we were not the only ones who were surprised. The United States Army was a little shocked, too.

Boyd, I came to learn as I got to know him, was a Florida boy, through and through. Born, bred and likely to die there, presumably of a gator bite.

However, unlike the other South Florida native in the show (Tom), young Boyd was nobody's sidekick. If he followed anything, it was his own blinkered imagination.

He was a tall drink of water, our Boyd. Well over six feet, with short dark hair and an expression on his face that was perpetually set at, "What did you just say?" This was not, I should be clear, because Boyd was slow. He wasn't. But he didn't approach life in what you could call a very serious way and, naturally, he assumed that you didn't either.

Originally, Boyd had joined the cast as a non-performer, functioning as an official/unofficial cast photographer. But after a couple of weeks, snapping pictures just didn't seem to satisfy him anymore, so he finally hit the thrift store:

Black jacket. White shirt. Black pants.

Joining the Transylvanians, in this case, didn't quite work. Boyd never seemed to fit in with everyone else, mostly because he was missing that essential element that makes for a truly top-notch ensemble member: He couldn't *blend in*. He was always just a half a beat off, or a second or two behind the big dance moves. And because of this, he was *mesmerizing*. You couldn't take your eyes off him. This, for a Transylvanian, was a problem.

Given his...what's the expression?...*stand-out-ish-ness*, there was little that Russ could do about Boyd. As cast manager, Russ essentially had two choices: Fire Boyd or kick him upstairs. Given how sweet and kind Boyd was, the likelihood of his getting booted out of the show was pretty low, so Russ decided to see if Boyd could actually become an understudy for anyone. And with Mark's exit and Billy officially taking over the role of Frank, there was suddenly a very large hole in the cast for Boyd to fill: Frank-N-Furter understudy.

And so, inexplicably, after only three months in the cast, Boyd had a shot at this extremely difficult and highly coveted job. As risks went, this was a doozy.

Up until this time, Billy had been the Frank-N-Furter backup whenever Mark was not around, and the part-time work seemed to suit him fine. Now that Mark was gone, though, Billy wasn't all that anxious to step into the role full time. He had always seen himself as merely a fallback, not a replacement. Besides, slathering all that makeup on every night took *forever*.

Per Russ's edict, every understudy had to suit up and play the role once a month, so we were all anxious to see if Boyd, when his turn at the plate arrived, could even begin to do what Mark, or even Billy, had done with the role.

I was playing Dr. Scott the night he went on and, consequently, had a front-row seat. I could hardly believe my eyes.

Until Boyd took the stage as Frank, I had always assumed that the primary job of the Rocky performer was to mimic, as closely and minutely as humanly possible, the actor on the screen. Boyd, for his debut as Frank-N-Furter, took another route.

He *interpreted* the role. And it was a sight to behold.

Boyd did all the blocking, sang all the songs and went through most of the same motions that Tim Curry had done when they filmed the thing, but Boyd...added a little something of his own to the part. It was subtle, yes, but distinctly noticeable.

And, strangely, it worked.

You felt compelled to watch him because, unlike most of us up there, you didn't know quite what he was going to do next. If Curry threw a look at the camera on the screen, Boyd threw a similar look out at the audience but, somehow, it was his own. He wasn't copying Curry's performance as much as he was using it as a springboard for his own.

Needless to say, he was a huge success. Within a week, Billy had stepped aside and handed complete control of the role of Frank-N-Furter over to Boyd.

Just like that (and from the least likely source imaginable), we had a new Frank.

Unfortunately for Billy, and for all of us, Boyd wasn't destined to wear the pearls for very long. His personal life was a mess, his finances were in shambles and his prospects of employment were extremely dim. Given these circumstances, Boyd finally decided to take the route that so many young men had taken before him:

He joined the Army.

We cautioned him against it, partly because we were worried that he would wind up battling on some distant shore (after all, there was a Republican in office), but also because...well, we knew him. Army life, what we understood of it anyway, did not seem to be the sort of thing that would agree with our free-spirited Frank-N-Furter performer.

None of us, save Doc, had ever been in the service, but we imagined that the Army was going to *expect* some things of our friend Boyd. We thought, for example, that the Army might be...disciplined. We weren't sure, of course, but we thought it might.

We also speculated that life in the Army could very well mean adapting to a regimented existence (in that Boyd would be part of a regiment, and all). Again, it was just a guess.

We further thought that Boyd could be expected to (and this was just wild conjecture) *do as he was told*. We were concerned that his introduction to the armed services could quite possibly be filled with mundane and routine tasks that, despite his protestations, were not to be altered in the slightest bit.

Mind you, these were just guesses. But we thought they were pretty fucking *good* guesses. And we also thought, just as a sidebar, that Boyd was completely and utterly incapable of performing the types of duties that the Army required as a matter of course.

In short, we were of the collective opinion that the Army was going to chew him up and spit him back out again, and imagined he might not enjoy that chewy, spitty experience. And we told him so.

Boyd was having none of it. He had made up his mind and, by God, he was going to have a future. He was going to sign up, ship out and shape up.

He was going to be all that he could be.

So, after only two months as Frank, Boyd announced that he was going. Bye bye Boydie.

Naturally, we had a big goodbye bash for him. We gathered at the Orphanage, roasted him unmercifully and teased him about how the drill sergeants were going to kick his ass. We made special mention of how miserable he would be without his long, sequined gloves to pull on every weekend.

Boyd promised to stay in touch and smiled through all the good-natured teasing. And then...he was gone. Off to boot camp. Frank-N-Furter had gone to war, God bless him.

Almost immediately, we began getting dispatches from the front (actually Boyd's base camp up in Georgia). He had arrived safe and sound and at first seemed to enjoy the change. As expected, they had begun conditioning Boyd and, from what he said, he appeared to enjoy the new routine.

As his letters continued to trickle in, however, they grew more and more despondent in tone. The regimen, which at first blush had seemed quaint and new, quickly grew tiresome, ponderous and very, very depressing. The Army, as it has been known to do for its entire existence, was sucking the individuality out of young Boyd and turning him into a soldier. And the experience was just killing him.

We did what we could to cheer him up. We wrote, we called, we sent him magazines, photos, mementos from the show. We said how much we missed him and begged him to let us know if there was anything we could do.

His responses went from sad to depressed. Then from depressed to *extremely* depressed. Ultimately, he appeared almost on the verge of suicide. We were scared to death for him.

Two weeks later, Boyd was home.

Walking into the Ultravision one night in his fatigues, Boyd announced cheerfully that he was done with Army life and that the Army was decidedly done with him. We were thrilled and amazed at this development but also more than just a little perplexed. What on earth had happened?

We all knew that getting *into* the Army, if you are an able-bodied, young American man willing to give it a try, is about the easiest thing in the world to do. You sign up, they look you over, they stamp you "approved" and off you go.

But if you become displeased with your decision and wish to rescind it...good luck, pal. Once they've got you, getting them to let you go is quite a trick. They *own* your ass and they take pride in ownership.

So in case you're wondering how to get *out* of your Army commitment once you join, here's a tip:

Have your friends send you pictures of yourself wearing black-and-silver high-heeled shoes, fishnet stockings, black underwear, a woman's bustier and a sassy set of pearls around your neck. Then take said photos and...share them with the boys in the barracks. And your sergeant. And your C.O.

It also doesn't hurt to get caught at lights-out with a pair of fishnets under your uniform.

Go ahead. Try that. They'll have you out the door faster than you can say, "Atten-SHUN!" (Perhaps not nowadays, in the new, more open-minded Army. But back then? That kind of thing did the trick every time.)

Boyd had been summarily booted out of the Army due to what they called his "moral depravity." For his part, Boyd did little to argue the point. He saw the open door and went through it as quickly as he could. They called it a dishonorable discharge, but Boyd saw no dishonor in it whatsoever. He was free.

The Army's loss, however, was our gain. We had our Frank back.

He just had to wear a long wig until his buzz cut grew out.

Super Heroes Come to Feast

"The Piranha is coming."

Tracey dropped this little nugget of information on me in a matter-of-fact tone and then stared at me as if I was expected to react in some way. Trouble was, I had no idea what she was talking about.

"What," I asked, "or who, is the Piranha?"

Tracey looked stumped. We were sitting together at the long table at Denny's and she leaned in close to answer me. "I was hoping you could tell *me*," she said. "I don't know what it means, either. All I was told was: 'The Piranha is coming.' Seemed like a big deal to Storme, anyway."

I glanced down the table and spotted Storme curled up in one of the diner chairs, grinning to herself. She looked like the cat that had just fucked up the canary's taxes real good.

"She told me to keep an eye on Ron during the cast meeting tonight," Tracey went on. "She's up to something, but I can't imagine what."

Before I could ask anyone else at the table what might be at the bottom of this little mystery, Russ called the nightly meeting to order. He dispensed with the busywork pretty quickly, told us to expect a new Brad steering wheel the next week (our old one had been stolen by an audience member, presumably as a souvenir of the show), collected the weekly dues and then began running through the cast for the following week's show.

"Okay, now as we know, both Boyd *and* Billy are going to be out of town next Saturday, leaving us without a Frank. Fuck you very much, fellas, for leaving me high and dry."

"You're welcome!" called out Boyd cheerfully.

"However," Russ went on, "I've had a couple of weeks warning about this development and I managed to put my hands on a one-night-only replacement. This particular understudy will come and watch the show on Friday and then step in on Saturday. There shouldn't be any problems." Russ smiled. "You know, I don't think we've ever had a special guest pop in and do the show. Should be fun. And this is one special guest, lemme tell you." His tone of voice had taken on a mysterious air.

"So? Who is it? Spit it out," said Sunday, clearly annoyed by Russ's attempt to build suspense.

Russ looked around the room dramatically and announced: "Charley. Charley Paretta."

During the course of the meeting up to this point, Tracey and I (and presumably a few others) had been watching Ron very carefully. He was sitting two seats to Russ's left and didn't seem to be paying much attention to what was being said, choosing instead to concentrate on what appeared to be a very tasty bacon cheeseburger.

At the pronouncement of this name, however, Ron suddenly looked as if he'd been jacked into a wall socket. His back went rigid, his eyes flew open and, for a moment, I thought he might actually be choking to death.

Andrea was the first to speak. "No shit," she said and a huge smile lit up her face. She looked over at Ron and rumbled a low chuckle. "Well. This should be interesting."

"Wow," said Sunday, and for the first time since I'd known her, she actually looked impressed. "Haven't seen that motherfucker in a while."

By this time, Ron appeared to be slowly regaining the ability to express himself. His mouth, at least, was opening and closing and something resembling sounds were coming out. Before he could actually form words, though, Cheryl called out, "Who the hell is Charley Paretta? Is he cute?"

"She's not a 'he,' Cheryl. Charley's a 'she.'" Russ informed her. Cheryl looked crestfallen. Ron looked like a beached tuna. "And she's agreed to come out of retirement and give us her Frank for one night only. Cool, huh?"

By now, I had gathered that Charley was the infamous Piranha. What's more, since the Hollywood veterans all knew her name, it appeared that she had once been associated with the show down at the Twin. Unlike every other member of Marshall's cast, however, Charley appeared to be neither despised nor, it seemed, unwelcome. This in itself was surprising. Most of the Twin actors were, by definition, Ultravision kryptonite. But what made the whole thing truly intriguing was the effect that this news was having on Ron.

In all the time I'd known him, I had never seen Ron appear to be anything less than unflappable. No matter what you threw at him, he seemed able to handle it. Andrea and Sunday, at various times, had unloaded both barrels of their infamous, biting scorn at him and he hadn't blinked.

But this. This was historic. Ron was actually *speechless*.

Russ looked around the table one last time, ready to wrap up the meeting.

"Anything else? No? Okay. See you next wee—"

"*Wait.*"

Ron had finally choked out a word. Russ froze, an amused smile dancing around his mouth. "Yes, Ron?"

"Who…" he stammered out. "Who's playing Brad?"

Russ appeared confused, but you knew he wasn't. "Saturday you mean?" Ron nodded. "Well, you are, of course."

"About time, too," Andrea murmured.

"You want me to…?" Ron looked as if he'd been kicked in the gut. He seemed unable to finish the sentence.

"Is that…going to be a problem?" Russ asked sweetly. Ron looked up and, for a second, he looked almost *scared*. Then he looked around the table. All eyes were on him. With an effort, he sat up straight and cleared his throat.

"No," he finally said, forcing a wan smile. "Not at all. Why should there be a problem?"

Russ nodded, satisfied. "All righty, then. See you Friday everybody."

He left Ron looking disconsolately at his plate, his appetite clearly destroyed.

I looked from Ron to Tracey. She sat, open-mouthed, like the rest of us.

"What the hell was that all about?" I whispered to her.

"I don't know," she said. "But I'm gonna find out." We both stood up and made our way over to Storme, who was cackling maliciously as she tucked into a chocolate sundae.

"Okay, spill," said Tracey, flopping down next to her. "Who is Charley Paretta?"

Storme grinned widely. "Nobody calls her that. Paretta. That's not her name." She tipped a spoonful of whipped cream into her mouth and dropped her voice. "She's *the Piranha*." Storme laughed quietly and shot a look over to Ron to make sure he wasn't listening. "Wanna know why?" she asked us coyly.

"She...likes to swim?" I offered. "She has good dental hygiene?"

"Fuck you, Jack," said Storme blithely. She turned her attention to Tracey. "Can you guess?"

Tracey crinkled her brow. Why would someone be nicknamed "the Piranha"? Because they're mean? Violent? Dangerous? There were lots of reasons, none of them good.

"Nope," said Storme, after Tracey had rattled off a few options. "Not even close."

"So? Why?"

"Because," Storme whispered conspiratorially, "she's a man-eater."

Charley "the Piranha" Paretta, it turned out, was something of a local Rocky legend back in the old Hollywood Twin days. Originally from New Jersey (the actual town was unclear), Charley was a bona fide RHPS veteran even before she arrived in Florida. She had been involved in one of the early Rocky casts back in her hometown and, like many of us, had worked her way up from the bottom. By the time her snowbird parents dragged her down to Ft. Lauderdale, she had reached the very pinnacle of Rocky achievement: performing the role of Frank-N-Furter for over six months, one of the few girls ever to hold the honor.

When she got to the Swamp, her arrival oddly coincided with Marshall's attempt to put together the show down at the Twin. And while some people might have seen this as a sign from above that destiny was pointing her toward the Hollywood cast, Charley had other plans.

She had been doing Rocky for so long, she no longer felt the need to get her Frank on every weekend and she certainly wasn't about to let herself be bossed around by a lowlife like Marshall. Besides, she wasn't the "reliable" sort and could hardly be counted on to show up every weekend and do the show like it was a *job*. That kind of dependability just wasn't in her.

Instead, she somehow wangled special permission from Marshall to make guest appearances at the Twin whenever she got the itch. Every few months she would show up, unannounced, and ask to do the show that night. Mark, as a courtesy, would step aside for the evening, Charley would strap on the bustier, take the stage and...things would get shaken up for an hour or two.

From what Storme had heard, this girl just burned up the stage. Not only was she hot-looking, she was utterly fearless. Where Tim Curry's eyes on the screen would flash, Charley's would practically shoot flames. She was predictable only in the sense that you knew she could be counted on to mouth the words that were being spoken on the screen by her character. Beyond that, everything was up for grabs. You never knew *what* she was going to do.

Especially, Storme told us, in the Brad/Frank bedroom scene.

This scene, when performed by two men, is sexually charged to begin with. After all, Frank actually seduces Brad during the course of a few minutes and winds up actually servicing him orally before the scene is over. Performing this on stage, live and in person, involves some strategic choreography of Brad's robe to mask the "naughty bits."

Of course, once you knew that it was all carefully staged and that nothing even remotely sexual was taking place, watching the scene live became routine. Just another part of the show.

Not, we were told, when Charley was involved.

Like everything else she did, Charley dove into the scene…ahem… headfirst. Storme had heard from a reliable source—Russ himself—that Charley made a point of performing the scene as written and would actually go so far as to service whomever was playing Brad on that particular evening. Russ had learned about this *first hand*, so to speak, and swore that it was gospel.

The legend of Charley the Piranha, Storme assured us, was no myth.

"Wait a minute," I said to Storme. "If it happened to Russ, it must have happened to Ron too, right? He was the full-time Hollywood Brad, wasn't he?"

"Yeah, funny thing about that," said Storme, "but whenever Charley would show up to play Frank, Ron would magically disappear. Previous commitment, feeling sick. Something always prevented him from playing the role that night. Weird, the coincidence, innit?"

"So, what, he's *afraid* of her?" asked Tracey. "That's not possible. He's not afraid of anything."

Storme slurped the last bit of ice cream from her spoon and shrugged her shoulders. "I guess we're gonna see on Saturday, aren't we?" She glanced down the table at Ron who was sitting very still, looking as though someone had reached into his chest and removed his soul. "Me? I can't wait."

Friday night rolled around and I got to the show early, anxious to finally meet the one person in the world who could rattle Ron's cage. What kind of exotic creature could she be? And what was it about her that could put Mr. Unflappable on edge?

By 11:15 she hadn't yet shown her face, so I drifted over to Ron's car to learn what I could from him instead. He had pulled up a few minutes earlier, glanced around and, seeing that our special guest hadn't yet made her entrance, was simply sitting there, listening to the radio and staring out the windshield. I sidled up next to him and he killed the music.

After a second of two of silence, he finally spoke up.

"Go ahead. Ask. You know you want to," he said, not even bothering to look at me.

"Okay, fine," I responded. "What's the deal with this girl, huh? Why so touchy?"

"You'll find out soon enough," Ron replied. "It's...hard to describe."

Not satisfied, I pressed on. "Well, I mean—is she just a real bitch or some gigantic skank or—"

"I said," he interrupted, "you'll see." He got out of the car and slammed the door as punctuation. Without a glance back at me, he made his way toward the theater. The conversation was clearly over.

Curiouser and curiouser.

Later, when we were loading the props and equipment into the theater, I caught sight of this girl standing with Russ. At first I figured it couldn't be the infamous "Piranha," as she looked about as harmless a young thing as you could imagine. Short, curly hair of a sort of mousy brown-blonde, freckled nose and an enormous pair of green eyes. I was soon proven wrong, though, when I heard someone call out, "Charley!" and saw her face light up in recognition.

She certainly didn't *look* like a marine predator.

Charley seemed relaxed, chatting casually with Russ who was, in turn, introducing her to various cast members as they made their way into the theater. Sometimes Charley would spot someone she knew from the old Twin days and they'd embrace. But mostly she just shook hands politely and took in her surroundings. She was clearly awed at the majesty that was the

258

Ultravision.

Once I finally finished helping to move all the props into place, I made my way over to get a close-up view for myself.

"Jack!" Russ called out. "Get over here. This is Charley. Charley, this is this year's reigning champ as Most Promising New Cast Member, young Jack. He's gonna be your Dr. Scott tomorrow."

"Hi!" said Charley sunnily, sticking out her hand. Her face split into a gracious smile and as we made our introductions it struck me how much she reminded me of Holly. Sweet, harmless and totally unthreatening.

Ron, I was thinking to myself, was completely off his nutter. This girl was a sweetheart.

Russ walked Charley around the theater, explaining where various scenes happened in our show and where she'd need to be when she played Frank the following night. Charley listened attentively, asking the occasional question. She met Boyd, who was performing Frank this evening, and they talked a bit, too. He looked a bit dubious that this tiny thing was capable of pulling off a Tim Curry impersonation, but then…that wasn't his problem.

Finally, the pre-show swung into action, the movie cranked up and we were off. Everything seemed to be going fine, but I did notice that Ron was almost imperceptibly tensed up throughout the entire proceedings. You probably couldn't see it from the audience, but as close up as I was, I could tell that he was wound as tight as I'd ever seen him. Hit this guy with a hammer, I thought, and he'd ring like a church bell. Weird.

The show finished up, the crowd applauded and we packed up for Denny's. Charley begged off. She wanted to rest for her big debut tomorrow. She left with a smile and a wave, saying how much she was looking forward to her big night with us.

And that was it. Charley the Piranha had shown up at the Ultravision and simply charmed the hell out of everyone.

"So…that's the Wicked Witch, huh?" I said to Ron as he was getting back in his car. I was needling him on purpose, due to the fact that he had so clearly proven himself to be an utterly paranoid fruitcake.

Ron didn't bat an eye. "What, her?" he said, jerking a thumb at Charley's departing vehicle. "That's not who I'm talking about."

"That's not Charley Paretta? Is that what you're saying?"

Ron looked at me sadly and shook his head. Clearly, I was a moron. "No, Jack. That's Charley Paretta. She's a nice girl, isn't she? I like her a lot."

He got in his car and turned the key. The engine rumbled to life.

"Tomorrow, you meet the Piranha. And I can't wait for you to tell me what you think of *her*."

Saturday night arrived and I got to the Ultravision parking lot a little late. While I had no specific expectations, I was definitely looking forward to this evening's show. I had never done Rocky with a female Frank-N-Furter and it was undoubtedly going to be a unique experience. After all, it's one thing to watch a guy flounce around in a sexy pair of fishnets all night. But a young lady? This I couldn't wait to see.

I looked around the parking lot for Charley, but didn't spot her. Russ was there, talking to a dark-haired stranger in a leather jacket. As I sidled over to Russ to find out if Charley was running late, the stranger whipped around and I stopped, frozen in my tracks. It was Charley.

And yet...it wasn't.

Instead of her natural curls, Charley now wore a shoulder-length, black, curly wig that matched Tim Curry's tresses from the film identically. Her black leather coat was also straight from the movie, an exact duplicate of the jacket Frank wears late in the film. And it was clear that, underneath, she had already changed into her Frank costume. A hint of bustier peeked out of the jacket and her legs were already fishnet-clad.

But what had really stopped me were her eyes.

I don't know how much time she had spent that evening trying to get the Frank-N-Furter makeup exactly right, but it had clearly been time well spent. Her eyebrows were now lush and black instead of girly and cute. Her lips were crimson and outlined by a faint sliver of black. And her eyes, which had seemed big and beautiful the day before, now stared out at me from a deep cavern of liner and eye shadow.

"Jack, isn't it?" she purred. "I remember *you*." She looked as if she wanted ed to *eat* me. It was terrifying.

I tried to say something, a greeting of some kind maybe, but the words just died in my throat. I couldn't rip my eyes away from her. The mousy girl from the night before had transformed into a fucking panther and she looked ready to pounce.

"Jack." Russ broke the spell, calling my attention away from Charley. "I think the theater's open. Better get started, huh?"

For a second, I hadn't the slightest clue what he was talking about but then my mind returned from whatever alternate universe Charley had sent me and I refocused. Muttering, "Sure, sure," I wandered off toward the storage closet. Before I left, I snuck a final glance.

There they were again. Those eyes.

"See you in a bit, Jack. Can't *wait* to start the show." I swear, her voice had dropped an octave from the previous evening.

I'd like to be able to tell you that I responded coherently to her. Some snappy rejoinder or witty remark. Instead, I made a sound that was more or less in the area of, "Bluh." Something impressive like that. And then I got away from her as fast as I could.

Suddenly, everything Ron had said made perfect sense.

I had finally met...the Piranha.

Thankfully, Charley stayed out of the theater during the pre-show. I don't know what kind of moron I would have made of myself if I had been asked to do the warm-up under her watchful eye. After all, you can't properly rev up a crowd by just saying "Bluh" repeatedly, so I'm glad I didn't have to find out.

When I went into the ladies room to get changed, there she was again. Sitting in front of the huge mirror, shoulder-to-shoulder with the rest of the cast, she was putting some finishing touches on her magnificent Frank makeup. Her leather jacket was carefully folded on the counter.

And then I saw it.

Etched in black and red ink on Charley's back, just below her right shoulder, was a tattoo. But not just any tattoo. It was probably the most recognizable tattoo in Rockyland.

In the film, as you doubtless remember, Frank-N-Furter has inked onto his right shoulder the word "BOSS." Below it is a red heart with a knife thrust through the middle, with a few drops of blood squirting forth.

Mark, Billy and Boyd (and everybody who ever played Frank) would take the time before the show each night to sketch the BOSS tattoo onto their own shoulders with magic markers. It was a time-honored Frank-N-Furter ritual.

But this one...this one was *real*. No magic markers for this girl. Hers was forever seared into her flesh. And this was in an era when young girls didn't often sport tattoos the way they do now. Back then, it was mostly bikers and merchant marines who got inked to that degree. This was a level of commitment you didn't see every day.

"Like what you see?"

The voice shook me out of my reverie. I looked up and found that Charley was staring at my reflection in the mirror, piercing me with her eyes like a butterfly on a corkboard. And her smile. It was otherworldly. The way she was grinning at me would have given Ford Prefect the heebie-jeebies.

I said something non-committal and brilliant like, "Huh-buh-gah-jah," and got swiftly dressed for the show, dashing out of the bathroom as though pursued by ninjas.

Back in the theater, the previews were still running and I saw, by the light of the "Blues Brothers," that Ron was just pulling on his jacket for the wedding scene. I made a beeline over to him.

"Um...I think I owe you an apology," I said.

Ron was unsurprised. "Oh, so you finally met her, huh?" I nodded. "Yeah, I thought you might change your tune after that."

"Well, she's so..." I started. I searched for the words. I came up empty. I gave up. "What *is* she?" I finally asked.

"Tonight?" Ron said, putting his final touches on his costume. "Tonight, she's Frank-N-Furter, body and soul, brother." He smiled nervously at me. "Wish me luck."

Off he went.

And all I could think was: *Via con Dios, mi compadre.*

Once the movie actually starts, the character of Frank-N-Furter doesn't show up for a good fifteen minutes. There are four full musical numbers, a whole lot of narration and a great deal of exposition to get through. This was fortunate, as it not only allowed us to get fully caught up in the performance, it also put some distance between us and our guest star.

In the interim between first seeing Charley in her transvestite getup in the parking lot and her first appearance on stage, the full impact of being in her presence had diminished significantly.

But as I lay on the floor at the conclusion of "The Time Warp" and heard the opening beats of "Sweet Transvestite," the anticipation began to grow anew. I could just make out Charley's tiny frame, off in the corner, facing the wall, her black cape swirled around her tiny shoulders. She was stomping her foot to the beat of the song while Tracey and Ron backed slowly toward her.

On screen, Brad and Janet are oblivious to the fact that, just behind them, Frank's elevator is creeping slowly down toward the first floor. When it gets to the bottom, Janet is the first to spy Frank through the gated door and reacts noiselessly, her eyes wide and her mouth agape in horror. Brad remains blissfully unaware of Frank's presence until, quite suddenly, the gate to the elevator flies open, Frank swirls around and Janet, screaming in terror, faints to the floor.

On our stage, Ron, as Brad, prattled on obliviously as Tracey's Janet slowly turned, pretended to see Frank through the elevator door, and silently began to freak out. Then the power chord struck, Tracey let out her scream and Charley whipped around.

Every Frank-N-Furter brings their own, special essence to the role. Mark's Frank had been a study in complete transformation. He simply embodied the character that Curry had created for the film. Boyd, on the other hand, was entirely his own person, a Frank-hybrid, if you will. He was still Frank, of course, but he added, as a bonus, his not-quite-in-focus view of the world as well. Billy's was more of a conventional impersonation, the straight guy playing the transsexual (but all in good fun).

Charley's Frank, however, was something else entirely.

When she flashed her laser eyes on Ron that night, I was half-expecting him to leap back in terror. Because if Charley brought anything to the role of Frank-N-Furter that I had never seen before, it was this:

Danger.

Charley's Frank wasn't simply sexy, she was *predatory*. This was a slinky, smokin' hot praying mantis that would happily welcome you to her bed, fuck your brains out, and then rip off and consume your goddamn head as a finale.

Charley finished the first couple of lines of the song and started trotting away toward Frank's throne at center stage, singing all the while. When she reached the throne, she whirled around again and struck a seductive pose. "I'm not much of a man by the light of day," she sang. "But by night I'm one hell of a lover." At this point, Charley smiled seductively, stepped forward and, with a flourish, threw off the cape.

Now, I knew that this girl only stood about five-foot-four in her stocking feet. She was this petite, little thing in real life. But on stage, at this moment, she looked like an Amazon. Standing there in her black corset, slinky underwear and thigh-high see-through stockings, she was the living embodiment of towering sexual desire.

Still, despite her obvious attractive qualities (and there were plenty of them), your first instinct upon seeing her was, inexplicably, to back away. This was not someone to enfold lovingly in your arms. The vibe that came off her was less "potential sex partner" and more "ravenous feral beast."

The crowd, predictably, was going bananas. Guys who normally refrain from cheering too loudly at Frank's entrance (for fear of appearing attracted to a dude) were now hooting lustily. By the time she climbed back into the "elevator" and disappeared at the end of the song, everyone in the room, men and women alike, mourned her absence.

Well, almost everyone. Because as each minute of the film ticked by, we got closer and closer to…The Scene. All eyes, when they weren't glued to Charley, were fixed on Ron. And he already looked like he wanted to jump out a window.

Generally speaking, the members of the cast (at least those of us who had been doing the show for months) didn't usually watch the entire movie. We'd participate in our scenes and then, during a break, we'd run to the bathroom, maybe make a phone call from the lobby, nip out to have a smoke. As long as you didn't miss your next entrance, you could do whatever you wanted.

Tonight, our eyes were riveted to the stage show. Even after the Rocky/Frank wedding scene, when most of the cast was done for the night (the Transylvanians having completed all that was required of them), nobody left the theater. The entertainment on hand was just too good to miss.

Charley was taking the role of Frank-N-Furter to new heights (or depths, depending on your perspective). She slinked her way around the lab, she fondled Rocky with obvious relish…every scene had an extra dash of red-hot spiciness that the guys who regularly played the role simply could not provide. At least not from where I was sitting.

Finally, the Narrator appeared and announced that Brad and Janet were being shown to their separate rooms. We were now three scenes away from Ron and Charley's long-awaited face-off and the suspense was delectable.

First, though, it was Tracey's turn. Charley, playing Frank (who, in turn, was playing "Brad"), rushes into the darkly lit chamber and climbs into bed with Tracey's Janet, supposedly to seek comfort for the night. They were bathed, thanks to Tom's spotlight, in a pink glow. Soon, the two are locked in an embrace and, as events proceed, Janet offers no resistance until...surprise! Janet pulls off Frank's wig and discovers that he has been masquerading as her fiancé. Frank, undaunted, continues to encourage her to give in to him and, after receiving the assurance that Brad will never know the truth, Janet succumbs.

Seeing Charley climb on top of Tracey and seduce her was great fun, of course, but it was only the appetizer. The main course was only a minute away.

Slam cut, on the screen, to Riff and Magenta cleaning up the lab. This is the scene where Riff chases Rocky down the elevator shaft and gets a little elbow sex, but no one was paying any attention to the players on stage. Knowing what was coming next, our full focus shifted to Ron. He stood, wearing a blue bathrobe, a pair of white briefs, white socks, dark shoes, and a forlorn expression.

Steeling himself, he strode up the ramp toward the bottom of the screen, lay down in his accustomed spot for the bedroom scene (where Tracey had been writhing about only a few moments before) and awaited his fate.

He lay as still as a corpse. He didn't look around in expectation or alarm, or appear panicked or distraught. Instead, he seemed resigned, ready to accept whatever came. Then Riff laid a big smackeroo on Magenta's neck, she moaned in delight, the spotlight switched to blue and...

....it was time.

An hour or so later, when the lights came up after the show, I looked around for him but...Ron was gone. I helped put the props away, asking everyone I saw where he could be. Nothing. He had just disappeared.

Giving up the hunt, I was stepping into Steve's car to head over to Denny's when I spotted Ron's car parked on the other side of the movie house, partially hidden. I could just make out a figure in the front seat.

I told Steve to head over to the restaurant without me and made my way over. Sure enough, there was Ron, sitting behind the wheel, staring through the windshield with an odd look of disbelief on his face.

I rapped on the passenger's side, trying to snap him out of his trance, but he didn't seem startled. It was like he was expecting me. He reached over and flicked the lock and I got into the car.

We sat, wordless, for a few seconds. And then for a few seconds more.

"So," I finally offered. "What was that like?"

Ron's eyes slid over to me and, after a beat, he said: "Lemme ask you something. What could you see?"

I thought back, searching my memory for any abnormality in the scene. At last, I simply said, "Not much, actually. I don't know what I was expecting but...it looked pretty much like it does every night."

"Really?" he said. He looked relieved. "That's good."

"I guess that means...nothing happened. Right?"

He allowed himself a sideways smile. "Not quite."

"So...what? What did she do?"

Ron shook his head like he wasn't going to tell me, but then just as quickly changed his mind.

"Okay, look. Let's get something straight right off the bat. That's a hard scene to feel sexy in to begin with, all right? I mean, when you're dressed like I am...in the robe, the tighty-whities, the socks and shoes...you're not exactly feeling like Casanova, you know?"

I interrupted him. "Hey, I've been meaning to ask you—Why the *shoes*? Brad just wears his socks in the movie. What's up with that?"

"That's self-preservation, brother. I played him without the shoes when first I started out. Ran around a movie theater in just my socks one night. It was fucking disgusting. I wanted surgical gloves to take the things off when I was done. It was *toxic*. After that, it was socks and shoes all the way."

"Aha. Insider Brad info. Got it. Go on."

"Well...you know the scene in the bedroom, how it goes. Frank gets in, snuggles up to me, we start to kiss. Then the wig comes off and I jump back. So tonight, the same thing happens with me and Charley but...about two seconds after she climbs on top of me, I see her reach for my underwear. And I think, 'Oh, shit. Here we go.' Luckily, the timing is perfect so I pull off her 'Janet' wig and jump back like I'm supposed to.

"Trouble is, I was not quite as quick as she was. Somehow, her index finger had hooked the top of my waistband, so when I jumped back...I made *another* entrance."

Ron looked over at me to make sure I fully understood and I nodded. I could picture it in my mind, but from where I had been sitting earlier, I couldn't see it from the house. His robe had covered everything.

"You mean...you were *at attention*? Right there?"

At this, Ron shifted a bit in his seat uncomfortably. "Well, no. Not at *attention*. How could I be? It was freezing in there."

I frowned slightly. It had *not* been cold in the theater. It never was. I almost contradicted him on this point but, it wasn't my story so who was I to argue?

"Besides, I was in character, right? I'm not *supposed* to be turned on by the whole thing, you know?"

"Oh, sure. Absolutely," I said in an understanding tone. I didn't really understand him at all, but I thought it nice to pretend that I did.

"Plus..." he said uncomfortably, "she had this...*look* on her face."

And then I got it. I knew exactly what he meant. I had seen the look myself and it had just as efficiently unmanned me. It was the look of the man-eater. The Piranha.

"I hear you loud and clear, brother," I told him. "Believe me."

"It was unreal, Jack. There I am, lying in front of this sexy, hot little nympho who's just ready to go to town, waiting for me to step up and...I got nothing. It was exactly what I was worried would happen."

I felt terrible for him and thought it my fraternal duty to try to comfort him. "Hey, big deal. It's over. Forget all about it."

"Oh, you think that's the end of the story?" He laughed. "No way. I'm not *near* done. Because when she sees what's going on down-stairs..."

"You mean, what's *not* going on."

"Yeah, thanks a lot. Anyway, when she sees that Mr. Happy isn't paying her the proper attention, Charley decides...she's going to help."

"Holy shit."

"Uh-huh. So when Frank starts kissing Brad, making his way down his chest and toward his nether regions, Charley starts doing the same to me. She's nibbling my neck, she licks my chest...she fucking bit my nipple, Jack."

"Wow. So did it work?"

"No, it didn't fucking *work*. It was horrifying! I think I actually got *smaller*."

"Jesus."

"Tell me about it. Hell, I even thought about trying to get away from her. Just ditch the scene and take off, you know? But she had this iron grip on my underwear *and* my robe. What am I supposed to do, slip out of them and streak naked out of the theater? Like that's an option?"

267

"A worm on a hook, huh?"

Ron stared at me. "You couldn't come up with a better way of putting that?"

"Sorry," I said. "So what did you do?"

"What else? I did my job. I just...played Brad. She tells me to give myself over to pleasure and I'm thinking, 'Talk to the guy downstairs,' but I don't say it. I just continue with the regular lines, doing the scene. And it seems to be taking for fucking *ever*. I mean, the whole thing is like a minute long, but it just seemed to go on and on..."

"And what's she doing?"

"Oh, God...she's licking my stomach, nibbling my thighs...she's having the time of her life. Then I say, as Brad, 'You promise you won't tell?' and she's supposed to say, 'On my mother's grave,' and she goes down on me, right? But instead, she checks to see if there's been any change in my condition since she started trying to get something going and she sees...zip. All quiet on the Western front, you know? And instead of her line, she just looks up at me and whispers, 'Awww.' Real quiet. Disappointed. Not like I'd let her down, exactly. More like I'd told her she couldn't play with a toy she really liked.

"And then that's it. The scene is over. And just as the lights wink out, she kisses me."

I gulped. "Upstairs or downstairs?"

"Downstairs. But don't get excited. It wasn't even sexy. It was more like you'd kiss a misbehaving kid who should know better. Then she released me, growled low in her throat and...took off."

He was looking out the front window of the car, remembering. Then he shook his head again.

I put my hand on his shoulder. "I'm sorry, brother. I wish it could have worked out."

Ron turned and looked at me in surprise. "Sorry for *what*?" He smiled and became animated again. "Listen to me: That couldn't have gone better, Jack. Honestly. That was exactly what I needed."

It was my turn to look surprised. "What are you talking about? Didn't she just humiliate you?"

"Hell no! You know what she did? She showed me *exactly* what I am. I'm not this fucking lady-killer, so great in the sack, so cool, so awesome that every chick should be drooling after me. I'm a kid, Jack. So are you. Sure, I'm a little troublemaker, a hell-raiser...all that shit. But I'm not a *man*. Not yet, anyway."

I couldn't quite believe what I was hearing. His lack of performance had somehow morphed into an object lesson.

"Anyway, that's what I took away from it. I thought she was going to go all Linda Lovelace on me. Right there. Live and on stage. And for the first time in my life, the prospect of getting blown actually scared the crap out of me. And I couldn't figure out why."

He smiled. "Now I know. I wasn't anywhere near ready for what she had to offer and so..."

"You...failed."

"Yeah. Hey, there's a first time for everything."

We sat in silence for almost a minute. Then he reached out and started up the car.

"You hungry?" he said.

"Starving."

"Me, too. These performances always give you an appetite, don't they?"

I looked over at him. "Who are you to talk? As far as I can see, only one of us was able to actually *perform* tonight..."

"Touche," he said, pulling out of the lot. Then he added: "Asshole."

The Devil's Eyes

Halloween is to Rocky what Christmas is to Jesus.

Dressing up in silly costumes and running around like a moron for a few hours? That was our stock in trade down at the ol' Ultravision. So the holiday and the movie went hand in sequined glove.

What's better—if you're running an RHPS show and the 31st of October happens to fall on a *weekend* (as it did in 1982), you're going to see a huge boost in attendance, guaran-damn-teed. On this night-of-nights, a lot of folks like to go trick-or-treating with the kids, hit a Halloween party or two and then, feeling buzzed and bored around 11:00, they wander over to the Rocky show because...why the hell not?

Russ had prepared us for the coming onslaught. The plan was, we would open the doors a little early, have an extended pre-show and then really give the folks a performance to remember. We had even conjured up some prizes for a costume contest to be judged right before the virgin sacrifice. There were two categories: Best Rocky Costume and Best Costume Overall.

Primed and ready, we opened the doors just before 11:00 to accommodate the bigger-than-usual attendance. From the line outside, we looked to top 400, the biggest night of the year since they'd opened the show in January. Not anything near the 600 available seats, mind you, but it was as close to a sell-out as we'd ever seen.

I got the nod to get things started and jumped up on the front row of seats to greet the guests.

"Good evening ladies and gentlemen, and welcome to 'The Rocky Horror Picture Show'!"

The crowd roared back. It was gloriously loud.

About 11:30, word passed through the cast (and eventually up to where I was running the pre-show activities) that Ron had not yet shown up. This was extremely unusual, as he could generally be counted on to be among the first to arrive.

Tonight? Nothing. No phone call. No warning. Just...nothing.

Before we had much time to worry about him, the news broke that Ron had been seen earlier that evening at a Halloween party in Ft. Lauderdale and that it looked as if he was having a grand ol' time. Hearing this, we all relaxed. Clearly, he had been unable to tear himself away from the party but he would, we presumed, be along any minute.

Ten minutes later, no Ron.

Ten minutes after that, with showtime rapidly approaching, *still* no Ron. Russ, his understudy, got into his Brad outfit and prepared to go on in case Ron was a complete no-show.

Back on the stage, we never let on that anything was amiss. We held our costume contest, handed out the prizes, deflowered our virgins. Just another day at the office.

Then we hit midnight, the chanting for lips began and Ron was still nowhere to be seen. We had no choice. We motioned for the show to start, Russ became Brad for the evening and we were off and running.

It was a terrific house: enthusiastic, energetic and *loud*. We weren't used to a house this size and everyone in the cast caught a contact high off the audience. Scene after scene, we were getting huge reactions to things that had gotten only smatterings of applause for months. We were *loving* this.

But through it all, Ron's continued absence made us more and more uneasy. We were all thinking the same thing: Sure, he might have been late to the pre-show. We might even have understood his showing up late to the actual performance. But for him not to show up at *all*? This was completely unheard of.

Finally, the film wound down and we got a healthy round of applause from the assembled guests. The audience filed out and we headed off to Denny's. The moment we arrived at the restaurant, we noticed that Russ had zipped off to a pay phone, presumably to try to dig up some news.

The waiters came around. We all ordered some grub, chatted about the show and how cool the whole evening had been, but it was a hollow joviality. We were all on edge, waiting for Russ to come back with good news about Ron and start the meeting.

Ten minutes later, the food had been delivered and Russ was still on the phone.

Twenty minutes after that, we had all finished up our meals, grown increasingly nervous, paid our checks and...still we waited.

It was getting really late, well past 3 o'clock. We should all have been long gone by then. Conversation had died completely. Nobody stirred or made a move toward the door. We simply had to know what had happened and we weren't going anywhere until we did.

Russ remained at his post at the front of the restaurant, the phone pressed against his ear and a stricken look upon his face.

Finally, he hung up. He paused, looking absolutely drained of all emotion, and then he looked up and saw everyone at our table, necks craning to get a look at him and glean from his demeanor some hint of what to expect.

Obviously, we were in for something bad.

Russ made his way back to the table, his hands pushed into his jacket and his head hanging low. Before he could even say a word, Tracey burst into tears.

"No," Russ said immediately. "No, it's not that. Ron's not dead. Okay?"

The cast exploded into a cacophony of relief. Holding our collective breath for the last hour hadn't been easy. We had been expecting the absolute worst but, miraculously, the worst had not occurred.

But Russ wasn't finished. After letting us celebrate for a second or two, he again called for our attention.

"Hold on, hold on," he yelled out. "It's not all good news." Again, the room went completely silent.

Russ again looked down as if he was having difficulty finding the words. This was very odd, as words were, generally speaking, his primary currency.

"He was in a car accident," he finally said. "No big surprise there, right? And, yes, he's in the hospital."

There was a sharp, collective intake of breath from all of us. Okay, so he wasn't dead. But that left a lot of options on the table. Maybe he was paralyzed? In intensive care? Had slipped into a coma? Anything was possible.

Sensing our anxiety, Russ pressed ahead. "Here's what I know: He was at this party, right? A costume party, I guess. And Ron was all dressed up, goofing around, having fun. Lost track of the time and didn't get on the road until late. He was hauling ass to get here and would probably have made the pre-show, but at Sample Road and Dixie Highway...he got hit. I guess it was pretty bad.

"This other guy, the guy who hit him, he was just wasted from what I hear. Flying along Dixie in a big Plymouth or something. Blew through a red light and T-boned Ron's car. Sent it flipping across Sample and into the gravel next to the train tracks. Ron's car was totaled. All the windows just blown out of the thing. A complete wreck.

"The drunk, the guy in the other car..." Russ looked around at us. "He's dead. Wasn't wearing a seat belt. Flew right out of the car. The paramedics didn't even bother trying to revive him. I guess...it was pretty obvious that there wouldn't be any point. And from what I heard, when they got a look at Ron's car lying in the median, they weren't all that hopeful about finding *him* in one piece either."

Again, Russ paused, pulled out a cigarette and lit it before speaking. No one else moved.

"Here's the thing, though," Russ's brow crinkled. "Does anyone here happen to know what Ron decided to be for Halloween this year?"

He looked around the table, seeing if Ron had shared his costume choice with anyone. We all returned his gaze with blank stares.

He nodded, as if he expected that we wouldn't have a clue. Then he said:

"Well, I guess Ron got a big kick out of the 'Excalibur' movie last year. You all saw it, right?" Most of us nodded. Where was this going? "Well, Ron decided that for Halloween this year, he wanted to be a knight. A Medieval knight. Had a big sword. A mace. A shield with a crest in the trunk. The works. Must have been a hell of a costume."

He took a drag, blew it out and continued: "So when the paramedics went to pull him out of the car, you know what they found sitting in the front seat?"

We all tried to conjure up a picture, and all at once it hit us.

Russ nodded. "Yeah. That's right. They looked in this car wedged sideways on the side of the road, glass everywhere, just a hunk of twisted metal... and they found a guy perched behind the steering wheel wearing a *full suit of fucking armor*. Breastplate, chain mail, everything.

"He actually said 'Hi' to them when they arrived. Asked if they could let him out. He was having trouble with the door, he said. So they pried it open and this motherfucker *walked out*. Stepped out of the goddamn car and walked around the scene of the accident like he was just a curious friggin' bystander. They practically had to wrestle him into an ambulance so they could look him over. He didn't want to be examined. He wanted to come *here*. He told them he wanted to go to the Ultravision and *do the show* after that. But they insisted, so..."

Russ couldn't help it. He laughed.

"So he's in the hospital. They did a bunch of tests. Nothing. Zip. Nada. He's the picture of health. They're releasing him tonight."

Russ looked dazed, but immensely relieved. He grinned at us.

"The car is fucked, of course. But I mean, seriously, can you believe that shit?"

That November saw a lot of changes in the Deerfield cast.

For one, Tracey finally moved out on her own. Fed up with her tyrannical mother and ready to breathe the fresh air of life as a single girl, Tracey stormed out of her house one day and, looking around, found herself in need of someone to share an apartment with. Fortunately for her, this event took place at almost the exact moment that Kenny began looking for a roommate of his own.

The stars must have been in perfect alignment that month, because it turned out that Felicia's mother had lost the tenants who rented the second half of the duplex she owned in West Lauderdale and the place was sitting empty.

Within a week, it was agreed: Tracy and Kenny would move into the apartment next door to Felicia. And when the Orphanage finally shut its doors later that month, Kenny and Tracey's place became the new Party Central.

Yes, the Orphanage was finally going the way of the dodo and while the cast wasn't particularly happy about this news, it had been a long time coming. When Russ finally announced shuttering the place, no one bothered to act surprised.

For one thing, the revolving door of roommates had been spinning a little too quickly for even Russ to handle. Troubled teenagers had blown in and blown out. Rent money was harder to rely upon than ever before. And, frankly, we had completely trashed the place.

Russ had gone through four cleaning services over the years and each one of them, having cleaned it once, had refused to return. The money didn't matter. This joint was beyond redemption. How bad was it? Listen, when you get members of the Rocky cast—whose tolerance level for just about anything raunchy and disgusting is as high as you can get—showing up to your house and becoming horrified by the state of your domestic hygiene... it's time to *move*.

Personally, if I had been Russ, I would have evicted all my roommates, tossed all my personal stuff in the trunk of my car and doused the place with gasoline. Flicking a match over his shoulder as he strolled out the door seemed to us a perfectly appropriate ending to the Orphanage's illustrious history.

Russ, however, kept a level head. He didn't burn the place to the ground but...he didn't exactly ask for his security deposit back either.

He established himself in a little two-bedroom place in Pompano and started rotating roommates in and out of his new apartment at about the same pace he had with the Orphanage. We still went to Russ's after the show every few weeks, but it was only to play poker. The place was way too tiny to substitute for the spacious confines of the Orphanage.

[Side note: The building formerly known as the Orphanage no longer stands. The owners leveled the place soon after Russ turned in his keys and there is now, directly across the street from the infamous Hollywood Bread Building parking structure...an empty lot. I like to think the landlord walked into the place after Russ was done with it and decided that the only thing to do was to knock it down, salt the earth and walk away. Another pet theory is that, after we abandoned it, the place got really depressed and committed suicide. It's possible.]

Also that November: Tracey and Ron finally became a couple. Well, at least they let it be *known* that they were a couple. They had been going out together and scromping for a few weeks, but we all pretended that we didn't notice.

I was skeptical of this pairing right from the get-go. Ron was a tomcat and not much inclined to obey the strictures of a monogamous relationship. And Tracey was a true believer in deep, honest, long-lasting commitment.

This was not likely to end well.

But the big news that November, at least as far as I was concerned, was meeting Alice.

Storme had decided to throw a party one Saturday night after the show and when we heard the news, we dutifully trooped down to her place when the cast meeting was over. Why not? No reason *not* to go.

But rather than just invite her Rocky friends, Storme had expanded the guest list to include some people from her high school class as well. Maybe she harbored some secret desire to see how the teenagers at Pompano High would react when thrust into the hard-partying midst of the Wild and Untamed Things cast. Hard to say. She had her reasons, I'm sure.

I had been at the party for about an hour or so when I noticed this girl sitting in front of the television in the living room, watching MTV along with a group of about six or seven others. I might not have noticed her at all, but she had this blazing head of red hair. I just had to get a proper look at her.

Unfortunately, she was angled away from me in a way that didn't allow for even the tiniest glimpse of her face. Slowly, and not a little awkwardly, I maneuvered my way across the room and positioned myself at an odd angle, perpendicular to the bedroom doorway, so that I could get a good look. I couldn't hold the position for very long (I was wedged between the Lay-Z-Boy and the wall), but I saw all I needed to see.

She had pale, almost translucent skin that was oddly free of the mass of freckles that usually comes along with the whole red-headed package. Her eyes were just enormous, so much so that in the few seconds I spent taking in her features, I could see the MTV vee-jays reflected perfectly in those brown pools.

Finally, I was finally forced to stand, as the pressure of leaning in my current viewing position was causing a disc to rupture in my back. But I had already decided that this beautiful young creature needed much closer examination.

I wasn't exactly a smooth operator in the Approaching Girls Department, but this situation didn't seem to call for much more than my sidling up and plopping down next to her as if what really interested me was the current video on the screen. This I did, finding myself staring up at the TV just inches away from this girl who, up to now, didn't seem to sense yet that I was zeroing in on her.

Trouble was, of course, that I wasn't at just any old party. I was at *Storme's* house. This meant that, just thirty seconds or so after I sat down, I heard a familiar voice call out:

"Hey, Alice. You're gonna want to keep an eye on that one."

The redhead jerked around and looked back at Storme who motioned to me with her chin in a "Yeah, *that* one" sort of move. Following Storme's gaze, the girl turned to look at me for the first time.

She cocked her head and took me in for a few seconds. "So I need to keep an eye on you, huh?"

How could I respond? "I guess so."

"Okay. So I'll watch out for you," she said jovially. Then she stuck out her hand. "I'm Alice."

"I'm Kevin."

And then I thought, *Kevin?*

Why the living hell would I introduce myself as *Kevin?* I was *Jack*, for Pete's sake. Practically everyone I knew (and *everyone* at this party) called me Jack. I was only "Kevin" to my family. What was this?

I didn't have an answer. It was simply that, for some reason or other, I didn't want her calling me by my Rocky moniker. I had no idea why.

"You in the show, too?" she asked. Apparently Storme had introduced her to some of my castmates.

I told her I was. She said she hadn't seen Rocky yet, but that Storme had described it to her. It sounded, she said, pretty weird. I wasn't about to argue with her.

Asked if she was planning to check it out for herself, Alice nodded and said that she was planning to try to come the following weekend. Friday, in fact.

My eyes lit up. The following Friday just so happened to coincide with my monthly performance as Riff Raff. With this in mind, I said that she had picked a good night to come and (casually, of course) mentioned who I would be playing that evening.

Of course, having not seen the film, she didn't know Riff Raff from Rhett Freakin' Butler, but she tried to sound impressed.

"Is that your regular role?"

"No, I'm the understudy, actually. But I get to play Riff once a month or so."

"Oh. So who do you normally play?"

I found it next to impossible to try to describe the character of Dr. Scott and after giving it a shot, I finally gave up. "You'll see when you see it," I said and left it at that.

I asked her how she knew Storme and it turned out that she and Storme went to the same high school. So we talked about that.

She asked me how long I'd been involved with Rocky and, given that it was a favorite subject of mine, we chatted about that for a while, too.

Then we talked about other things...our families, our school lives, our plans for college.

We talked for a long time.

When we were done, we looked around and noticed that we were the only ones still awake. Everyone else had dozed off hours earlier and, to our surprise, we saw that the sun had begun to peek over the horizon. We had been talking all night long and hadn't realized it until this minute.

"I should go," I said. I stood up, but then I realized I didn't have a ride home. "Crap."

"What's wrong?"

"Oh, nothing," I said. "I just...I should have grabbed a lift with Steve. He must have left without me."

"Where do you live?" Alice asked.

"Deerfield," I told her. Storme's house was in Pompano and I lived about ten minutes away by car.

"No problem," she said. "I live in Lighthouse Point. I can give you a ride."

"Great."

We made our way quietly out of the house, trying not to wake anyone up. Crossing the room, strewn with prostrate teenagers, was like picking our way through a minefield. We eventually made it outside.

The lawn was littered with vehicles but Alice knew just where she was parked. She stopped in front of her car and got out the keys to unlock it.

When I saw the vehicle she was preparing to get into, I froze. Alice turned around, surprised.

"Something wrong?"

"This..." I said. "This...is *your* car?" I could hardly believe it.

"Yup," she said. "Pretty cool, huh?"

Cool didn't even begin to describe it. Alice drove a car that would have made grown men weep. There wasn't a set of wheels like it within ten square miles. This pretty little redhead was about to step behind the wheel of a mint-condition, bright-red 1965 Chevy Malibu convertible with a snow-white rag-top, four white-wall tires, original seats and sparkling bright chrome rims.

And, somehow, I was being offered a ride in this amazing automobile. I could hardly believe it.

"Where the hell did you *get* this thing?" I stammered out. "It's incredible."

"A friend of my Dad's was selling it and the price was right. I still can't believe it's mine." She smiled. "Get in. It gets better."

I jumped into the front seat. She slid the key in the ignition and the car started to rumble. It was like a giant cat come to life. She put it in reverse and backed out of Storme's driveway and into the street. With a quick look over to me, Alice grinned and gunned the engine.

"Hold on," she said. And she hit the gas.

We shot out of that neighborhood like a goddamn cannonball.

Less than five minutes later, we pulled up in front of my house. It felt like we had barely touched ground. My knees were weak. And whatever was left of my insides had been left back in Storme's driveway.

The brief trip home had been an unforgettable experience. All of 16 years old, Alice piloted her car like a NASCAR veteran.

When we pulled up, I didn't want to get out of the car. Given that it was 6 in the morning, I had little choice.

I tried to stall. "Thanks for the ride."

"Sure. Happy to."

There was a pause. I should have just gotten out, but it just didn't seem possible. I had unfinished business here. I couldn't even bring myself to look at her. I just sat there.

Then, almost imperceptibly, I sensed that Alice had shifted in her seat and had inched the tiniest bit toward me. I wasn't sure if that was the signal I'd been hoping for, but I was willing to take the risk. I turned my face up to hers and she was staring me dead in the eyes.

I moved forward.

We kissed.

And just like that, we fell in love.

At least, it seemed that way to me. I had never felt a connection like this before. I couldn't explain it, couldn't define it. All I knew was, I had a hold of her at this particular moment and that was good enough for me.

After a few blissful minutes, we finally detached from each other and made hurried plans to reconnect that week. We spoke in excited whispers, as if worried that we would break the spell. We exchanged phone numbers. We kissed again, more at ease, less frenzied.

Then we disengaged. Reluctantly. I opened the car door. I got out. It wasn't an easy thing to do.

"Talk to you later today," I said.

"Okay," she replied and hit me with this dazzling smile. "Get some rest." Then she put the car in gear and pulled away. I watched until she disappeared around the corner.

"Wow," I said to myself. And a few seconds later: "Wow."

When Worlds Collide

Russ was pissed. Half of the damn cast seemed to be going out of town for Thanksgiving, including me. My father had arranged to fly my brother and me to New York for the holiday and it would be the first time in almost eleven months that I would miss a show. Upsetting, but what could I do? Family first and all that.

As Russ scrambled to make sure all the roles would be properly covered for the weekend, word quickly got around that I wouldn't be the only cast member in NYC for the big holiday. Tracey was heading up to New York to visit her father and so was, of all people, Sunday. It was a little hard to believe that we *all* had divorced fathers living up north in the same city (and that each of our mothers had decided to spend their post-divorce lives down in the Swamp), but we quickly got over the coincidence and had a brief pow-wow on how to take advantage of our proximity to the big city.

We almost immediately decided that if we did anything in New York together, we absolutely had to see…The Show.

Now, for every Rocky Horror fan, young and old, there was one place that was considered the Rocky Mecca, the center of all things RHPS. This was the famed 8th Street Playhouse in New York City, where the longest-running Rocky show lit up the stage every weekend night. The president of the Rocky Horror Fan club, Sal Piro, was the Master of Ceremonies in this revered hall and it was the goal…nay, the *dream*…of every Rocky aficionado to make a pilgrimage there at least once. Of course, RHPS began its strange and storied journey at the Waverly Theatre. But by 1982, Sal's cast had long since packed up and moved to 8th Street to set up shop as official Rocky Headquarters.

And so it was decided. Tracey, Sunday and I would meet up in New

283

York City over Thanksgiving vacation and visit the world-famous 8th Street Playhouse to pass judgment on the pinnacle of Rocky life in America.

The trick, for me, would be to convince my Dad to let me go.

See, my father still thought of my brother and me as being roughly 5 years old. We had never lived with him and, tragically, he hadn't had the chance to watch us grow into the fine young men that we thought ourselves to be. He only knew us from the weekends and holidays we had managed to spend together over the years.

Our mother, of course, was a different story. She knew us top to bottom and, based on this familiarity and trust, she unhesitatingly allowed me to spend my weekends in Rocky's warm embrace. But Dad? He looked at us and saw a couple of kids in short pants clutching a pair of all-day suckers. How could we convince him that we were mature enough to manage ourselves on a night out in New York City?

First, I enlisted my brother as a covert operative. Two heads being better than one, and misery loving company and all, there were many advantages to having an ally in this fight. And a fight it would surely be.

Dad's overprotectiveness was fierce to the point of ridiculousness. He got antsy if we offered to walk down to the corner store to pick up a newspaper. And he lived on the Upper West Side. It wasn't like he lived in the Bowery surrounded by drug addicts and pimps. This was one of the nicer neighborhoods in Manhattan. If he didn't allow us to roam the streets up here (where the greatest danger was the threat of being accosted by an East Coast liberal railing against Reaganomics), how were we ever going to get him to release us into the wilds of Greenwich Village without a chaperone?

And right there we struck upon the solution. A chaperone. We would have to fake a chaperone. But who? David and I conferred and came up with the obvious choice:

Sunday's father. We would convince our Dad that the entire evening would be spent under the close supervision of Sunday's *pater familias*.

Next, we had to make up a totally safe-sounding yet plausible scenario surrounding our protector. The setup, as we rehearsed it, became: He would never leave our side, he had been to the show already with Sunday a number of times, he knew the neighborhood really well and, to really bring it home, he was a former cop.

A complete fiction? Sure. But it sounded *great*.

With all of that in our favor, how could he refuse?

284

"No. No way. Not happening." This started on Tuesday and continued through the week, even during our lovely Thanksgiving meal. By then, we had almost run out of time. My brother and I had only twenty-four hours to change his mind in time for the Friday show, forty-eight if we were going to make it on Saturday.

The battle raged over turkey and stuffing.

"Dad, seriously. I'm 17 years old." I was, too. Seventeen. Think about that. "Next year I could join the *Army* if I wanted to, but you won't let me go downtown for one night? *One* night?"

"You don't know the area," he said. "I do. It's the Village. Down by NYU. Washington Square Park. It's crazy down there. Dangerous. Forget about it."

"It's not like we'll be *alone*," I stressed. "Sunday's dad will be there the whole time."

"Oh, that's comforting. *Sunday's* dad. Who names their kid Sunday? Who is this guy? Does she have a sister Tuesday? A brother October? No way."

David took a crack at it. "Dad, Kevin does this every weekend down in Florida, no problem. What's the big deal?"

"The big deal is, this is New York City, boys. This isn't Deerfield Beach. You guys could walk out of here and I'd never see you again."

"What's the worst thing that can happen?" David posed. And clearly, this was the wrong question to ask. You could see our father thinking of all kinds of worst things that could happen.

"Plenty. Now stop asking."

He held firm through dinner and all of Friday, and before we knew it, Friday night was upon us. Sunday and Tracey called. I said, "Maybe to-morrow. I'm still working on it." They were amazed that our father was so intractable. Their own dads couldn't *wait* to get them out of their respective homes. Ours, though, was being way too...parental.

So Friday night passed, permission to go was not issued, and David and I remained at home.

And we were *pissed*.

Saturday morning around that apartment was pretty damn chilly, let me tell you. My Dad wasn't really prepared for the frosty attitudes we displayed. Having not spent a whole lot of time around sulky teenagers, he hardly knew what he was in for. And he was about to get a double-barrel full of brooding.

David and I ratcheted up the Sulk-o-Meter to full blast and let him have it.

We slumped at the table during breakfast. Poked at our food. Looked despondently at nothing in particular. And we didn't say a word.

"C'mon, boys," he cajoled. "Eat your breakfast."

"Not hungry," we mumbled. Oh, we were good at this.

Dad let the mood hang for a minute or so and then tried to change it.

"Hey, what do you want to do today?" he said perkily. "Head over to the park? Catch a movie?"

"Nothing."

He looked alarmed. Two teenagers in the middle of New York and we wanted to just sit around doing nothing? Were we sick? What was the matter with us? (He hadn't really connected our mood to the previous evening's refusal of permission. Dads can be a little slow.)

Now, the key to successful sulking is *lethargy*. Energetic sulking doesn't do the job. To really get your sulk on, you've practically got to go boneless and melt into the couch. After breakfast, David and I wandered over and wilted like tender orchids into the cushions. It was pathetic. Dad was completely thrown by this display.

Finally, the light dawned.

"Hold on. Is this about that show last night? The movie?"

"No. Whatever. Who cares?"

We withdrew further into our protective post-pubescent shells. Dad was on the outside looking in with a puzzled expression. This was a new experience. Moodiness was not our natural state. He was getting a little freaked out.

"Be fair now. I couldn't let you go. It was too dangerous." He tried to say it with finality, but he couldn't muster it.

"S'allright." Our vocabulary was devolving as well. Soon we would move on to monosyllables. That would drive him completely batty.

Dad considered. He knew he was really letting us down, but his protective instinct was not about to be defeated this easily.

"I wish I could take you myself, but I have a very important phone call tomorrow morning and I have to get up early and prepare." Dad's business, putting together trade shows for big-dollar clients, meant a lot of odd hours. We didn't doubt that he was telling the truth. But we were also, in this scenario, completely without sympathy.

"'Kay," we said. We stared at our shoes. We sighed dramatically. We deadened our eyes.

He was weakening. We could tell. David finally laid down the trump card.

"Listen," he said. Then he sighed. "If you think..." he took a big gulp, like this was *really* hard for him to say. "If you think I'm too young or whatever, Kevin can go without me." Dad and I both stared at my brother. He was the picture of Young Despair. "Really," he said miserably. "I don't care."

With this enormous concession, David sat back on the couch with his eyes misting over. He wasn't going to cry. He was going to hold it together. He was going to be *strong*. But it was obviously killing him, admitting that he might be less mature than I was.

I had to hand it to him. It was a masterful performance.

Rushing to the breach, I took up the gauntlet he had thrown down. "No, David," I said, firmly defending him, the way a brother must. "It wouldn't be fair. Of course you're old enough. We both are." Here, I tried on my martyr hat. "No," I declared. "Either we both go or..." I let my voice waver a bit, "...or neither one of us goes."

And I slumped down into my chair as well.

There was nothing more to say. It was all in our father's hands now. Everything depended on these next few moments. The Guilt Sandwich had been lovingly prepared. Would he bite?

Shaking his head as if he couldn't believe what he was about to say, Dad furrowed his brows and finally managed: "He'll be with you the *whole time?*"

I leaped into action, every hint of listlessness suddenly evaporating. "Yes! The whole time! He will. And he even said he'd walk us to the train after."

"Train?" Dad looked horrified. "You're not taking the *train* home." He was revving up the protectiveness, assuming control once more. He said firmly, "I'll give you cab money. You'll take a *taxi* back here. The *minute* the movie is over. Understand?"

We nodded energetically. And that was that. It was settled.

I was on the phone to Tracey and Sunday within minutes.

We were on our way.

It was agreed that we would meet at Sunday's place in midtown and proceed from there. Tracey was coming from Queens and we certainly weren't going anywhere near the outer boroughs, so Sunday's was the logical choice.

Even though Rocky had never really been his thing, David was pretty excited about the prospect of hanging with us for the entire night. I thought it mostly had to do with the fact that (a) he would be cruising around the Village after-hours at the tender age of 15 and (b) he would be doing so in the company of two smoking-hot young ladies.

I had to agree with him. Both of those prospects sounded pretty good to me, too.

We were given permission from on high by our Lord Father to take the train to Sunday's and, thanks to his unbelievably explicit directions, we found the apartment without a problem. We buzzed-in downstairs and hopped on the elevator up to Sunday's New York digs.

Nothing Sunday had ever said to me about her father (which hadn't really been much) could possibly have prepared me for the experience of stepping into his apartment that night. David and I did our best to remain cool and aloof, but it was a jaw-dropping sight.

When I pictured a New York apartment, I generally envisioned a place like my Dad's. Small, slightly cramped but, all in all, tolerable, given that putting up with the tight confines meant you got to live in one of the greatest cities in the world. I never dreamed that New York apartments came in any size besides Extra Small.

This place, Sunday's father's joint, was enormous. "Cavernous" was a word that sprang to mind. It went on for miles in all directions. In a city that measured its worth in inches of floor tile, this place was a palace. The Madison Square Garden of apartments.

And it wasn't just the size that knocked the wind out of you. The place had *windows*. And they were *everywhere*. Looking out from their living room, you'd swear that you could see into virtually every other apartment in the city.

The decor was modern, elegant and very intimidating, but the forbidding nature of the place was offset by the playfulness the current inhabitants had brought to it. For one thing, there were at least three working pinball machines lining the living room wall. Actual, real, *functioning* pinball machines. In their fucking *house*.

The artwork was kooky. Silly, but unpretentious. Like the owners had bought it because they actually liked it, not because it was an investment. And there were pictures and sculptures and little, hidden art pieces all over the place.

Finally, and maybe most important to my brother, there was the stereo.

In every home I had ever entered, be it an apartment or a house, I had discovered that the best way to get a feel for the person who lived there was to pay close attention to what was coming out of the speakers. The quality of the sound system was important, of course, but the musical selection was the real indicator.

No music at all? That meant that you were likely dealing with a very understated and probably very uninteresting person.

Classical music = educated, stuffy but artistic.

Jazz = Asking for trouble.

Smooth jazz = Mind-numbingly boring.

Blues = Either incredibly deep or astonishingly shallow. It went both ways.

Zydeco = Probably stoned.

Rock and roll = If classic rock was playing and they were over 40, it meant they were nostalgic middle-aged folks pining for their youth. If *modern* rock and over 40...

...actually cool. You rarely ran into that.

We did at Sunday's.

Her father didn't come out of the kitchen wearing a pair of silk pajamas and offering us hits off his wizard bong, nor did he walk in pulling off his necktie and bitching about his awful day at the office. He strolled in, relaxed and mellow, offering us each a warm handshake.

He was a silver-haired, middle-aged guy with a wide smile. He was deeply tanned and wrinkled the way guys who spend too much time lounging about Central American beaches are wrinkled. He didn't actually smell of cocoa butter, but I would have bet that he had requested that some equally tanned woman assist him in smearing it on his person in his recent past. We Floridians can sense these things.

In an attempt to be cool in front of his daughter, the first thing he did was offer us a beer. We declined, but it was nice to get the offer anyway. He made small talk, asking politely about the Rocky show in Florida. I did my best to be polite as well and took special care not to say anything that could be misconstrued as inappropriate or incriminating. Sunday would have wrung my neck. Her father seemed positively *charmed* to meet us.

Sunday, on the other hand, looked supremely uncomfortable and not at all thrilled to have us hanging around the apartment, poking around in her personal life and, worst of all, conversing with her father. I could hardly blame her. I wouldn't have been all that happy about her meeting *my* Dad either.

These two worlds of ours didn't often collide, and we liked it that way. Real life was over here and Rocky life was somewhere else entirely. Unfortunately for Sunday, the twain were meeting right in her dad's living room and it was decidedly unpleasant for her.

This meant that when Tracey finally arrived, we set a new record for quick exits. Sunday wanted to get gone, and so, gone we got. We said our goodbyes to Sunday's father and skedaddled.

"Jesus, I couldn't wait to get the fuck out of there," Sunday said once we were out on the street. "Guy can talk your ear off, can't he?"

"He seemed pretty cool to me," I said, earning an incredulous look from Sunday. Nobody likes to hear good things about their parents.

Tracey was practically euphoric. "Which way?" We were to take a subway down to Washington Square and then walk over to the theater. We had allowed ourselves two full hours of lead time, expecting the crowd at the theater to be huge on a holiday weekend.

We rode the train and the torrent of our conversation never ebbed. We talked about the how Thanksgiving had gone, our respective families and how great it was to get out of Florida and into civilization. Then David and I recounted the difficulty we had endured in securing the necessary permission to come. Sunday and Tracey were amazed that we had put up with our own father's stubbornness.

"If my father had told me I couldn't go to a midnight show, I'd have walked right out the door. No question," Sunday said. And I believed her. She wasn't a big one for parental control of her life. Tracey was in total agreement. They lived their own lives. Their parents no longer drove the bus.

David and I, for all our supposed wild-and-crazy South Florida lifestyles, were about as Victorian as these two could imagine. We were considered absolute wimps for having obeyed our own father.

We got to the Village in almost no time at all and were standing in front of the theater by 10:30. To our amazement, there was almost no line. Three or four people were queued up, but that was it. No down-the-block group of fanatics clamoring to be the first in the door like we had expected. Hell, the Ultravision line was longer than this. Here we were, at Rocky Central, and no one seemed all that interested. It was disappointing.

Maybe, we told ourselves, we were just too early for the real crowds to show up. Probably it was a New York thing, showing up late. We made little comment on it and took our places at the back of what line there was.

Lucky for us, it was a fairly warm night by Northern standards. Being Florida folk, we were horribly chilled by temperatures that dipped below 50 degrees. Considering that it had snowed the previous week and had gotten down into the teens only a short while before, we had it unbelievably easy.

A little after 11:00, we saw some of the cast members arrive. There was, of course, no huge parking lot like we had down South, so the New York cast generally were dropped off or showed up on foot. They were hard to miss. Some came pre-dressed in their all-too-familiar Transylvanian outfits but the majority were in their civvies, slipping in the door to go get changed. Even out of costume, it was easy to see who they were. Their attitude was pure Rocky.

We were on the lookout for two people in particular, the only two Rocky personalities who were nationally known. The first was the aforementioned Sal Piro, known for both his founding and presidency of the official Rocky Horror Fan Club and for his brief appearance in the movie "Fame." In the film, Piro is featured in a scene from the live Rocky show that had been shot at this very theater. So, as Rocky celebrities went, he was the Big Kahuna.

The second Rocky legend was the 8th Street Playhouse's famous long-time Frank-N-Furter, the renowned Dori Hartley. We had seen pictures and read interviews with Sal and Dori over the entire time that we'd been involved in Rocky and we felt sure we would recognize them on sight. In fact, Dori had appeared in a lightning-fast cameo in the Tim Curry video "Paradise Garage" that we danced around to every weekend.

The two of them were as close as it came to Rocky royalty.

But of course, this was late 1982 and, by now, the show had been running in this theater for years. When we didn't spot them, we reasoned that Sal and Dori had either retired from the Rocky game altogether or were taking a well-deserved break from the show. In any case, seeing the two of them was not the real purpose of our visit. We were here to check out the show and, naturally, see how we measured up to them.

Or, rather, how they measured up to *us*.

At about 11:30, they opened the doors and we finally piled in. As show-time approached, the crowd had grown to a pretty respectable size, the line outside the theater stretching down the block. But by my educated count, they still only drew about 200 people. If that seems like a lot, remember—we were in the middle of New York City, one of the biggest metropolitan areas in the entire hemisphere. Given that there were more than 200 people living on that block alone, this was not quite the throng we had anticipated.

None of us had bothered to bring any props or throwable objects, by the way. No newspapers, toast or cards. We weren't tourists, after all. We were veterans. Regulars. That sort of thing was for civilians. Still and all, it was a thrill to walk into the lobby, finally setting foot in the place where it all started.

And while the theater was a lot smaller than our playing space down in Florida, that was to be expected. This was a Greenwich Village movie theater sitting atop the most valuable real estate in the world. Naturally, their stage was going to be a lot tighter than where we performed. That said, it was still a pretty nice theater and the fact that they had actual aisles that went up *through the audience* made it look like a fun joint to put on the show.

Their pre-show was fun, but there was nothing about it that made me feel like I was letting anyone down during my own warm-up at the Ultravision. Many of the chants and callbacks sounded pretty familiar too, and it dawned on me that many of the audience-participation bits I had been doing in Deerfield had likely originated in this very room.

Finally, the moment came. Like virgins at their first show, we chanted: "*We want lips! We want lips!*"

The lights went down. The screen flickered to life.

And what do you know? We got our lips.

What do you want me to say about The Show? That we were blown away? I'd love to. But we weren't. I'm sorry, but it's the truth.

Did we have a good time? You bet we did. We shouted our time-honored South Florida lines at the screen (some of which were new to the New York crowd) and we picked up some lines from the 8th Street crowd to bring home with us. We saw some great performers, some okay performers, some clever solutions to staging challenges and some scenes that fell completely flat.

All in all, it was an impressive display, no question about it.

But did the 8th Street Playhouse Rocky cast teach the three of us a lesson in how the live Rocky show was supposed to look?

The hell they did.

Now, in all fairness, we were seeing this cast after they had been doing the show for a number of years. The original cast at 8th Street had long since hung up the fishnets and, this night, we were clearly looking at third- and fourth-generation cast members. The people they had were solid. Serviceable. Maybe not the best we'd ever seen but, hey, after all that time, maybe we didn't get to see their A-game. Perhaps this holiday weekend, four years into their run, it was unfair to judge them. A couple of years earlier, in their prime, maybe then they would have rocked our world.

Maybe. I'm only trying to be fair.

All I can say is, Sunday, Tracey and I went back to Florida with our heads held high. All this time, right up until our trip north, we had proudly believed that there wasn't a Rocky cast anywhere in the world that could measure up to what we were doing twice-weekly at the Ultravision.

We thought, prior to that evening, that the Wild and Untamed Things had the best live Rocky show in the country.

Now?

We *knew* it.

Spaced Out on Sensation

In defense of our friends and colleagues in New York: Doing Rocky can get to be a drag after a while.

I know it sounds like Rocky blasphemy (if there is such a thing), but the truth is that performing the same show, week after week without any variation at all, can be draining and demoralizing. This is true of live theater, rock music and dolphin acts. Doing each and every piece of Rocky choreography, by rote, each and every night leads inevitably to boredom and stagnation. You think Keith Richards *likes* playing "Satisfaction" at every single concert while he's on tour? No. He fucking hates it. But he does it because that's what the people want. And, you know, for all the money and stuff.

Fortunately, the people who perform the Rocky show on a regular basis know that atrophy can set in after constant and mindless repetition. And their solution to this malady is: Mix things up every once in a while.

Now, what I'm about to describe didn't happen that often. We generally did the show exactly the way it was meant to be performed and worked every night to nail the characters as perfectly as we could.

But every once in a great while (say every three months or so) Russ would announce at a cast meeting that we were going to have a Very Special Rocky Horror Show. This meant that, for one night and one night only, the rules went out the window.

These Event Nights were as diverse as they were rare. And they came in all shapes and sizes. In the time that I spent as a Rocky cast member, we enjoyed the following Event Nights:

SWITCH NIGHT

Pretty simple: All the boys played the girls' parts and vicey-versey. We had a female Frank and a male Janet so...something for everyone. The female Rocky wore an ace bandage wrapped around her...attributes. And the male Magenta strutted around in a man-sized maid outfit, which was always a crowd-pleaser.

This was the most popular and most common of our Event Nights because it was fairly simple to do, involved the same blocking as our regular show and needed very little rehearsal to pull off.

Besides, seeing Andrea play Frank was enough to ensure that I would die a happy man. As if that weren't enough, I got to see Kenny play Magenta too, so...let's just say that switch nights never failed to be an enjoyable alternative to the regular routine.

PUNK NIGHT

Let's call this one a failed, but worthy, experiment.

Punk was all the rage in those days (and had been for a few years), so we decided to give it a go. All the characters in the Rocky show would become punked out and Mohawked, complete with torn shirts and safety pinned jeans. What could go wrong, right?

Well, for one thing, it just made everyone *angry*. Brad and Janet were pissed off, Frank was pissed off. Even Rocky, that mindless goop, was all in a lather.

And two hours of nothing more than seething, hacked-off Rocky actors is no way to run a railroad. We tried it. It sucked. We moved on.

Kinda like early '80s punk, come to think of it...

BLUES BROTHERS NIGHT

Okay, this one was pretty high concept: Instead of doing the regular Rocky show and performing the characters on the stage exactly as they appear on the screen, Russ concocted a plan to have us play our roles as if each of us was one of the various characters from the Belushi/Aykroyd comedy classic, "The Blues Brothers."

This show, lemme tell ya, was the definition of bizarre. Russ and Kenny played Jake and Elwood Blues who, in turn, played Riff Raff and Magenta.

296

With me so far? Ron and Tracey played Matt "Guitar" Murphy and Aretha Franklin as they might have conceivably portrayed the characters of Brad and Janet. I played Dr. Scott as the Henry Gibson Nazi leader from the film (the German connection making this a natural choice). Boyd played Sister Mary Stigmata (if you remember, the nun who ran the orphanage) as she would theoretically appear as Frank-N-Furter. And it just went on from there.

It was, to say the least, extremely strange. But a hell of a lot of fun.

I truly hate to think that anyone came to see the Rocky show for the first time that night, because if they did, they likely never returned. It was crazier than paintball for the blind.

And yet, somehow...it worked. Well, *worked* is probably a little strong, but it was pretty hilarious to watch. I mean, instead of doing Elbow Sex, Jake and Elwood would face each other and sing "Stand By Your Man" accompanied by the appropriate Blues Brothers choreography. Completely whacked-out, but we practically wet our pants.

SHE NIGHT

If you're *not* someone who grew up in South Florida during this time period, you're probably thinking this referred to an all-girl Rocky show. Nuh-uh.

Instead, it refers to the Home of Rock, WSHE radio, 103.5 on your FM dial.

The tag line: "SHE's only Rock and Roll."

There were other rock stations in South Florida (Y100 was probably the alternate choice if SHE was playing something you didn't like), but for true rock fans, there was only one station worth listening to in the entire region.

We knew the SHE DJs as well as if we'd gone to school with them: Joe St. Peter, Skip Herman, Nancy G., Neil Mirsky, Drew Mellow and, in the mornings, the one and only Sonny Fox. From the time we woke up until we dropped off at night, in Broward and Dade counties anyway, WSHE was about the only thing pouring out of teenager-controlled radios.

And then, one day...a miracle happened.

Russ, our cast manager extraordinaire, got in contact with a buddy who knew a friend who was acquainted with a guy down at the radio station and between them all, they came up with a plan:

The Ultravision would host "SHE Night" at the Rocky show.

One night only.

Be there.

This idea could not have come at a better time. Russ had been looking a little nervous at the cast meetings about a month or so before this plan was hatched. One night, when he had downed a few beers and his defenses were low, he finally let spill that the attendance was starting to fall off, making the management of the Ultravision a trifle concerned about the show's future prospects. As warm-up guy, I had noticed that we weren't packing them in as we had, but I never gave it a thought.

Frankly, I was a little shocked at both his candor and his anxiety. Russ usually kept things pretty close to the vest.

"The management. They're worried," he said, looking plenty worried himself. "Who can blame them? I mean, it's not that the crowds have been *bad*. We're getting twice the attendance of the Twin. But it ain't cheap cleaning up the theater after our crowd has been in there. Rice, toast, cards, all that shit. It's a pain in the ass. To justify it, the crowds have got to be big and *stay* big."

"They aren't thinking of shutting us down, are they?" I sincerely hoped he couldn't hear the panic in my voice.

"Nah," Russ said, clearly lying. "We're fine. We could just...you know. Use a little bump. That's all."

After that, he clammed up and tried to appear cheerful. But I knew.

When he finally announced the Big Event, I was fully aware that this experiment was more than just a one-off, "let's break up the monotony" night. This show could mean the difference between shutting it all down and staying alive.

SHE Night at Rocky was to be promoted on the air for the entire week before the show, courtesy of the full lineup of DJs on staff. As a bonus, the station agreed that, for this event, two of their on-air personalities would show up at the theater and personally judge the pre-show Time Warp contest that Russ had on tap for the night.

This was huge. South Florida's premiere rock station promising to spread the word all week long about our little Rocky show and actually *pay* DJs to drop by and become a part of the proceedings.

It was a marketing bonanza. A publicity miracle.

And it was *free*.

As the big week approached, news of even more perks started trickling in:

Following the Time Warp contest, record albums would be given away as prizes to the winners, courtesy of the station. WSHE swag (bumper stickers, T-shirts, beer cozies, anything the station had on hand) would be distributed to the crowd as promotional giveaways. Every day, the news got better and better. It got to the point where I wouldn't have been surprised if they announced free blow jobs for the first twenty customers. It was *that* good.

We put our heads together and, for this one night, decided to do a totally new pre-show warm-up. We would turn the microphones over to the DJs, of course, to welcome the crowd and supervise the contest. But then, before running the previews, we would give the folks a one-of-a-kind show.

Kenny, Andrea, Sunday, Boyd and the rest of the Transylvanians would get up on stage after the DJs had turned things over to us. They would then cue the projection booth to flood the theater with *audio only* and perform a live version of "The Time Warp" and "Sweet Transvestite," using pirated audio from the California production of the Rocky show at the Roxy Theatre.

One. Night. Only.

With all of this in place, we were praying (some of us more than others) for a fairly decent crowd.

We had no earthly idea what we were getting ourselves into.

Russ gathered the troops early that week and laid it all out for us. First, as I wouldn't be doing my regular pre-show in deference to the SHE DJs, I would join the rest of the Transylvanians in trying to handle crowd control. In other words, we were supposed to keep the adoring fans back and off the stage while the DJs did their work. Who knew what kind of fruitcakes would show up?

Then, after the contest and right before the previews, the music would kick in and we would do our musical numbers, as agreed. Kenny, Sunday and Andrea had prepared their own choreography for their number. For his, Boyd decided to just go with the flow and wing it. Tom, up in the lighting booth, was tasked with following the performers with his spotlight, even though the theater would still be fully lit. This was to be a brand-new Rocky experience. We'd have to see if it would be a bomb or a hit.

Following our new opening, everything would go back to normal. We'd switch on the previews, roll the Curry videos, segue into the Rocky flick and do our regular show. That was it. Russ made sure that everyone was up to speed and knew their various assignments. We were as ready as we could possibly be.

As promised, the radio station promoted the show heavily every day leading up to that weekend. I think the announcers were selling some line of bullshit about it being the fifth anniversary of the first live Rocky show or something, but we knew better. This piece of fiction was concocted purely to promote the event itself (and probably originated with Russ). But we really didn't care one way or the other. Just get asses in seats, that was our only concern.

Every Rocky cast member spent the week with the radio faithfully tuned to WSHE, and it was both thrilling and bizarre to hear the various DJs talking up the show on the air.

"This Saturday night at midnight at the Ultravision Theatre in Deerfield, your hosts, WSHE radio personalities Nancy G. and Joe St. Peter, will be live and in-person at 'The Rocky Horror Picture Show'! Get your tickets now for this soon-to-be sold-out show this Saturday night only. Prizes will be distributed to the winners of the Time Warp dance contest, so pull on your fishnets and come on down and do the Time Warp again!"

It was as if they were promoting a rock concert, they gave it so much air time. We couldn't believe how much they were pushing this event.

Russ, by all appearances, had performed a Rocky promotional miracle. Whether it would pay off remained to be seen.

The night of the big show, we were all instructed to get to the theater at least a half hour early and set up our gear as quickly as possible when the feature film let out. The Ultravision management let us pre-load our props and costumes just outside the door so we could be ready to go as soon as the regular patrons had vacated the premises. We were itching to get started.

Even at 10:30, a crowd was starting to form in the Ultravision parking lot. We all knew that, on a regular night, there might be twenty or thirty cars parked in the lot by 11:30 or so. Tonight, there were over a hundred and it was still ninety minutes to showtime.

And they just kept arriving.

Finally, the late movie let out and we bustled into the theater and got ready. We moved at lightning speed, so that we would have plenty of time to get into costume and makeup before the crowd made their way in. The feeling was electric.

While we were setting up, the DJs arrived and the cast started buzzing. We had been listening to Nancy G. and Joe St. Peter for years on the radio, but this was the first time most of us had ever laid eyes on them. In the small world of the South Florida celebrity circuit, being a rock and roll disc jockey made you a *huge* star. And suddenly, there they were.

Nancy G. was a lot taller than we expected, but just as hot as we'd hoped. Most female DJs have slinky, sexy voices, and Nancy certainly had one of those, but it was rare to see someone live up to their sound. She looked fantastic, with her light-brown hair pulled back off her shoulders, a pointy model's chin and these beautiful, glittery eyes.

Joe St. Peter, on the other hand, had a look that said, "Good evening. I play rock and roll on the radio for a living. What do *you* do?" Black, curly hair. Neatly trimmed beard and a black leather jacket. Dark cowboy boots and a completely relaxed demeanor. The whole time he was there, he sported this huge, pleased-to-meet-you grin.

As excited as we were to see these living legends in our theater and in the flesh, we were also pretty well terrified to go near them and left Russ to handle the hosting duties. We had a show to prepare for.

I was scheduled to do Dr. Scott that night, which meant doing my regular Transylvanian job and then switching into the doctor's outfit and hopping into the wheelchair. My pre-show prep, therefore, was very short and I found myself in the theater when the doors opened and the crowd began entering.

And entering.

And *entering*.

To the point, frankly, where it actually started to get a little scary.

I had been to the Rocky show at the Ultravision almost from the very beginning and I still remembered the first few weeks of the show. Back then, when curiosity about the whole Rocky phenomenon was at its highest, the crowds had been pretty huge. We had welcomed 300 people a night, easy.

Since then, we had drifted down to about half that size, sometimes barely breaking a hundred patrons a night. Not bad, actually, for a show you did every weekend, twice a week, for almost a year. And, excuse me, pretty fucking awesome for a movie that had been in theaters for upwards of *five* years. But there had been a significant tapering off, it was impossible to deny.

Halloween, of course, was the exception. The crowd topped perhaps 400 people that night and was a huge hit, no question. But we never, in our wildest dreams, ever expected to see a bigger crowd than that. It had been gigantic. Unsurpassable.

Well, I'm here to tell you: SHE Night, when it hit, put every other crowd to shame.

By the time we finally cranked up the new and improved pre-show, the crowd was over 600 strong. They were packed into the auditorium like processed tuna in a can and there wasn't a single seat left. As if to confirm our suspicions, we then got the official word from the box office:

We were sold out. Completely. First time ever, there wasn't a ticket to be had. People wanting to see "The Rocky Horror Picture Show" in Deerfield Beach, Florida, had been *turned away*.

When we heard that, our collective blood pressure shot through the roof.

The chanting began at about ten to midnight.

"Rocky! Rocky! RO-CKY! RO-CKY!" They were itching for the show to start. We were getting pretty keyed up ourselves.

Finally, when it looked like everyone was seated (it actually looked like everyone in the state of Florida was seated) and the energy level hit its peak, the DJs, presumably used to this sort of thing, called the evening to order.

Joe St. Peter picked up the microphone and hollered:

"Goooooood evening ladies and gentlemen, and welcome to SHE Night at 'The Rocky Horror Picture Show'!"

The sound that came off the crowd was a force of nature. It was like being punched in the chest, it was so loud. Watching this enormous throng of people jump to their feet and whoop with joy, it crossed my mind that if they decided to storm the stage and eat the cast, we would have had little recourse but to sit back and allow ourselves to become tasty, nutritious snacks.

St. Peter went through some of the preliminaries, thanked the management and everyone for showing up and then, in Rocky parlance, asked if there were any virgins among the assembled crowd. More than half the people in the audience answered him in the affirmative. It was incredible for us to discover that the majority of this throng were here for the first time. Clearly, the marketing strategy had worked wonders.

The initial welcome over, St. Peter introduced his partner, Nancy, who received a warm welcome herself. She deftly segued into the Time Warp dance competition and invited a select group (the first three rows) to the stage. The two of them encouraged folks not to rush to the front and, miraculously, they complied. People, it seems, will do anything a disc jockey tells them to do.

When finally assembled, the participants numbered seventy-five or so, and as Nancy G. called out the steps ("Jump to the left! Step to the right!"), they all attempted to show us their best moves. It wasn't exactly pretty, but it looked like they enjoyed themselves.

Finally, they were done and the judges conferred. After a minute or so, a stack of record albums were distributed to what appeared to be a random group of "winners." Everyone else got some type of WSHE swag (there were no "losers") and the patrons took their seats again.

It was close to midnight. The mood was contagiously ecstatic. The DJs talked up how cool it was to be there with the best rock and roll fans in the country (huge applause) and then they told everyone to hold on to their hats, the show was about to begin.

And with a nod to Russ, we were on.

Russ turned and signaled the booth and, within seconds, the theater was filled with the opening guitar riff from "The Time Warp." No picture on the screen, of course, just the music. But to anyone who knew the score of the film as well as we did, the sound was decidedly different. This was, after all, the music from the live show in L.A.

For their stage performance, the director in California had clearly chosen a much more punchy and faster beat for this number. And when the sound hit the audience, the energy level in the theater jumped about three notches.

Tom swiveled his spotlight from the WSHE disc jockeys to where Kenny was pre-set on the stage as Riff. Upon seeing the first actual Rocky character of the night framed in his own pool of light, the crowd, primed and ready, went crazy.

To this day, I don't know who the singer was that did the Roxy show in L.A., but I'll tell you this: His voice was *amazing*. Don't get me wrong, O'Brien is the all-time Time Warp lord and master and all that. But this dude in California could fucking *sing*.

Kenny threw himself into it, parading across the stage as a newly unleashed being, free of the confines of having to do the song exactly as his on-screen counterpart had performed it. Then he passed the ball to Andrea, who took it and ran. They both tore into the number with an enthusiasm unlike anything I'd seen from either of them before.

303

Then they hit the big intro, swung into their Elbow Sex and the entire Deerfield cast stepped forward and hollered: *"Let's do the Time Warp again!"*

Every member of the Wild and Untamed Things, each and every one of us, was a Transylvanian that night. And for the first time ever, we performed the Time Warp as one; jumping, stepping and pelvic-thrusting to a version of the song we had never heard before.

It was a thrilling experience, doing something so familiar and yet so completely different. The mood, the energy, the driving beat...it elevated the experience to an entirely new level.

And it was while I was doing it, in the middle of actually performing the dance itself, that it hit me:

We were making it our own. We weren't being forced to match someone on the screen who dictated the way we moved. We were doing *our* version, the "Ultravision Time Warp," if you will, which consisted of whatever each of us, individually, thought this performance should be.

We could do *anything* with the song. Anything at all.

So we did. We bumped and ground against one another, we flailed our arms in the air, we ran around the stage. There were no *rules*. Rules? Those would be back soon enough. For now, the Rocky show was ours and no one else's.

And the audience couldn't get enough.

Finally, the song wound down, we sang our final chorus and we collapsed to the stage, completely exhausted.

The applause was thunderous, deafening. But we weren't done yet.

When the music for "Sweet Transvestite (Roxy Version)" kicked in and the spotlight hit Boyd at the top of the ramp, I thought the roar of the crowd might actually blow out the back of the theater. These people went positively *bat-shit*.

Boyd, being a sentient being, couldn't help but be caught up in the wave of adoration that hit him. To us, he looked three stories tall as he strutted down the ramp and started making his way down the aisle. Rather than follow his regular blocking, Boyd used the entire theater, stepping up onto the armrests in the audience to address the crowd. When he threw off his cape to reveal the sexy outfit beneath...

...I'll betcha they heard us in fucking *Miami*.

Boyd seemed to be everywhere at once, working the crowd and they, in turn, showered him with love. His every move, even the tiniest gesture, was met with a chorus of hooting and cheering.

He was a star.

Eventually, the number spiraled down to its final few moments and Boyd once again perched himself at the top of the ramp, center stage. He was, it seemed, pinned to the screen by the beam of light and the audience responded to him like 600 incredibly turned-on lovers. If it was at all possible for an entire *room* to have an orgasm, Boyd was giving them one.

Then "Sweet Transvestite" came to a close with its final power chord, the spotlight went black and the theater lights immediately dimmed, signaling the start of the film. The SHE Night audience, already whipped into a frenzy, roared out their excitement.

It was like that all night long. As each new character appeared, the crowd welcomed them aboard with a huge sonic embrace. When Riff Raff made his first appearance on-screen, Kenny got the biggest ovation of the night. Well, until Frank showed up again, of course. Boyd was, upon his entrance, treated to the kind of welcome that Lindbergh got in Paris.

Each of us, Andrea, Sunday, Billy, even li'l ol' me in my wheelchair, as we hit the stage were treated to a tumultuous round of entrance applause. We drank it up like sweet nectar.

It was intoxicating.

Better than any drug.

We were mainlining uncut, pharmacy-grade adulation. And it was zonking us out of our *minds*.

At the end of the night, we took our curtain call and the applause seemed to rise up over the house like a tidal wave and come crashing down upon us, smothering the cast in a rush of love. By now, the army of people filling the house was no longer as frightening as it had been when they had first crammed their way into the theater. With the intimidation factor gone, there was nothing left but pure enjoyment.

And then it was over. Our little Rocky Woodstock had come to an end and it was time to pack up our gear, debrief at Denny's and simply marvel at the experience.

Russ was glowing, as proud of us as I'd ever seen him. We'd been faced with a high-pressure, do-or-die situation and had somehow pulled it off. Better than that—the size of the crowd (and their obvious enthusiasm) practically guaranteed that we would get a huge bump in attendance over the next couple of months, something that never fails to mollify a nervous theater owner.

Though we didn't know it at the time, this evening would also mark the high point of the Ultravision Rocky show. We had enjoyed great nights before that one and many wonderful nights afterward, but nothing would ever compare to the pure energy, the raw enthusiasm and the mind-blowing rush of that huge crowd eating up everything we did with a big-ass spoon.

Over the next few weeks, a number of full-time cast members, most of whom had now spent almost a year away from their old home in Hollywood, began to walk away from the Deerfield cast. Andrea left first with Tony in tow. Tom, naturally, followed suit. Sunday was next out the door. Even Billy left. One by one, the original Ultravision cast faded away.

Storme took over Magenta. Steve became our full-time narrator. Cheryl was the new Columbia.

And very soon afterward, after almost a year of waiting, my big moment arrived.

Kenny announced his departure in December of 1982 and symbolically turned over the Riff Raff reins by presenting me with his combat boots in a brief ceremony after the show. He told me that he would be keeping the skullcap and tails, but the boots were all mine.

"Have fun, Jack," he said, grinning wide. "He's yours now." Kenny seemed almost relieved to be done with it.

It was a whole new cast. The only Hollywood veterans left were Donny, Russ and Ron. Everyone else had turned in their keys. We still saw them a lot, of course, down at Tracey and Kenny's place or at one of our outings, but the word had come down from the mountaintop.

The old guard was finished with their work. There was a new Rocky gang in town.

And we were it.

Say Goodbye to All This

So that was 1982. It had been the greatest year of my life. And the way things were going, 1983 looked poised to top it.

I was going out with the prettiest girl I'd ever met, my redheaded young goddess with the bitchin' car. I was finally playing the role of my dreams, kicking it as Riff Raff every Friday and Saturday night at the Rocky show. My friends were the coolest people on the planet and knew more ways to have fun than ought to have been legal (and quite a few that were decidedly *not*). My senior year was in full swing, I was starting my final semester of high school and, as Class President, I quite literally ruled the school.

Even better, after graduation I'd be looking at three blissful months off—my last summer at home—and then the real adventure: my first year at college.

Life, in other words, was a bowl of cherries. And I was making cherry fucking *pie*.

As a cast, we spent almost all of our free time either at Kenny and Tracey's place, Russ's apartment or Storme's house. By then, all of my high school friends, save Dean, had completely ceased to exist. It was all Rocky, all the time.

Classmates threw parties. I didn't care.

Clubs at the school beckoned. I ignored them.

Organized sports? Who had time?

307

The only reason my grades stayed above sea level was because my Mom would have yanked the plug on the show if I'd let them slide. So there I was, a full year after having joined the cast, and my enthusiasm had not ebbed in the slightest. Instead, my devotion to the show had multiplied exponentially.

Rocky had become my entire world.

This became clear one night when I found myself at Denny's after the show locked into a conversation with Ron, Tracey and a new cast member named Sam. Only a three-week rookie, Sam was trying to get his mind around what it really meant to be a true Rocky devotee. He was having fun and everything, he said, but he didn't quite grasp what we got in return for our dedication. And he was deadly honest about it. He thought our unwavering allegiance to the show was a bit...ridiculous.

And then, after expressing his confusion over why we considered the show to be such a big deal, he made the mistake of saying the dreaded words:

"After all, it's just a movie. Right?"

Ron's face fell, but he seemed ill-disposed at the time to school this kid on what an egregious Rocky *faux pas* he had committed. It isn't easy to try to explain the inner meaning of life as a Rockette, so I could hardly blame Ron for giving it a miss. But schooled this kid must be, so I did my best to explain:

"Lemme tell you something, Sam. And I'm not just blowing smoke at you. This is the truth: Rocky is not (all evidence to the contrary) just about dressing in crazy costumes, getting up on stage and pretending to be some character in a movie. If it were, just about any movie would do the trick. You could do Rocky versions of...'Grease,' you know? Or 'Wizard of Oz.' Anything. Hell, it would be just as easy to get dressed up as Danny Zuko or Dorothy or the Tinman or whatever and do this kind of show, wouldn't it?"

Sam nodded. This seemed to encourage me to expand on the topic. "So if it was just about performing a live version of a movie, then ask yourself: Why this one? Why is this the *only* movie on the planet where people show up, week after week, get in costume and perform the show the way we do? I mean, why '*The Rocky Horror Picture Show*'?"

Sam looked as if he didn't have an answer. But Ron did:

"Because this movie is not about all that surface shit. It's not about being a nympho or running around half-naked or fucking everybody you see. I mean, it looks that way, at first, and that's part of the original charm, I suppose. It may be what gets people (especially teenagers) to check out the movie or think about joining the cast. But it's not what makes them *stay*. The essence of this movie and, by extension, the point of doing the live show every weekend, is..."

Ron looked at me. "Go ahead. Your turn," is what Ron's look said to me.

I took a breath and picked up where he left off. "It's about getting rid of your fear. That's the worst thing about being our age, right? The fear? The high school anxiety, the peer pressure bullshit. Scared of being embarrassed or laughed at or bullied or...well, just scared of being...different.

"Shit, that's what Rocky's all *about*. Embracing your...differentness. Seriously, if you're looking for a formula to make a 17-year-old kid less self-conscious, you could do a hell of a lot worse than letting him strut around in a bra and fishnets every weekend, lemme tell ya.

"Around here, the rule is: Let go. Just lose your fear, dump it, and then you can do *what* you want, *when* you want, without giving a shit what other people think of who you are."

"Or what you look like," said Ron.

"Or your ambitions or your love life or *anything* you want to do. Any-thing."

Ron said, almost under his breath: "Don't dream it. Be it."

I nodded. "Goddamn right. It's easy to go through life scared. Or emo-tionally fucked-up. Or disappointed."

Sam spoke up. "Disappointed in what?"

This surprised me. "In what? Hell, in everything, man! Disappointed in yourself. In your life. In your girlfriend, your parents, your husband, your wife, your family, your friends, your job. It's the easiest thing in the world, hating your life, right?"

Sam was really listening now. It was encouraging.

"But you know what's hard? Changing all that. Doing what you actually *want* to do instead of what you're *supposed* to do. Not being afraid of some-one calling you a loser or a dreamer or a faggot or a weirdo or a fuckup.

"And that, Sam, is the message of this dumb fucking movie. And that's why we do it. Every weekend. And that," I said, leaning close, "is why the show works."

I climbed down off my soapbox. Sam was quiet, taking in what I had said. I figured it was best to leave him alone with what I had just hit him with. My thought was that he would either swallow the Gospel of Rocky as I had preached it to him or dismiss me completely as a brainwashed nutcase.

(Either option was entirely valid, really. I wouldn't have blamed him either way.) So I figured I was done.

But when I got up from the table and turned around, Russ was standing there. He'd been listening the entire time.

He didn't react, at first. He just looked at me very seriously. He seemed to be sizing me up. Then he looked as if he'd made a decision.

"Come here, Jack. I gotta talk to you." Russ motioned me to a private booth and sat me down.

As was his way, he didn't waste time.

"Listen," he said. "I want to offer you a job."

"A job?"

"Don't get excited. It doesn't pay anything."

I smiled. I hadn't expected that it would.

"Here's the thing," he said. "I want you to be cast director."

I was a bit taken aback. I'd never even heard of such a position.

"Cast...what?"

"Director," he said. "It's the perfect job for you, Jack. You…get it. What we do here. You believe in it. And best of all, you can *say* it." He puffed on his cigarette. "So?"

I was totally flummoxed. "What does a cast director....do?"

Then it was Russ's turn to look perplexed. "You know what? I dunno. I guess we'll have to figure it out as we go along." He stared off for a moment, deep in thought. Then he said, "For starters, you'd be in charge of who plays what. You make the assignments. Main characters, understudies, the works. And new hires. Any cast members we get from here on in, you're their new boss. Think you can handle that?"

I considered the offer. It was more responsibility than I'd ever imagined I would have in this cast. It might even involve pissing people off, assigning them to positions they didn't particularly want. But I simply couldn't see myself looking Russ in the eyes and saying, "No thanks. Not interested." Because that would have been a *huge* lie.

"Sounds great," I finally stammered out. "Starting when?"

Russ grinned. "Starting right now." He stood up and called for everyone's attention.

"Listen up! I want to announce a new position. And I've asked young Jack here to take it. Please welcome the new cast director."

I was expecting a collective "Huh?" but, instead, the cast applauded. I was apparently the only one in the room who didn't see this coming.

The spring semester flew by. I got letters back from the colleges where I'd applied and discovered that I had been admitted to three of the four schools I'd written to. In fact, Dean and I had both been accepted by virtually all the same New York schools and were trying to figure out which one to pick. It was an enviable position, I knew, having a selection to choose from.

After wrestling with our various choices, Dean and I finally settled on a state school, part of the SUNY system, about ninety miles due north of New York City. We would go together. Strength in numbers. We were all set.

But we weren't in any hurry. We were still in high school, after all. College didn't start up until the fall. We had plenty of time to—

Boom. Graduation Day. Just like that. School is done. Real life begins. Here's your hat. What's your goddamn hurry?

We couldn't believe it. We thought we'd have more time to prepare. We thought we'd be ready.

We thought wrong.

The whole final semester seemed to take no more than a week, really. On Monday we were back from Christmas break. Tuesday we studied. Wednesday was prom. Thursday was finals. Friday, they handed us our sheepskins and kicked us out the door.

Before I could wrap my head around it, I was forced to come to terms with the fact that I was now a high school graduate looking at my last summer before college.

So, you know: Gulp.

I feel the need to preface the following by saying that, despite what we had accomplished over the previous year and a half, the Deerfield cast took nothing for granted. We did not, by any means, *coast*. We were still hump-busting every weekend, trying to fill the high-heeled shoes of the performers who came before us and, so far, it seemed to be working.

Russ and I had been running the show in tandem for about four months by the time summer arrived, and we had developed a system that ran smoother than a cashmere Camaro. Our A-list cast was as solid as it had ever been and our understudies were prepped and ready for anything. The money flowing in from the cast dues was steady (which kept our props and costumes in tip-top shape) and the attendance, though decidedly down from the weeks following SHE night, was still impressive.

So when you're feeling as sure-footed as we did heading into that summer of 1983, the last thing you're expecting is to have some schmuck grab the edge of the rug and *pull*.

Three weeks after graduation, I was living the dream.

I had spent the entire previous year busing tables and salting away whatever cash I could with an eye toward having a wad of money in my pocket when I left for college. That plan disappeared about three seconds after I got my diploma. In the time it takes to say, "impulsive wastrel," I had quit my job and planned to do nothing over the next three months that didn't involve blowing, dollar by dollar, the tidy sum I had amassed.

Alice and I were going stronger than ever. She was everything I had ever imagined in a girlfriend: beautiful, smart, sexy and able to pilot her vintage Chevrolet like she'd invented the damn thing. She had even joined the cast briefly and proved to be a terrific Magenta understudy (inappropriate flaming-red hair notwithstanding).

I was spending whatever time I didn't spend with Alice hanging out down at Kenny and Tracey's place. Like the Orphanage before it, their apartment had become the gravitational center of the entire cast. You could try to ignore the attraction, but the pull was irresistible.

In addition, I had finally been invited to sit in on the Dungeons and Dragons games that Donny hosted on a weekly basis. This was not an easy group to break into, but my time had finally arrived to become one of the Chosen Few.

To my disappointment, however, my entire D&D experience was an unqualified disaster. Don't get me wrong: I loved the game. But for some reason I had, without question, the worst luck of any player in D&D history. Certainly worse than any of the veteran players had ever seen.

This was a game, after all, that relied primarily on the roll of the dice. Everything, absolutely everything, depended entirely on whether you got a good or bad roll.

To my horror, every single character I attempted to play was dead within a few days. They would inexplicably die the most catastrophic and improbable deaths anyone had ever seen. The dice seemed to *hate* me.

If there was a 1 percent chance that my sword would shatter and I would get a fatal shard through the eye, or that I would trip on a dead Orc and skewer myself on my own pointy amulet, that's exactly how it went down.

It became something of a joke. If our group of warriors entered a room and there was something sharp sticking out of the ground, you could pretty much guarantee that my head would be impaled on it sooner or later. It was a virtual certainty.

No one involved in the game could figure out why my luck ran so bad, and my fellow players would involuntarily cringe every time I reached for a twelve-sided die. I eventually just walked away, unable to endure their looks of pity.

Mostly, though, I went to Kenny and Tracey's for the company. The Rocky stalwarts still saw one another at least two or three times a week, despite their having left the show. And though dozens upon dozens of cast members had come and gone over the months since the Ultravision show began, there was still a core group of about twenty of us who remained as close as ever.

Kenny, Ron, Tracey, Felicia, Iris, Donny, Russ, Steve, Sunday, Andrea, Tony, Tom, Billy, Boyd, Storme, Cheryl, Mark and me.

Half of us still performed the show every weekend, but most of the original Hollywood transfers had retired. They had put in their time. They were done.

Not me. I was still going strong.

One night in mid-June, Russ walked into Denny's looking as if someone had punched him in the gut. He sat apart from us, off in the corner smoking and drinking coffee, putting off the cast meeting until the checks had been paid and the entire cast was eyeing the door. We knew something was up, but couldn't imagine what it could be.

313

Sensing that he couldn't put it off any longer, Russ finally ground out what must have been his tenth cigarette, walked dazedly over to the table and called the meeting to order.

"Listen, um..." he started. "You need to know..." He paused again then simply appeared to lose steam. Finally, he managed to stammer out: "I don't know what to say."

At this, everyone in the room had red flags flying. Russ struggling for words was ominous indeed. What the hell was up?

He stared at the floor for about a minute, unable to speak. Nobody moved. At last, he seemed to come to his senses and looked up.

"Well, what *can* I say? It's over. We're done."

A murmur flitted across the table. What did *that* mean? Over? Over how? What was over?

Russ squared his shoulders and finally spit it out: "Look, I had a talk with the Ultravision management after the show. They had asked for a meeting, so I went to see them. It didn't take long. Turns out they can't afford to keep the show going anymore, so...they're pulling the plug."

And with these words, the table went up for grabs. We couldn't believe what we were hearing. We didn't even know that there was a *possibility* of the show coming to an end, so it was inconceivable for us to believe that this outcome, our utter demise, had already been decided.

Russ had his hands in front of him defensively as the questions rained down. He raised his voice.

"Settle down. *Settle down*. I'll tell you what I know."

We all found our seats and fell back, deflated.

"Here's what they told me: Apparently, the studio that owns the film— the actual film that we watch every night—they take this *huge* cut of the door. Even bigger than I thought they did. Because of the cost, the theater has to keep attendance really, really high in order to justify not only the money they pay the studio, but also the cleanup. I mean, we all know what a fuckin' mess the place is after we're done."

No question about that. The theater was trashed every night. We all had wondered, at one time or another, how they managed to clean it when we were through.

"Well, apparently, we're not hitting our numbers. We haven't for a couple of months, actually. And it isn't us, don't get me wrong. The management, they love having us around, doing the show week after week, all that. But the fact is that the profit margin isn't there. And without that..." He shrugged. "So they're cutting us loose."

Steve piped up. "This is non-negotiable?"

Russ looked insulted by the question. "Steve, if it was negotiable, don't you think I would have negotiated with the man?"

There was no arguing with that. Russ was a horse trader from way back. If there was a deal that could have been struck, he would have made it happen.

After a second or two, Tracey seemed to find inspiration. "What about another special event? Like a SHE Night Part Two or something?"

Russ shook his head. "Too late for that. They already made up their minds. We're done."

This pronouncement took a few moments to sink in. We all sat there with dazed expressions, unable to grasp the enormity of this news.

Finally, I looked up and asked the question that was on everyone's mind.

"When, Russ?"

Russ sighed and shook his head.

"Next week," he said. I felt the blood drain out of my face. My mind was a blank, as if my power cord had been yanked. I was speechless.

Felicia was the first to respond. Her voice was choked with emotion. "Next *week*?" she said. "That's it?"

"I'm afraid so," said Russ. He looked defeated. Like I'd never seen him before. He was *beaten*. "Next Saturday, we do the last Rocky Horror show at the Ultravision."

And with that, he threw some money on the table for his share of the check, picked up his cigarettes and walked out the door.

I'd like to be able to tell you that the big Ultravision farewell was this enormous, celebratory, we-packed-'em-in-like-sardines blowout the following week. But the fact is, partly because of the short notice and mainly due to how depressing we found the whole thing, we went out with a whimper rather than a bang.

The crowds were okay for our last two shows, but nothing that would have swayed the minds of the Ultravision management into keeping it going.

They had done pretty well, all told, in hosting the Rocky show. No doubt a pile of money had been amassed in the previous year and a half. But they clearly felt that the experiment, successful though it had been, was over. In their opinion, it was time to move on and we had no say in the matter.

As far as quality goes, that last weekend featured two of the best shows any of us had either seen or performed. We certainly didn't let the quality flag on our way out the door. But, maybe because we were being kicked out rather than deciding to end it ourselves, there was no satisfaction in having done a great job for our final performances.

We were performing the best Rocky show in the nation. And our reward was to be shown unceremoniously to the exit.

And though we considered it, we ultimately decided against putting together a huge gathering of all the veteran cast members for our final show at the Ultravision. No one had the energy or inclination to organize it. We just showed up, gave the crowd the best goddamn Rocky shows they'd ever see for the rest of their lives, packed up our gear and walked out the door for the last time.

Tears were shed. Promises of fidelity and pledges of long and lasting fraternity were demanded and surrendered by all present. The final party, hosted at Storme's, lasted until the sun was high in the sky that final Sunday afternoon.

Looking back at what we had accomplished during our tenure at the Ultravision, it was easy for us to refer to it as the end of an era, but this "era" had really only lasted about eighteen months from beginning to end. The first Ultravision Rocky show had occurred on New Year's Day, 1982, and the run had concluded in June of the following year. In the long and storied history of Rocky, that is a drop in the bucket.

Still, when we looked back on all that had happened during our brief residency in that magnificent theater, it was difficult to believe that we had crammed so much into so short a period.

It had felt like years. A lifetime.

And now it was over.

Well, sorta.

Because as much as I would like to report that the Ultravision cast, once the final curtain came down, collectively graduated from Rocky Horror and preserved our legacy by leaving it all behind after that weekend, that is sadly not the case.

Like a junkie trying to make the high last as long as possible, we did whatever we could to get our Rocky fix.

When word came round in the following weeks that another Rocky cast was starting up at different theater, we jumped at it. It didn't seem to matter much that it would be in Plantation, Florida, at the tiny, little Mercedes Cinema. We all signed up. Doing the show in a little venue, in our opinion, was certainly better than giving it up entirely.

That was the theory, anyway.

We soon found out, after arriving at the Mercedes, that the magic was almost entirely gone. We were trying to start a fire with wet timber and the show must have looked about as pathetic as it felt.

First off, the theater simply wasn't suited for the show. The Mercedes was a forerunner of the new trend in movie houses: the Megaplex. When we got there, we were asked to perform Rocky in a joint that sported no less than *six* miniature theaters, the largest of which could fit, at most, about 200 people. The "stage" was the narrow area between the front row and the screen, which loomed so high above us we could barely get a peripheral look at our own characters without snapping our necks.

I guesed that the Mercedes management negotiated a better rate from the studio than the Ultravision, given that the theater was so miniscule. Naturally, with very little overhead besides the cleaning bills, drawing only fifty people a night meant that they could keep it open forever if they wanted. And if they made money off the show, what did they care if the live performance was utter crap?

The Ultravision veterans, however…we knew better. We knew what this show could be, and had been, if the circumstances allowed it. As a result, we realized that doing the Mercedes show was like ordering up a cheeseburger after the gourmet restaurant had closed. Sure, we could still eat. But it was a *fucking cheeseburger*. We missed our filet mignon Ultravision *steaks*, goddamit.

But that item was no longer on the menu.

We stuck it out for as long as we could, a few weeks at most but, pretty soon, we just wandered away. An inglorious end to a glorious experience.

Rocky, for us, was no more.

My last night as a Floridian was in August of 1983. My flight to New York was scheduled for 10 a.m. and I had spent the previous few weeks making my long goodbye.

The previous weekend had been spent in the loving arms of my Rocky brothers and sisters. They had toasted my anticipated success as a college boy, promised to stay in touch during my absence and were convinced (though certainly not through my doing) that I would one day return. It appeared difficult for them to believe that anyone would prefer to live somewhere other than the Swamp. I tried not to argue the point.

That night, several of my Rocky cohorts presented me with certain tokens to carry with me on my travels. Russ gave me one of his bow ties, as a show of respect and admiration. Sunday gave me a Queen of Spades playing card, with a hand-printed admonition that I should always return as her Jack. Ron gave me his pair of Riff gloves and exacted a promise that I would never return to Florida without them. And Tracey, my loving bride, proudly presented me with one of her most prized Rocky possessions. As a result, before I left my house to head off to school, I packed Tracey's one-and-only Janet bra in my bag.

I'd like to say I was the only guy headed off to college with a bra in my suitcase, but we all know that isn't true, don't we?

The night before I hopped my plane to New York, Alice drove over and, for the first time, spent the night with me at my place. My mother, of course, didn't object. She knew what was what.

Alice and I made love that night for what turned out to be the last time. When we woke up and got dressed to leave, she insisted on wearing, and keeping, the shirt I had worn the previous day.

My mother thought it was best not to drive me to the airport. It would have been far too emotional a goodbye if she did. Alice would drive me, it was decided, and my brother would tag along, too.

I kissed my mother goodbye and waited to receive some words of wisdom upon my departure. She had none to offer besides this:

"Be happy, kid."

To this day, it's the best advice I've ever received.

During the previous year and a half, my house had become a non-stop swirl of activity, thanks to my mother. People were always stopping by. I would sometimes come home on the days she wasn't working and find my mother deep in conversation with one of my friends from the show. Sometimes they weren't even there to see me. They had come to talk with my Mom.

The attraction, I suppose, was that my mother didn't judge. And she had a capacity to listen, the rarest quality possessed by human beings. Most of us don't know how to listen for two goddamn minutes. My mom just loved to hear people talk.

So they came. By the carload. And were received with open arms.

I left Florida missing almost nothing about the place itself. When I got on that plane, all I would miss would be a very select group of people.

Chief among them, though, would be my mother. There was no one else like her. At least, no one I had ever met.

She was this really cool lady.

Have I mentioned that?

Alice, David and I trooped through the airport in complete silence. We knew better than to try to speak.

After I had checked my bags, they both offered to walk me all the way to the gate, but I thought it was best to say goodbye before I headed through security. Sitting around for another half hour at the gate waiting to board the plane wasn't going to do any of us any good. Better to get it over with.

I hugged my brother. He cried. I cried. I told him to watch out for himself. He said I should do the same. Then I let him go.

I turned to Alice and she fell into my arms. I held her for as long as I could. Time, however, has an unfortunate tendency to fly whether you're having a good time or not.

We parted. I kissed her goodbye for the last time. I walked to the escalator, started up and turned back to look at the two of them.

319

The last view I had of David and Alice was as I ascended, seeing my brother's arm protectively draped around Alice's shoulder.

Finally, as I drifted up, I lost sight of them. Then I turned, looked up and began to make my way to my new home.

My life in the Swamp was over.

New horizons awaited.

Blue skies.

Time Warp

May 26, 2007
Pompano Beach, Florida

I place my foot onto the armrest of the chair in the front row and haul myself up as I had done hundreds of times before. Not quite so easy as it used to be, but I can still do it, goddamn it.

I bestride the chair. I clear my throat. I gaze out at the huge crowd.

And then I yell at the top of my lungs:

"*Welcome, ladies and gentlemen, to 'The Rocky Horror Picture Show'! Sit the fuck down, we've got a lot to do and very little time to do it!*"

In response, the crowd roars its welcome.

It is certainly nice to be home again.

"*In case you haven't heard,*" I continue, looking out at the hundreds of upturned faces, "*you've arrived on a rather...special night. This evening, for the first and last time, the one-and-only cast known as the Wild and Untamed Things, from the famous Ultravision Theatre in Deerfield Beach, is here to perform our 25th Anniversary Show. So get. Fucking. Ready.*"

I look around the room, and there they all are:

Ron. Tracey. Russ. Donny. Kenny. Felicia. Sunday. Andrea. Tony. Tom. Storme. Cheryl. Iris. Mark. Boyd.

Twenty-five years older. But as ready as ever.

It should never have been possible. Yet, it's happening.

But hold on. Before we continue with this particular event, it's probably best if we back up a second to explain exactly *how* it came to be.

Since the day I left for college, lo those many years before, I had some-how managed to live up to the promise I made to myself when I was a kid:

Once I got out of Florida, I was never going back.

Well, not to *live* anyway.

And I had gotten out. What's more, I somehow managed to *stay* out. But that didn't mean I couldn't visit every once in a while, did it? No rule against that.

So, over the years, I had managed to sneak back every year or so to revisit the place. (Well, not the *place*. I still couldn't stand the Swamp itself.) But I did, as you can imagine, have many, many reasons to make the trip down.

Sadly, my girlfriend wasn't one of them. Alice and I didn't even last until Christmas break of '83. I think she knew, deep down, that I was never coming back to Florida and, for my part, I knew that she was never going to come up north and join me in New York, so we inevitably drifted apart. It was emotional, heartbreaking, overly dramatic, complete with all those crippling, devastating feelings that accompany the end of your relationship with your first true love.

Those feelings, by the way, last for a long time. Right up until the mo-ment when you meet your *second* true love and you say, "Hey, wait a min-ute..." Then, inexplicably, they're gone.

But while my relationship with Alice eventually went ka-flooey, I still had my mother, my brother and roughly twenty or thirty of my nearest and dearest down south who were exerting their irresistible gravitational pull on me. I certainly didn't see the harm in zipping down every once in a while to visit.

Ultimately, though, when it came to the Rocky cast, I knew that attempt-ing to keep that elusive connection alive was a pointless endeavor. Sure, we would stay in touch for a short time. A few months. A year maybe. But in the end, the tenuous hold we had on one another was destined to peter out.

What, did we think it was going to last forever? Impossible. And realis-tically, I knew that it wouldn't. It couldn't. People start up careers, get mar-ried, have kids. They grow up.

Maintaining that bond would have taken a lot of work. It would require a level of commitment that this group of misfits couldn't possibly muster.

So eventually, as adults do, we would put away our childish things. We would move on.

Well, to put it succinctly: Fuck that shit.

Despite the distance, despite the years and despite the divergent personal lives, we did it. We stayed together, we stayed in touch and we were as close, twenty-five years later, as we had ever been.

How did we do it? How did we possibly keep that spark from fizzling out?

Well, for one thing, we had Felicia. And thank the gods above for her. As mailing addresses and phone numbers led to e-mail addresses and cell phone numbers, it was Felicia who kept us all connected. She became Rocky News Central, our unofficial Den Mother, keeping everyone up to date on the happenings of the others. And when too much time passed between reunions, it was Felicia who would put out the word:

It's time. It's been too long. What should we do and when can we do it?

Schedules would be consulted. Dates agreed upon. Then a spot would be chosen, security deposits made and, in my case, flights would be reserved.

And so it would be, every two or three years. We would converge on some unsuspecting destination. Key West. Ft. Lauderdale. Hollywood. Orlando. The location mattered not one bit. All we needed was a place to go in order to take part in the Great Reversion.

Because for that weekend, we were no longer 25, 30, even 40 years old. Nope. Not us.

We were all 17. Eighteen, tops. At least that's what we told ourselves.

The truth was, our masquerade was pretty convincing. Well, internally anyway. We probably looked like relics to the outsiders, but to us, we were as we were at the beginning. And it was only for the weekend, we bargained with ourselves. That's it. We'd soon go back to our normal lives, our families, our jobs. All we asked was for seventy-two hours of uninterrupted '80s nostalgia and mild substance abuse. That's really all we needed. And then we were good for another two years.

All that was required was the itch. And before we knew it, we were there, ready to scratch.

Then, one year, the big one loomed in the distance. Twenty-five years. A quarter-century. We could hardly let this historic milestone pass without a get-together, right?

I got word early in the planning stages since I had the farthest to travel. May in Florida, Jack? Can you make it? My response: I'm there. But...what are we going to do to mark the occasion? Any special plans?

The wheels started turning. Soon, the accommodations were booked. Storme had set us up in a fantastic timeshare on the Hollywood Boardwalk. Four rooms. Plenty of space for us to spread out.

Tracey was the coordinator—assigning rooms, gathering deposits from everyone, arranging for whatever supplies were necessary. The two of them, Storme and Tracey, had to crack the whip sometimes to get us to pony up the necessary cash, but the word quickly spread and the message was: "We're not teenagers anymore. You want to play, you got to pay." And so the money flowed in to cover all expenses, of the malted, distilled, fermented and herbal varieties.

And still the questioned loomed: Sure, we'd see each other. But what would we *do*?

Russ, as usual, provided the answer. It would simply be up to us whether or not we took him up on the opportunity.

There was, he discovered, a Rocky show running in South Florida. Not at the Twin, of course. They had died even before the Ultravision show gave up the ghost. No, this show was in Pompano at a theater called "Flippers Cinema."

It was hard to believe: After all these years, the RHPS phenomenon had managed to survive and attract cast members. Even now, almost 35 years after the movie first opened, teenagers still signed up, troweled on the makeup, and spent their weekends jumping to the left, stepping to the right and pelvic thrusting to their heart's content. Thus, the weekend we would gather together in Florida, a midnight showing of Rocky Horror would take place, complete with newspapers, rice, toilet paper...the works.

After conferring with the management of the Flippers Rocky show, the question Russ posed to us was this:

Were we willing to do a reunion show? We were being offered a 25th anniversary full-on Rocky Horror Picture Show performance. It was ours for the taking. Did we have it in us?

As befitted a group of people this wildly diverse, the responses to this inquiry were decidedly mixed.

Kenny, Mark, Andrea, Sunday...they were out. Dress up as Riff, Frank, Magenta, Columbia? No. Fucking. Way.

But see, for them, they had no reason to suit up again. Each of them had quit doing the show long before the Ultravision had pulled the plug on the rest of us. They had reached their personal limits and walked away by choice. On their own terms.

Some of us, however, hadn't been given the opportunity to quit. Some of us, in fact, had been thrown out on our asses. This meant that a small group of us still had a score to settle. Or, at the very least, we had one more show left inside of us.

I heard most of the discussions secondhand. Apparently, it went something like:

"Wanna do the show?"

"Jeez, I don't know. Who's doing it?"

"Tracey is. And Ron says he is if Tracey's in it."

"Is Jack doing it?"

"He says he would."

"What about Tony?"

"No way. He's done."

"Mmmm. I dunno. You?"

"I dunno."

And so on. Back and forth.

Finally, it was decided. We would do the show, but with a skeleton crew. The following people were slated to participate:

Ron would play Brad.

Tracey would return as Janet.

I would reprise Riff Raff.

Storme would take on Magenta.

Cheryl would suit up as Columbia.

And Russ would fill in as Floor Show Brad.

The rest of the cast would be rounded out by the Flippers' regular cast.

It should be noted, by the way, that the first one to sign up had been Tracey. Our Janet Supreme for the last year of the Ultravision show, Tracey so loved Rocky that she had gone so far as to dress up her two pre-teen daughters as Columbia one Halloween. And no one called child services to have her arrested.

Tracey's kids, when they became old enough to realize what their mother had been up to all those years ago (and having met a few of us in the meantime), made a few demands on their mother. Actually, it amounted to one simple request: Whenever a Rocky reunion seemed to be in the works, the two of them were to be informed as to when and where we were all getting together. Armed with this knowledge, the young girls could make every effort to be as far away from us as humanly possible and consequently be spared the embarrassment of having to watch all those old people do the Time Warp.

We agreed that this was an entirely understandable request.

We nailed down the third Saturday in May as the official show date. The Flippers cast manager was never anything less than magnanimous about hosting us and the cast was incredibly generous in offering us their parts for the night. And of course, this being a Russ Production, a marketing campaign to draw a decent crowd for the event was set in motion almost immediately.

Once the cast list had been agreed upon and forwarded to the Flippers folks, we began to plan how to put the whole thing together. After all, we could hardly just stroll in the door and begin performing the show after all these years. We had to rehearse.

As it was, we were scheduled to convene at the timeshare on Friday in Hollywood and then perform the following night. After shooting ideas back and forth, we decided to spend Friday simply enjoying one another's company and then devote all day of Saturday to prep for that evening's show. Everything was in place.

Then, a small bump in the road:

Someone had suggested that Andrea and Sunday, while unwilling to perform their old roles, at least step forward to do the opening number. For one night, it was proposed, would they be willing to trot out their old "Science Fiction / Double Feature" choreography? For old times' sake?

The answer was swift and final: Forget it.

Cajoling was attempted. Such efforts were definitively shot down by the both of them. No way. They'd show up, watch us do the show, enjoy the movie, no problem. But perform? Not a chance.

Those of us who knew them knew better than to argue.

For the cast members planning to participate in the show, some homework was in order. After all, we were trying on characters we hadn't worn in a quarter-century. But this time around, we had snappy new modern conveniences to assist us.

DVDs, downloadable versions of Rocky, YouTube videos...the source materials available to help us prepare were endless. Frankly, during the planning stages, it was difficult not to come across like a curmudgeonly old whiner: "*You kids today. You got it so easy. Why, in my day...we had to learn Rocky in the <u>theater</u>. No rehearsal at all! And people beat us with <u>sticks</u> while we learned it. And we had to pick our own sequins right off the <u>tree</u>!*"

To be honest, I'd have killed for a video of Rocky back in the early '80s to play at home and hone my craft. Andrea would certainly have been spared one THWOCK in the head with a feather duster, you can bet your ass on that.

So there I found myself, in my Chicago living room the week or so leading up to the big reunion, cramming for my Rocky final exam. I brought home a copy of the movie, popped it in the player, flicked the play button and went back in time.

I'd like to say that conjuring up my inner Riff after all those years was as easy as getting back up on a bicycle. I'd *like* to say that, but here's the difference: When you haven't ridden a bike in a long time, you simply get on, grab the handlebars, pedal unsteadily at first and then—bam—you get the hang of it. That's it. You're done.

Playing Riff Raff? Slightly different experience. Because it's the details that'll kill ya. How much time is there, for example, between the door creaking open and the first "Hello" to Brad and Janet? Three point eight seconds? Gotta feel that timing in your body. The routine before stepping onto the elevator? You pour the glass of champagne, take a swig, drop the bottle, step in the elevator, slam the door, hit the button. Timing, timing, timing.

Then there's the Time Warp choreography. Oh, it comes back to you. But it takes a while.

So, study I did. Night after night, watching that unwatchable movie until I had it *down*.

After all...I couldn't disappoint the team.

The flight from Chicago to Florida that Friday morning was uneventful. I wish I could say the same about the rest of that day.

Ron and Tracey picked me up at the airport and gave me a lift to Hollywood. The two of them had broken up years ago and had each married (and divorced) along the way. But, despite their separate, personal emotional roller coasters, they had managed to stay close.

They looked terrific, too. I suspected that, like me, they had gone on "Rocky diets" the minute they agreed to do the show. Couldn't very well have a portly Brad or a Riff Raff with a poochy belly, now could we?

Instead, we looked dynamite. Middle age could go suck it.

Rolling up to the timeshare, we checked in and dropped off our bags, soon discovering that we were among the first to arrive. There was only one person there before us:

Donny.

I'd like to say that he looked terrific, too, but he didn't. He was bigger than ever and didn't look all that healthy. Not that you'd guess it from his demeanor. From the moment he laid eyes on us, his face lit up and beamed his joy across the room like a beacon.

I was starving after my flight so we grabbed lunch in the lobby restaurant, the four of us. Talk flowed easily, as always. None of that awkward bullshit that sometimes plagues friends and relatives who have been apart for a long time. We caught up on one another's lives, our kids (those of us who had them), our careers and our enthusiasm for this weekend.

Afterward, we retired upstairs and awaited the arrival of the rest of our merry band. But soon after lunch, I began to feel queasy. Then downright awful. Then really fucking sick.

Clearly, the lovely shrimp luncheon I had enjoyed downstairs was not doing me the favor of enjoying me back. It was, in point of fact, attempting to claw its way out of me using the nearest exit available. I very soon discovered that the only comfortable position was lying flat on my side, in the bedroom, with the lights dimmed.

It was horrible. Not being sick, necessarily, though that sucked, too. But missing out on the reunion—that was just killing me. I could hear people arrive and get swept up in the welcome from the next room, but I couldn't bring myself to get up. Every so often, I would get a visitor. Cheryl popped in to say hello. Storme dropped by to tell me to get my ass up and stop being such a pussy. Then Russ. Sunday. And, finally, Andrea.

"Hey, Jack."

I opened my eyes. And I boomeranged back to my sixteenth year of life.

"Hey."

"Not feeling so good, huh?"

"Not at the moment. Getting there, though."

"You need anything?"

"I'm okay. For now."

She smiled pityingly at me. "All right. You need anything, give a holler." She started to go and stopped. "But Storme's right. Get your ass up soon, willya?" She smiled again and left.

I allowed myself another twenty minutes of quiet and solitude to make sure everything was settled.

And then, taking their advice, I got my ass up.

The party had moved down to the bar. I went down to find them and it didn't take long. This group was hard to miss.

Almost everyone was there, the entire crew from the old Deerfield cast, save Billy, Boyd and Kenny. But the three of them were not completely AWOL. They were each planning to be at the theater tomorrow. Couldn't miss *that*.

The rest of the cast had taken over three tables in the lounge and the scene looked eerily similar to our post-show Denny's gatherings back in the day.

Storme spotted me as I staggered to the table. "Jack, you look like shit."

"Thanks, Storme. I aim to please."

Donny waved me over to a chair between him and Ron. I took a seat and was offered anything my heart desired. Under normal circumstances, I would likely have tried to match everyone drink-for-drink, as was our custom on these occasions, but I settled for soda water instead. I was feeling a little fragile.

Luckily, the bar was situated near the ocean and the breeze that blew in off the water was wonderfully rejuvenating.

After a few minutes of catching up and our usual fuck-with-one-another banter, the conversation turned to the following night's event.

Russ was the Answer Man.

"We've got the guy who does their Frank coming by tomorrow afternoon to meet with us. I asked him if he could come in the morning to rehearse but he's unavailable. So we're on our own in the a.m."

I slipped on my cast director hat.

"Okay, who can play Frank tomorrow for the rehearsal in the morning?"

After a brief silence, Sunday piped up. "Fuck it, I'll do it."

"You've got the tits for it."

"Bet your ass I do."

We ran through the cast list again. Flippers was fielding a Frank, an Eddie and a Dr. Scott. We'd provide the rest. We'd have two rehearsals, one in the morning, one in the afternoon. In between, we'd chill by the pool, grab some dinner and head over to the theater around 11 to get the lay of the land.

Russ, going through his checklist, asked if I was willing to do the pre-show.

"Absolutely," I said.

Sunday chimed in: "You've got the tits for it."

I grinned. "Bet your ass I do."

We retired upstairs and the real party began.

For some reason, the room that Ron, Tracey and I shared became the central gathering spot. We all crammed in, lit up, popped open various beverages and hung out. Old stories were recounted, as at every reunion. New developments remarked upon. Eventually a poker game broke out.

I tried to keep up, but Jack the Grog was alive and well. After my bout with botulism earlier that day, I thought it best to retire early.

Hey, I had a show to do. Better be ready. I drifted off with the familiar sounds of a Rocky party bubbling around me.

Ron woke me up, of course. I still wasn't entirely sure he slept at all. He had run out for bagels and coffee, and after a bracing breakfast, Tracey, Ron and I popped an RHPS disc into Tracey's portable DVD player and reviewed our bits.

Though Ron and Tracey had asked me for feedback on their performances, I had little to offer them in terms of direction. They donned the characters of Brad and Janet like some people slip on comfortable shoes. They didn't need my help.

When the hour was finally considered decent, the phone started ringing. It was the rest of the crew clamoring to get together downstairs. We had determined that the only place with enough room to do a full rehearsal was in the lobby of the building. Russ (of course) had spoken to the management and secured us a large area just off the back entrance where we could run through our cues. The place even had a TV and a DVD player we could use for rehearsal purposes, so when we got to the lobby, we shifted some furniture around, fired up the movie and got going.

I would like to report that everything went smoothly and got better as we went along, but I'm afraid that the diametric opposite occurred.

We bumped into one another almost constantly. Our timing was for shit. Instead of having the luxury of knowing the movie so well that we could look into one another's eyes during the scenes, we all found ourselves searching out the TV, sneaking peripheral glances every chance we could. Storme was the only one who seemed to be enjoying herself and we suspected that her occasional "smoke breaks" were the reason.

The rest of us were having fun, but we were also beginning to freak out. The idea that we could show up at the Flippers Cinema and leave behind a huge, stinking turd of a performance was looking more and more like a very real possibility.

We soldiered on. The only bright spot, it seemed, was Sunday's performance as Frank. Where the rest of us were tense and anxious, she was relaxed, easygoing, playful and on the ball. After all, she didn't have to stand up in front of a crowd that night and do this thing for real. Naturally, she was having a blast.

Lunch break. Then back to work. At some point, the Flippers Frank, this young, dark-haired fellow named Dan, dropped by. He had the basic Frank look down—shoulder-length hair, aquiline features, a barely detectible attitude. Seemed like he might work out just fine.

Dan had been informed that the Great and Powerful Wizards of Rocky, the legendary Deerfield cast, had decided to come to his theater and show him and his crew what was what. So he was here to rehearse a few numbers with us and see what exactly we brought to the table.

We went through a few scenes, got some basic blocking down and tried to get a feel for the kind of Frank he would be. He was good (not Mark or Boyd good, but pretty damned good all the same). As for what he thought of us, if he was unimpressed he certainly didn't let it show.

After zipping through the scenes with Dan once or twice, we decided that we either knew the damned thing or we didn't. Accordingly, we broke for dinner and decided to show up at the theater and let the chips fall where they may.

No pressure. It was just another show, right? Nothing important on the line. We were just there to have fun and we had nothing to prove to anyone. In the end, it was no big deal.

Uh-huh.

The theater was located in an outdoor strip mall. This was, as you can imagine, a bad omen for all the Ultravision grads who still remembered trading our happy life at the Big Theater only to be sequestered in the rinky-dink Mercedes. Despite the similarities, we did our best to withhold judgment. Looks, after all, could be deceiving. We hoped.

We hung out in the parking lot, the traditional South Florida Rocky pre-show ritual, and attempted to determine who among the crowd was in the cast and who were simply audience members. There seemed to be a lot of young Goth chicks pouring out of various cars, and hanging on their arms were equally pale, sunken-eyed, emaciated Goth boys. It was definitely a different crowd than we remembered from the '80s. And the younger they seemed, the older we felt.

Russ finally spotted the cast manager for Flippers and introductions were made. Jeanette looked like the perfect type to run a Rocky show. Short and tough-looking with close-cropped dark hair, she sported a no-nonsense demeanor mixed with a welcoming, friendly-as-can-be tone. She was, we realized, a female version of Russ himself.

She and Russ ran through the roster, cementing exactly who would be performing what role that night. Andrea and Sunday were asked, one final time, if they would be gracing us with their rendition of the opening number and they both shook their heads emphatically. Wasn't going to happen.

"Huh," said Donny, leaning up against Russ's car and lighting up a smoke. "That's a shame. I would have liked to have seen that." He drifted into the theater and we followed him.

I suppose I should mention that for that entire day, Donny had simply sat off to the side as the rehearsals and the meals and the day's activities spun around him, saying little, a beatific smile plastered across his face. Once the cast had gathered, he was as happy as could be.

It happened every reunion. When the entire group was together in one place, Donny was in heaven.

And while I'm sure he would have agreed to do Eddie in a red-hot minute if it were possible, Donny's performing days were obviously behind him. With the weight he was carrying, he had trouble just getting around. Time is not kind to big men.

Walking into the theater was a huge relief to all of us. Flippers was certainly no Mercedes. While it was nothing close to the Ultravision's size, the place was pretty impressive nonetheless. For one thing, they had an actual stage area up front. It was a spectacular development, seeing all that space between the front row and the screen. We'd have all the room we needed to actually perform the blocking we'd prepared.

There were two aisles that cut the main seating area into thirds and the aisles were remarkably wide. Plenty of room to play. What's more, we estimated the theater held about 300 people and from the looks of the crowd gathering outside, there was a chance that we would need every seat.

We had little time to take in our surroundings. Set-up was upon us. As I crossed up one of the aisles to find the bathroom/dressing room, I saw Russ talking to an older guy with a notepad. Russ gestured me over.

The guy turned out to be a reporter from the *Sun-Sentinel* newspaper who had done a feature on the Ultravision show back in 1982. Russ explained that, after all this time, the guy had returned to cover this performance as a sort of "Where Are They Now?" segment. It seemed a little unreal that this evening was actually worthy of even a scintilla of media coverage, but the reporter certainly seemed to think so. After answering a few questions, I made my excuses and finally sidled off to change.

Again, my progress was interrupted, this time by running into Kenny. He was one of the three remaining Deerfield cast members who hadn't yet made an appearance. Billy and Boyd had yet to show themselves. I threw my arms around Kenny in welcome (no easy task, the guy has a good foot and a half on me) and wound up whacking into his camera. He explained that he would be serving in the role of official/unofficial photographer that evening and promised to get plenty of great shots.

I made my brief hellos and dashed off. Showtime was rapidly approaching.

To my horror, the bathrooms (both the men's *and* ladies' rooms) had no mirrors. It was inexplicable. For the first time in my life, I found myself in a public toilet with no *fucking reflective surfaces*.

I didn't want to panic, so I talked myself down. No matter, I reasoned. Who needed mirrors? I mean, I didn't need to get the Riff blush affixed to my face until well after the pre-show and besides, the makeup didn't make the Riff Raff. It was the man *behind* the greasepaint.

I slipped on my old Transylvanian jacket, still festooned with twenty-five-year-old hilariously clever buttons and toodled back out to the stage.

The Flippers cast buzzed about, introducing themselves, getting to know all the middle-aged folks who had barged into their theater. I made my way offstage to try to see what kind of props they had that I could use. Candelabra? Laser gun? Wine bottle? What was handy?

I ran into a girl near the exit who appeared to be all of 17 years old. She was in the act of pulling props, costumes and various oddly shaped gadgets out of a shopping cart. The sight of her really took me back to my old Transylvanian days. Clearly, this was the person to talk to.

"Hey," I said as I sidled up. "How you doing? I'm Jack."

She glanced up at me with a bored expression and then, without a word, thrust a keychain into my hand.

I looked at it for a moment, bewildered. "Is this...for me?"

"Read it," she said, continuing with her work. I glanced at the string of keys and saw that they were attached to a strap. The strap had some writing on it along the edge:

"*Sorry boys,*" it said, "*I eat pussy.*"

334

Cute, I thought.

"Hey," I said to the girl. "As much as I'd love to see you indulge in your little hobby, I don't really have the time. I've got a show to do. You in charge of props?"

It was her turn to look perplexed.

I tried to clarify. "I'm not interested in getting into your pants, sweetie. I just need to know where the Riff Raff shit is kept. Okay?"

"Oh," she said, getting my drift. "It's all right here."

"Cool."

I loved the idea that this girl thought she could shock me. At the same time, I understood her instant antipathy. She was cute and probably got hit on quite a bit. To ward off the creeps, she had developed a fool-proof dirtbag repellant.

"Let's try again," I said. "I'm Jack."

"I'm Bobbi."

"Nice to meet you. Hope you enjoy the show."

Bobbi helped me gather together what she figured I'd need to do Riff. They seemed to be fully stocked with Rocky props. My arms full of necessary items, I moved into the theater and took a few minutes to place them strategically around the stage where I could find them.

Once everything was in place, I finally had the leisure time to really drink in the atmosphere.

I hadn't been to a showing of "The Rocky Horror Picture Show" with this group of people since I was 17 years old. We had met, off and on, during the intervening twenty-five years, but in all that time, we never felt compelled to do, or see, the show as a group. Not once.

And now, I knew, we would never do it again. This was it. Our final show.

Deep down, those of us who had been thrown out of the Ultravision before our time wanted some kind of closure, some do-or-die opportunity to finally get the release we were denied back in the day. Well, here it was. Our golden opportunity. It was now up to us whether we were going to blow it.

There was only one rule and it was a simple one: Don't. Suck.

By now, the audience had been turned loose into the theater and the seats were filling up fast. Jeanette found me and asked if I was ready to get the party started.

I nodded my assent. I walked to the front of the theater. I placed my

335

foot on the armrest.

And I stood up.

The crowd seemed pretty responsive, though I admit that my pre-show muscles had atrophied somewhat since my early days. At one point, when the crowd's buzz threatened to drown me out, the young girl who normally did the Flippers warmup hauled herself up onto a chair next to me and hollered in a deafening tone: "*Hey, shut the fuck up motherfuckers and listen to the man!*"

That, I'm happy to say, did the trick.

Resuming my duties, I made sure to thank the Flippers management and the current cast for generously offering us the use of their theater for the night. I gave everyone a brief history of the Ultravision cast, but didn't bother to go around introducing everyone in attendance. Time was short.

Finally, we ran through some chants, breaking out some of the old classics. We hauled the virgins up onto the stage and I let the Flippers regulars run them through their paces. Then I got the high sign from Jeanette, signed off for my final pre-show and went to collect my Riff gear.

Unlike the Ultravision show, the management at Flippers wasted no time with previews or music videos prior to the movie. They zipped straight to the main event. The crowd barely had time to chant, "*We want lips!*" before...there they were.

The familiar music started. The lips swelled to fill the screen. The spotlight in the back of the theatre flickered to life.

And to my absolute shock and amazement, Sunday and Andrea were revealed, in their customary positions, ready to lick those lips one last time.

I couldn't believe my eyes. These were not the type of women who changed their minds easily. What in the world had happened?

The answer was seated in the front row.

Gazing up at them, as he had so many times before, Donny looked perfectly serene and at peace. It was like watching a penitent kneeling before the altar. Donny was in church and, by God, he was getting a lifetime's worth of religion.

The girls...hell, the *women* went through their quarter-century-old choreography like they had just performed it yesterday. They had lost none of the precision they had honed back when they were kids. If anything, age had only enhanced their performance.

By the time Sunday and Andrea were finished, the Flippers cast and everyone else in attendance had finally gotten their first taste of Rocky Horror, Deerfield-style. The ovation afterward was suitably deafening.

Still stunned at what I had just witnessed, I zipped away to change as quickly as possible. I didn't want to miss Ron and Tracey.

Throwing on my gear, I managed to smear some blush onto my face, pull on Amos n' Andy and rush back to the stage just in time for the beginning of "Dammit Janet."

I had spent the last fourteen hours watching Ron and Tracey do everything possible to recall the roles they had brought to life as kids. Now, rehearsal was done. It was go time. They were the first of the Deerfield cast members to assume their former lead roles in the show and whatever we did the rest of the night, they would be the ones who set the pace.

I think it's fair to say that the Wild and Untamed Things were holding their collective breath.

For starters, they both looked incredible. Tracey had dragged her old Janet costume out of storage and still fit into it, even after banging out two kids. The expression you're looking for is, "Fuck yeah!"

Ron, who wore his hair close-cropped these days, had ordered up a special "Brad wig" and had it shipped into town just for the occasion. It was hilariously appropriate, providing what you might call a "Clark Kent" look, and it gave him a closer resemblance to Barry Bostwick than he'd ever pulled off before.

But what really made their performance so terrific was their timing. As teenagers, they had been good. As adults, suddenly taking this endeavor *very* seriously, they were spot on. Ron's days of fucking around on stage were forever gone. For once in his life, Ron was going to do everything letter-perfect and he couldn't have asked for a better partner.

Before I knew it, they were in the car on their way to the castle and it was time for me to get into position.

The suspense leading up to Riff's first entrance is simply delicious. First, the car gets a flat. Then the young couple decides to walk to the castle. Brad kicks the tire. They head off into the rain. And then, almost unobtrusively, the music kicks in.

Janet sings the first verse. The rain pours down. (The audience, true to form, supplied their own weather system.) Then Janet and Brad join together for the first chorus. The motorcycles rumble past them. The camera zooms in on the castle.

And then, ladies and gents:

It's Riff Raff time.

The Flippers spotlight, I should mention, was not the most reliable machine that ever existed. By the time I made it to the stage, it had completely flickered out and the residents had scrambled to illuminate us with handheld flashlights. These seemed to work just fine and, in truth, if you're playing Riff Raff, being lit from below by a pair of flashlight beams is almost *exactly* what you want for your entrance lighting.

So as the camera caught the on-screen Riff Raff framed in the window, the Flippers flashlights clicked on below me and lit up my face.

Now, of course, when you're playing Riff Raff, you don't get your enjoyment simply by playing the role. With Riff, you get to savor the whole package. And at this particular moment, that package included:

Richard O'Brien's entrance applause.

Tonight, however, just this one night, if you don't mind, Richard:

It was for me.

By the time the show finally came down, the Deerfield cast had stored up enough memories to last us another twenty-five years.

For me, just answering the door and seeing Ron and Tracey standing outside the castle for that one last time was worth the trip down to the Swamp. But the hits just kept a'comin'.

Kicking off the Time Warp. Laying a big hickey on Storme's neck during our Elbow Sex scene. And seeing the Flippers Eddie practically throw Cheryl through the ceiling during "Hot Patootie."

We drank it up, all night long. We savored it.

To put it plainly: We got what we came for.

Kenny snapped a thousand or so pictures. The crowd gave us a rousing reception at the end (the Flippers show featured a curtain call, which we hadn't been expecting, and the ovation was much appreciated).

One of my favorite moments of the night occurred during the Floor Show. About twenty minutes after the movie had started, I got a tap on my shoulder. It was Billy. He had been working, couldn't get away until the last minute, something like that. Some real-life bullshit. But here he was at last. I thought it was a damn shame that he wasn't able to participate in the show itself, particularly because he was still in excellent shape and, despite his advanced years, could easily have pulled off the role of Rocky.

What I didn't see coming was that, as the show wound to a close, Billy tapped out the Flippers Floor Show Rocky and stepped into the part at the last possible minute, bringing the full number of Deerfield participants to seven out of twelve main roles. Pretty impressive turnout for a bunch of old fuckers.

I know it's hard to make a nostalgic moment out of watching two of your buddies roll around on the floor wearing ladies underwear and enjoying an orgy with a group of perfect strangers, but seeing Russ and Billy dive into the Floor Show, well...there was more than one of us who wiped away a tear or two.

Maybe you had to be there.

We reconvened in the parking lot afterward. Jeanette and the rest of the Flippers gang were effusive in their praise, which was nice of them. They told us that it was the biggest crowd they'd ever hosted at their theater and seemed convinced that the old Deerfield cast had the magic ability to make a group like that show up whenever we made an appearance. (We did nothing to disabuse them of this notion.)

Jeanette was incredibly complimentary, going so far as to offer us the option of joining their cast, if we liked, or at the very least taking over the show once a month from then on.

It was a magnanimous, generous gesture. And we turned her down flat.

We knew, each of us, that what had happened that night was a once-in-a-lifetime experience. Trying to recreate it, even for a single additional night, would only be a letdown to everyone concerned. It was important that we enjoy our last night on stage together and then make *sure* it was our last.

We had been lucky, we knew. The planets had aligned just perfectly for us. We would never have another opportunity like that, where the clouds would clear away just long enough for us to see where we had come from and where we were. Best to be satisfied with the gift we'd been given.

We were officially retired from the Rocky game.

The Flippers cast invited us to their local Denny's that night, but we demurred. That was their place, not ours. We piled in our cars and headed back to our little timeshare apartments to enjoy our last night together.

We arrived back at the apartment feeling as if we'd run a marathon. Tired, but satisfied.

Donny took a seat in the corner of the communal two-bedroom suite and patiently began construction on his herbal origami tubes. He may have had softball gloves for hands, but he was an artist, no doubt about it. He remained mute as the rest of us rehashed the evening's events. Then at last he stood, inspected his handiwork, nodded in satisfaction and made his way out to the balcony. He paused in the doorway to make a simple announcement:

"The shotgun booth is open."

Smiling, we all followed him outside.

Epilogue: To Absent Friends

There is exactly one person from my high school graduating class with whom I am still in any kind of contact. Dean, a guy I first met when I was 13 years old and who I have now known for more than thirty years, still manages to keep in touch with me and I with him. He was the best man at my wedding and remains the only friend I had from South Florida who I never saw wearing fishnet stockings.

Other than that, I haven't the slightest idea what anyone from Zion Lutheran has been up to after all these years. And to be honest, I don't much care, either. High school was an experience, but it wasn't the most important thing to happen to me during that time of my life. Not by a long shot.

Rocky was everything. It had saved me from the soul-crushing life of the typical South Florida teenager. Before RHPS, I had faced an existence of conformity, of drug-addled complacency, of MTV-addicted lethargy. But instead of spending my weekend nights in the bong-smoke-filled basements of my loser, stoner buddies watching music videos and waxing rhapsodic over last week's fantastic bong-smoke-filled weekend, I instead got dressed up as a hunchbacked butler and danced the Time Warp again and again and again.

"The Rocky Horror Picture Show," without question, had saved my life. And for that, I will be forever grateful.

Curiously, I was the only one of the Deerfield cast to move out of Florida. All the rest of them, each and every one, stayed well south of the Georgia border. Some got out of *South* Florida (some even tried life up North for brief spurts before moving back), but in the end, for every Wild and Untamed Thing besides your humble narrator, the Swamp was, and remains, home.

Don't ask me to explain. I suppose the place must have *some* appealing qualities. But, aside from my friends, I can't seem to pinpoint any of them.

My Florida friends get on my case sometimes for living in Chicago and enduring the brutal weather we get here. And the winters can be brutal indeed. But I counter their criticism by asking them how hurricane season was this year and that usually shuts them up for a while.

So...what happened to all of them, my good friends down in the Swamp? Well...

Some of them eventually got married. Some did not.

Some of them are still with their respective spouses. Some are not. It happens.

Some got married, divorced and *re*married. That happens, too.

And a lot of us had kids. I mean a *lot*. Come to think of it, we could easily field a Rocky cast of our own, if we were so inclined.

We are not, as it happens, so inclined.

When our reunions occur (and they still do), it is as if no time at all has elapsed since we last laid eyes on one another. Months, years apart. It doesn't matter. We're family, so who gives a shit how long it's been?

And that's how each of us sees the other members of the group: as real, flesh-and-blood family. And since we consider one another family, it's only right that we treat one another accordingly.

So, in true familial tradition, we rag on one another incessantly, yell at one another constantly and love one another unconditionally.

This year marks thirty years since I first set foot on the Ultravision stage with my black jacket, white shirt and black pants.

Thirty years. A generation and a half. It's a little hard to believe.

To celebrate, we are getting together, as we always do, to mark the occasion. We don't know where and how we will meet, but it doesn't matter. Wherever we are, we'll have a gay old time. After all, we'll be together. That's all that matters.

I would love to be able to fill you in on what's going on with everyone individually, by the way. I'd really enjoy telling you what happened to them over the years and could, if I wanted to, run down the list of what all of my

Rocky brothers and sisters are doing right this minute.

But I think that both they and you would agree that I've said plenty about them already, right? A modicum of privacy is the least I can offer them after outing them in these pages for their teenage misadventures.

Before I call it a day, though, there are a just a few former castmates whose lives I'd like to follow up on, briefly, if you wouldn't mind.

In time, Alice and I—having lost touch for many years—actually managed to connect with each other out there in the ether. Social networking was invented for that sort of thing, I believe. She is, I'm pleased to report, happily married and doing terrifically well. Ironically, she is the only person I knew from my days in South Florida who lives in the wintry north.

She's here. In Chicago. She and her husband live about three miles away from my house.

Can you beat that?

My relationship with Ron, the clear personification of my id if there ever was one, has only strengthened over the years. He is my friend, my compatriot and my spider-brother to the end. He lives in Orlando now, is recently remarried and has become, since the Rocky days, a full-time actor. He appears in films, commercials and also makes a decent living...

...wait for it...

...driving a *stunt car*.

Seriously. I couldn't make that shit up if I tried.

Mr. Accident is a goddamn professional stunt driver.

Smoke on *that*.

Four and a half years ago, about six months after our twenty-fifth reunion, I got a call from Felicia announcing that Donny had died. It was not an unexpected piece of news. He had been unhealthy, then ill, then seriously ill, for many years. Felicia said he had finally had a heart attack and went without any serious pain. I sincerely hope that is true. He deserved none, God knows. He was one of the kindest, gentlest, most caring human beings who it has ever been my privilege to know. Smart, funny, compassionate and loyal. That was him. We never had a cross word between us, Donny and I. Not one. I love him dearly and miss him more than I can say.

At this writing, Donny is the only one of all of us who has gone.

Well, the only member of the cast, anyway.

Because, finally, there is the Ultravision Theatre. Whatever became of that venerated old cinema house, eh?

Well, the building is still there. You can see it to this day, sandwiched between 10th Street and Hillsboro Boulevard, on the west side of Federal Highway in Deerfield Beach, Florida. Go ahead. Check it out.

But don't look for a movie theater. They haven't shown movies in the place since we performed Rocky there all those years ago. Very soon after we were tossed out, the business folded. Like almost all of the old-school movie houses, the Ultravision management was forced to shut its doors, making way for the new generation of teeny-tiny super-googol-plexes.

It kills me. One of the greatest cinemas I've ever seen in my life and the place doesn't even show movies anymore. Nope.

You want to know what they did with the place? I'm not kidding:

It's a church.

Yeah, that's right. Some genius decided to convert the Ultravision Theatre, home to some of the most decadent, perverted, sexually outrageous and depraved behavior I have ever witnessed in my life, into a *house of God*.

Well, good luck to them. I wish them all the best. If they feel they can sanctify the joint after turning it over to us for almost two years, I say—be my guest.

But I've got some news for them:

No amount of scrubbing is going to cleanse the place and make it acceptable in the eyes of the Lord after what we did there. Not a chance. I don't care if it stands as a holy shrine for another thousand years. It will always be *our* place of worship. Not theirs.

So call it what you will, the Grand Temple of the Unification of the Spirit of the Nazarene or whatever. It will always be the Ultravision to me.

Whenever I'm down in South Florida for one of my biennial pilgrimages, I always try to stop by and pay a visit to the old place. And I always go alone.

I like to pull up in the parking lot by the north-side exit doors, where we used to truck in the props on our stolen wheelchairs. Once there, I park as close to the theater as I can and shut off the car. Sitting there, the engine ticking as it cools down, I close my eyes and bow my head.

And if I sit there long enough, I can hear it. The tiny echo from years past coming from deep inside:

"*We...want...lips...*"

You can just make it out. Just on the edge of consciousness.

"*We...want...lips...*"

Very faintly.

But I swear, if you try, you can hear it just as plain as day.

"*We...want...lips...we...want...lips...*"

Go on. Stop by. Park by the back door. Give a listen.

You'll see.